JOHN WHALLEY
COLLEEN HAMILTON

THE TRADING SYSTEM AFTER THE URUGUAY ROUND

Institute for International Economics
Washington, DC
July 1996

John **Whalley** is Director of the Centre for Development and International Economics Research and Professor of Economics at the University of Warwick and a Research Associate at the National Bureau of Economic Research.

Colleen Hamilton has collaborated with John Whalley on a number of projects in the field of international trade, having provided research support for the International Trade Group of the Macdonald Royal Commission on the Economic Union and Development Prospects for Canada and for The Ford Foundation project on Developing Countries and the Global Trading System (in particular, assisting in the drafting of the project's final report, *The Uruguay Round and Beyond*).

INSTITUTE FOR INTERNATIONAL ECONOMICS
11 Dupont Circle, NW
Washington, DC 20036-1207
(202) 328-9000   FAX: (202) 328-5432
http://www.iie.com

C. Fred Bergsten, *Director*
Christine F. Lowry, *Director of Publications*

Cover Design by Michelle M. Fleitz
Typesetting by AlphaTechnologies/mps
Printing by Automated Graphic Systems

Printed in the United States of America
98 97 96   5 4 3 2 1

Library of Congress Cataloging-in-Publication Data
Whalley, John
    The trading system after the Uruguay round / John Whalley, Colleen Hamilton.
        p. cm.
    Includes bibliographical references and index.
    1. General Agreement on Tariffs and Trade (Organization).   2. International trade.   3. Tariff.   4. Commercial policy.   5. World Trade Organization.
I. Hamilton, Colleen.   II. Title.
HF1379.W5   1995
382—dc20   95-12617
                                       CIP
ISBN 0-88132-131-1

Marketed and Distributed outside the USA and Canada by Longman Group UK Limited, London

We would both like to acknowledge the continual and unending support given to us by Tom Bayard throughout this project; this book is dedicated to his memory.

Contents

Appendices

Preface

The Institute did considerable work on the Uruguay Round of global trade negotiations from its inception through its conclusion. At the request of then-USTR Bill Brock, Gary Hufbauer and Jeffrey Schott provided one of its initial blueprints in *Trading for Growth: The Next Round of Trade Negotiations* in 1985. To deal with two of the most difficult sectoral problems, Dale Hathaway wrote *Agriculture and the GATT: Rewriting the Rules* in 1987 and William Cline coauthored *The Future of World Trade in Textiles and Apparel* in the same year. When the talks stalled in midterm, Schott produced *The Global Trade Negotiations: What Can Be Achieved?* and edited *Completing the Uruguay Round* in 1990. When the negotiations finally concluded, Schott evaluated the outcome in *The Uruguay Round: An Assessment* in 1994.

This new book by John Whalley and Colleen Hamilton looks back at the accomplishments of the Uruguay Round more than two years after its completion and seeks to draw lessons from the round, along with recent regional and other related initiatives, for the future of the global trading system. Its objective is to assess the implications for trade policy in the years ahead. In its analysis of how the Uruguay Round outcome affects prospects for commencement of a new round, it thus completes the cycle of Institute studies that began over a decade ago with the launch of the Uruguay Round itself.

This book had a difficult evolution because I initially asked Professor Whalley to write it when the Uruguay Round appeared likely to meet its initial deadline of late 1990. He faithfully produced a complete manuscript but publication obviously had to be postponed when the completion of the Round itself was postponed, eventually for a full three years. Hence the author was required to do far more than the usual updating and revising, for which I am deeply grateful.

The Institute for International Economics is a private nonprofit institution for the study and discussion of international economic policy. Its purpose is to analyze important issues in that area and to develop and communicate practical new approaches for dealing with them. The Institute is completely nonpartisan.

The Institute is funded largely by philanthropic foundations. Major institutional grants are now being received from the German Marshall Fund of the United States, which created the Institute with a generous commitment of funds in 1981, and from the Ford Foundation, the Andrew Mellon Foundation, and the C. V. Starr Foundation. A number of other foundations and private corporations also contribute to the highly diversified financial resources of the Institute. About 16 percent of the Institute's resources in our latest fiscal year were provided by contributors outside the United States, including about 7 percent from Japan.

The Board of Directors bears overall responsibility for the Institute and gives general guidance and approval to its research program—including identification of topics that are likely to become important to international economic policymakers over the medium run (generally, one to three years), and which thus should be addressed by the Institute. The Director, working closely with the staff and outside Advisory Committee, is responsible for the development of particular projects and makes the final decision to publish an individual study.

The Institute hopes that its studies and other activities will contribute to building a stronger foundation for international economic policy around the world. We invite readers of these publications to let us know how they think we can best accomplish this objective.

C. FRED BERGSTEN
Director
June 1996

Acknowledgments

This book was started in 1989, when the Uruguay Round was supposed to end in 1990. For a while it looked like neither endeavour would conclude, and we are grateful that both finally came to an end.

We are especially appreciative of the support and guidance given by C. Fred Bergsten, Director of the Institute for International Economics. Many thanks are also due to the participants in the various study groups on drafts of the manuscript held throughout the past few years. A number of individuals have been most generous with their comments on earlier drafts, including John H. Jackson, Bob Stern, Bob Hudec, Patrick Low and Julius Katz. Their comments, while invaluable, in no way make them accountable for any remaining errors or misconceptions—we accept responsibility for all of those.

In addition, our thanks go to Paula Mosurinjohn and Connie Nevill for typing the many variations of this book. On a personal note, Colleen would like to acknowledge the ongoing support and unlimited patience of her husband Bob and the understanding of her children Jenny and Mike.

1

Introduction

The Uruguay Round negotiations produced a large, complex array of agreements to address long-standing sectoral problems, further cut tariffs, create a permanent trade body, strengthen dispute settlement procedures, and provide new trade (or trade-related) arrangements in services, investment, and intellectual property. The Uruguay Round broadened the coverage of the rules that underpin the trading system. It also tried to strengthen the application of trade rules and achieve a major new market opening (see also chapter 3; Schott 1994; UNCTAD 1994).[1]

But liberalization in such areas as agriculture, textiles, and tariffs may prove less substantial than at first appears, and the extent of system strengthening is difficult to judge. The creation of a permanent trade body, the World Trade Organization (WTO), may generate new momentum for further liberalization, but at the outset it merely repackages previous General Agreement on Tariffs and Trade (GATT) arrangements, with little immediate or obvious impact on how well the trading system works. New dispute settlement procedures may prove important, but their impact remains unclear. New trade rules in antidumping have been criticized as codifying present practices rather than disciplining them. And agreements

---

1. Also see the discussions of the decisions in the round in the complementary Institute volume (Schott 1994) and the recent UNCTAD (1994) report. A useful summary of the initial decisions is to be found in the GATT press summary on the Final Act, released in December 1993 (reprinted in *The World Economy* 17, no. 3, June 1994), although there are some modifications in the subsequent April 1994 text adopted at Marrakesh. Also see the press summary of the earlier Dunkel text—the draft Final Act (reprinted in *The World Economy* 16, no. 2, April 1993).

in services, investment, and intellectual property mark only the beginning, not the completion, of new liberalization.

Yet great things are claimed for the Uruguay Round: that it will significantly open markets, generate new trade, prevent market closing, and improve global economic performance.[2]

Which view lies closer to the mark? How should the Uruguay Round be evaluated and what will its long-term consequences be? This book aims to map the course of the evolving global trade system and answer these questions.

Central to the question of where the trading system is going is the question of exactly where it has been. The general perception is that the grounding of the global trading system in strong nondiscriminatory trade rules has been critical to the global growth and prosperity achieved since 1945 and will be equally central to economic performance after the Uruguay Round. In fact, trade growth has in most years outstripped global income growth. Economists and policymakers see the system of global trade rules—embodied in multilaterally negotiated GATT accords and bilateral and other regional trade arrangements—as key to exploiting the gains from trade and thus as pivotal to improving the standards of living for people around the world. The system is credited with providing a stable, predictable global trade policy environment. Furthermore, it is viewed as a key defense against a reversion to retaliatory trade protectionism and any future implosion of world trade comparable to that of the late 1920s, when it fell by over 50 percent between 1929 and 1931 and by almost 70 percent by 1933 (Kindleberger 1973).

But this conception of the trading system as synonymous with the rules and principles that govern countries' use of trade-restricting border measures—rules embodied first in the General Agreement on Tariffs and Trade and now in the World Trade Organization—is an outdated notion. Even if the trading system was ever this limited in scope, which is doubtful, it has evolved away from this model. And as a result of the Uruguay Round, this evolution has accelerated dramatically and, in our view, will continue to do so.

The trading system is no longer largely about border measures; services, including telecommunications, show no respect for borders but are nonetheless included in the rule regime. The system is no longer just about trade in goods; investment measures and intellectual property protection now form part of the system. The system no longer even deals solely with trade; trade measures can be linked to nontrade issues such as intellectual

---

2. Peter Sutherland, director general of GATT, described the Uruguay Round in a September 1994 speech as the biggest trade liberalizing package in history, worth $755 billion of extra annual trade (*Financial Times*, 3–4 September 1994), and in October released GATT estimates of global gains worth over $500 billion annually by 2005 (*Financial Times*, 4 October 1994, 5; *Focus GATT Newsletter* 111, 1).

property and the emerging issues of labor standards and the environment. Basic principles such as nondiscrimination, which countries follow by according most-favored nation (MFN) status to their trade partners, has been more and more loosely applied.

Thus the idealized picture of the global trading system, set apart from other policy systems and supported by the twin pillars of nondiscrimination and national treatment, is even further from actuality after the Uruguay Round than it was before it. The intertwining of trade policy with nontrade issues will continue. The system now must also take into account the trade implications of domestic policies such as competition policy. And impurities in the system such as regional arrangements, present before the round, will spread further.

We argue that the round's effects and wider implications for the system may not have been fully understood. In terms of short-term access generation, these impacts are likely more modest than often claimed, but in the longer run the tariff bindings and added transparency in such areas as agriculture and developing-country tariffs offer significant potential for further liberalization. And while substantive immediate progress was not achieved in new areas such as services, momentum has been established for future liberalization.

How significant are the opportunities for increased trade created by the round? Are there avenues through which even further liberalization can be achieved? Will regionalism accelerate, and with what consequences? Can liberalization in fast-growing economies be locked in and enhanced? What does the enmeshing of trade and nontrade issues portend, and is this trend inevitable, or even desirable? And if there is another round, do environment and competition policy really make the best candidates for lead negotiating issues? We make four main points in connection with these questions.

Substance of the Round and Its Implications

We argue that the significance of the Uruguay Round over the next few decades may lie less in the direct effects of its barrier reductions and more in the future opportunities for liberalization it created in the key access areas of tariffs, agriculture, and textiles. This flies in the face of much of the discussion of the Uruguay Rounds results. In 1994 the GATT estimate of annual gains from the round by the year 2005 was $500 billion (*Focus GATT Newsletter* 111, 1). Projections of these gains made during the negotiations were also sizable, although many of these estimates were made well in advance of the round's conclusion, before the extent of actual liberalization was known. Some more recent model-based evaluations of the round find smaller gains (see chapter 4). Others magnify previous estimates by appealing to scale economy, procompetitive, and dynamic effects. Key assumptions underlie these calculations, and these can be challenged (see chapter 4).

In earlier evaluations, the majority of model gains occur in agriculture and textiles. In agriculture, "dirty" tariffication—that is, conversion of nontariff barriers to overly high bound tariffs—and tariff quotas accompanied by selective safeguards limit actual gains. In textiles, much of the liberalization is delayed until the final year of a 10-year phase-out, and a new regime based on antidumping duties is a threat. In tariffs, averaging procedures provided incentives to make large percentage cuts in small tariffs in order to meet tariff-cutting targets with minimal liberalization.

While we argue that the immediate market-access benefits are not as significant as first thought, we also argue that the round's contribution to future liberalization may be large. The conversion of previously complex and unbound protective measures (e.g., variable levies and waivers) into bound, transparent, and negotiable tariffs offers scope for future liberalization, as do initiatives to broaden system coverage and strengthen institutional arrangements (Tangermann 1994). Outside agriculture, many larger developing countries have also bound their tariffs, with substantial expansion in coverage.[3] Again, the bindings may be at levels too high to influence current trade patterns, but negotiable instruments have been created where few existed previously.

In services, substantive liberalization may be small, but the major step of initiating a multidecade process to deregulate services internationally has been taken. Add to this the expanded coverage of the system in other areas (intellectual property and investment) and the creation of a permanent World Trade Organization, as well as substantially strengthened dispute settlement procedures.

In sum, the Uruguay Round preserves the forward momentum for future trade negotiations that previous rounds have provided and has helped shape the agenda for subsequent rounds.

Entanglement with Nontrade Objectives

The Uruguay Round has not only substantially enlarged the coverage of the trading system in services, investment, and intellectual property, it has entangled trade policy with nontrade issues in ways the original trade rules cannot address. Domestic policies and their effects on trade enter the global debate with increasing frequency, and trade policy is some groups' vehicle of choice for eliciting compliance with nontrade objectives. During the Uruguay Round, the boundaries between trade and other policies have

---

3. François, McDonald, and Nordström (1994) report data showing that developing countries have moved from 22 percent of tariff lines bound before the round to 72 percent of lines bound after the round. For transition economies, bindings cover 98 percent of tariff lines.

become less distinct, and the objectives set for trade policies have been more widely debated and have grown more diffuse. Furthermore, instrument substitution—the replacement of GATT-restricted trade measures with other, sometimes more distorting practices, including domestic policy instruments—has become more common.

Negotiations on services dealt with barriers to trade affecting nongoods flows and disciplines to head off new protective barriers. Investment talks focused on trade-related aspects of investment, such as export performance requirements tied to foreign investment, with an objective of limiting the use of trade measures for nontrade purposes. And in intellectual property, the objective was to explicitly allow use of trade to enforce internationally agreed intellectual property rights (Whalley 1989b).

Other trade linkages, though they were not directly discussed in the round, have already figured prominently in discussions about the agenda of subsequent trade talks, most notably trade and the environment, trade and labor standards, and investment. These discussions clearly point to a wider role for domestic and social policy concerns in trade negotiations and wider use of trade as an enforcement mechanism rather than as policy measures whose design solely reflects trade concerns. These entanglements are more symbolic, focusing on cases and issues whose resolution will not affect the overall performance of the trading system, but as we will argue, this seems poised to change (see chapter 5).

No other round has raised the possibility of a *weakening* of global economic performance due to systemic changes; this is a clear departure from the past. This outcome is attributable in part to the round and is a central issue for any discussion of the post-round system. To the extent that this growing entanglement of trade and nontrade policy ultimately elevates trade barriers and reduces trade, the trading system (judged solely on economic performance criteria) will erode as more gains from trade go unexploited. But on the other hand, if this use of trade policy improves social conditions, then enhanced social performance can be claimed from this use of trade policy.

Regionalism after the Round

Both during and after the round, policymakers and other observers voiced concerns that the world was dividing into three trading blocs (centered on Europe, Asia, and the United States) locked in trade conflicts that would weaken the trading system and eventually undermine the global economy. We believe that the threat of new regionalism after the round is less severe than feared and that if the world is in fact headed toward blocs, there may instead be two groups—the Asia Pacific and Europe—rather than three.

In our view, the round reduced the threat of regionalism. This is because small countries have driven most of the new regionalism by seeking safe-haven arrangements, which have only limited effects on trade flows, and the imperative of finding safe havens is diminished with the round's conclusion (see chapter 6). In addition, larger countries used the threat of regional negotiations to pressure other large countries during the multilateral negotiations, and small countries quite consciously sought regional talks to increase their own regional negotiating leverage. The fear of a breakdown in the round further induced small countries to seek some form of safe haven with at least one large power. Again, the conclusion of the round itself, rather than its substance, will slow the spread of regional arrangements.[4]

We contrast this view of the new regionalism in the trading system with the older regionalism that preceded it: the latter being market- and trade-creating (as in Europe in the 1960s and 1970s), and the former driven by smaller countries seeking firmer guarantees of market access in large-country markets. In this new regionalism, including the North American Free Trade Agreement (NAFTA), there is little new liberalization in the larger country, but for their part of the bargain smaller countries significantly alter domestic policies. Because concessions are asymmetric, the new regionalism thus tends to be more redistributive toward larger countries than it is trade-diverting. Consequently, we do not see blocs based on these new arrangements as cohesive units pitted against other larger blocs. They are instead more of a transfer mechanism that leaves trade patterns (usually concentrated with one large power) largely unchanged and thus do not represent a major threat to trade performance. If there is a need to discipline these regional trade agreements, it may thus be more on distributional grounds.

The WTO and the Future of the Trading System

Much has been made of the new institutional arrangements resulting from the Uruguay Round, specifically the creation of the WTO. However, we see future multilateral trade negotiation and trade management under the WTO as being very much business as usual, with only limited short- or medium-term impact (see chapter 7).

The WTO is meant to eliminate the confusion and complexity accumulated in the GATT over seven negotiating rounds. Previous GATT ar-

---

4. This is not to minimize other factors fueling regionalism, such as the desire to move faster regionally than multilaterally, as has been expressed in the Asia Pacific Economic Cooperation (APEC) forum. This sets the stage for competitive liberalization, an interplay between multilateral and regional trade liberalization in which progress in one forum prods the other to action.

rangements have largely been rolled over into the WTO. This includes provisions on antidumping, safeguards, countervailing measures, subsidies, and balance of payments, as well as separate arrangements on government procurement, dairy, bovine meat, and civil aircraft. With the Uruguay Round, this list now also includes agriculture, textiles and clothing, trade-related investment measures, intellectual property, and the General Agreement on Trade in Services (GATS).

The dispute settlement mechanism has changed noticeably from its earlier form—probably the major short-term departure from previous arrangements. Instead of the old requirement that panel reports be adopted by consensus, panel reports now can only be rejected by consensus (subject to an appellate process), and strict time limits apply to the various steps. In turn, dispute settlement covers the three areas of goods, services, and investment, and in the goods area the disagreements covering intellectual property protection are included. Rights to a panel are now virtually automatic, whereas requests for panels could be blocked before.

Aside from dispute settlement (which might well have been incorporated in the GATT), it is unclear how significant the creation of the WTO is on substantive grounds. But a number of global economic agencies have seen the potential for a weakening of their role due to the creation of the WTO: the UN Conference on Trade and Development (UNCTAD), the World Intellectual Property Organization (WIPO), and even the Organization for Economic Cooperation and Development (OECD). In a climate of reexamination of the Bretton Woods institutions, the creation of the WTO may thus prove a catalyst for wider institutional change.[5]

Some economists have argued that the precise form of an international institutional arrangement is of less consequence than the fact of the mutual agreement that produced it. They argue that what matters is the creation of a focal point for cooperation and that achieving and preserving such cooperation is the key to a well-functioning trading system.

If it is true that the fact rather than the form of cooperation matters, the key to future global trade tranquillity may lie outside the WTO. Today there are more countries of significant economic size; hence the incentive for countries to retaliate is smaller and more limited than in previous decades.

The round process under the WTO will likely be business-as-usual. GATT rounds had become progressively longer, more difficult to conclude, and with longer gaps between end and launch; the WTO will not change this.

What the Uruguay Round has done is to create opportunities for reciprocity-based liberalization in a future round. As has been true in the

---

5. Recent publications have marked the 50th anniversary of the Bretton Woods institutions by looking at their effectiveness and future role in a changed global economy (Walters 1994; Bretton Woods Commission 1994; World Bank Group 1994; Bordo 1995).

past, however, a new round will be difficult to start, for three reasons. First, the opportunities for further liberalization that the Uruguay Round created, while significant, are also limited, particularly in sectoral coverage. Major liberalization may eventually follow in agriculture, developing-country tariffs, and services, but this by no means accounts for all remaining trade barriers. Something further will be needed to achieve liberalization in other areas.

Second, much discussion at present is centered on issues in which conventional exchanges of reciprocal concessions are unlikely to yield much. Trade and environment issues provide one such example. Containing regional trade arrangements is another area in which the thrust of trade discussions is defensive, not reciprocity-driven. Taking past rounds for a guide, it thus appears that a future round centered on trade and environment and competition policy is a nonstarter.

Third is the length of the process. The Uruguay Round took seven years to launch and more than seven to conclude; a future round could take even longer in both senses. Because the Uruguay Round will take 10 years to implement in both agriculture and textiles, a new round will likely take at least 10 years to launch. Each successive GATT round has taken significantly longer than the preceding round to conclude as well, and this trend will likely continue.

Put simply, the WTO does not change much in the medium term. To be sure, it tidies up the legal difficulties of a provisional GATT with separate disciplines and codes. But it is an illusion, in our view, that it will produce some form of revolutionary change in global trade policy—some sort of turbocharged GATT for the 1990s that can quickly usher in new negotiated liberalization. The issues will not be affected, the policy instruments at issue will be the same, the players will be the same, and so will, ultimately, the negotiating and management processes.

Summary

The Uruguay Round has been called a departure from earlier GATT rounds in being relatively little concerned with tariffs and more concerned with strengthening the system and restoring its consistency with multilateral principles. But the round's results in the rules areas (antidumping, countervailing duties and subsidies, safeguards) are modest, except for the commitment to eliminate voluntary export restraints (VERs), which falls under safeguards. The round contains little of substance in services and investment, and the short-run impact of a permanent WTO to replace the temporary GATT may prove to be small.

It is in the market-access areas of agriculture, textiles, and tariffs that the larger changes were achieved, and these areas also provide the unfinished business that would be the core of a new round. Although it may or may not yield the immediate market-access benefits many had hoped for at its launch, the Uruguay Round has laid a foundation for achieving significant new liberalization in the future in previously restricted areas such as agriculture and services. As such, the Uruguay Round may come to be recognized for its continuity with the past, rather than constituting a break with it. At its heart, the Uruguay Round, like previous GATT rounds, has proved to be a reciprocity-driven negotiation with attachments. It could eventually lead to another reciprocity-driven round, and its most enduring contribution to the trading system may be to make this possible.

2

The Trading System before the Uruguay Round

To gauge the long-run impact of the Uruguay Round on the world trading system, it is necessary to examine both how well the underlying global economy has performed and how the system governing it has evolved.

It is inevitably difficult to assess whether the trade policy system has had an effect on global economic performance. To measure the effects, microeconomists tend to focus on the gains from trade and improved resource allocation, which are difficult to measure, while macroeconomists look at output growth, unemployment, and productivity. In terms of all these characteristics, the long-run performance of the world economy has remained remarkably strong in the postwar period. At the same time, the trading system has been moving away from the central principles its creators established to anchor it in the 1940s—namely, national treatment, nondiscrimination, and transparency of border measures.

The global economy has changed considerably in the postwar years and endured a range of shocks and adjustments. Through it all, there has been persistently strong trade growth and, on average, good long-run income growth in the major global economies. In fact, the changes in trading arrangements achieved in earlier negotiating rounds appear not to have significantly affected overall economic performance in either direction, perhaps because the negative effects of voluntary export restraints (VERs) and other trade-restricting instruments have offset the gains from the negotiated tariff cuts. Whatever the reason, one hypothesis we will explore is that the Uruguay Round is no different than the previous rounds in that it will have relatively little impact on economic performance.

This is not to say that the Uruguay Round will have no impact at all. Beyond the incremental changes in economic behavior in the more conventional sense of impacts on welfare, consumption, production, and trade,[1] the Uruguay Round will affect the probabilities for future liberalization and trade conflicts. We return to this idea in later chapters.

Another hypothesis is that the trade policy system has been key to the sustained strong performance in the postwar global economy, not because trade and income growth depend on its ability to cut tariffs and sustain key principles, but because the General Agreement on Tariffs and Trade (GATT) provided a focal point for multilateral cooperation and thus prevented a reversion to the destructive, protectionist retaliation of the 1930s. In this view, the Uruguay Round decisions could be as important in preserving global cooperation as in keeping markets open.

Postwar Trade Growth

Before an evaluation of the impact of the Uruguay Round on the global economy, it is important to look at key indicators of economic performance. As noted earlier, the postwar period has seen strong and persistent growth in global trade; only two years of negative growth, 1975 and 1982, have been recorded since 1960 (table 2.1). World trade growth in real (volume) terms averages 6.2 percent per year over this period. Annual trade growth was 8.5 percent during 1960–70. In the 1970s it grew at 6.4 percent, and between 1985 and 1992 it was 5.0 percent. Strong growth in global trade is also evident in the late 1980s, following the recession of 1981–82.

Strong trade growth also is reflected in changes in the share of trade in GDP for major OECD countries as well as the associated growth in trade as a fraction of consumption in these same countries. As table 2.2 indicates, US trade shares approximately doubled between the early 1970s and the late 1980s and have more than doubled since the 1950s. Trade shares for the European Community (EC) taken as a single trading bloc have edged up slightly since the 1960s, but once internal EC trade is added in, a substantial increase in trade share is observed, although not a doubling, as in the US case. Trade shares in Japan oscillate on the import side due to exchange rate volatility and show relatively little change over the whole period.[2] Trade shares for the smaller OECD countries—Canada, Australia, New

---

1. In conventional microbased trade models in which countries are modeled with production sets and preferences for representative consumers, if production frontiers are close to linear and/or indifference surfaces have little curvature, there will tend to be large effects on trade volumes by changing, say, a tariff, but only small effects on welfare.

2. The net effect is that each of the major trading areas now has trade shares in the 10 to 15 percent of GDP range. The United States has substantially opened its economy and has integrated more in world markets, the European countries have opened substantially to each other's trade with a reduction in non-European trade, and Japan has remained at roughly unchanged levels of openness.

Table 2.1 Growth of world trade volume in OECD countries, 1960–94

Year	Volume indices of exports from OECD countries (1980 = 100)	Annual real growth rates (percent)
1960	24	
1961	n.a.	
1962	27	6.1
1963	29	7.4
1964	32	10.3
1965	34	6.3
1966	37	8.8
1967	39	5.4
1968	45	15.4
1969	50	11.1
1970	54	8.0
1971	58	7.4
1972	64	10.3
1973	71	10.9
1974	76	7.0
1975	73	−3.9
1976	81	11.0
1977	85	4.9
1978	90	5.9
1979	96	6.7
1980	100	4.2
1981	102	2.0
1982	101	−1.0
1983	104	3.0
1984	114	9.6
1985	118	3.5
1986	121	2.5
1987	128	5.8
1988	137	7.0
1989	147	7.3
1990	155	5.4
1991	159	2.6
1992	166	4.4
1993	164	−1.2
1994	179	9.1

Sources: Authors' calculations based on UNCTAD, *Handbook of International Trade and Development Statistics 1986, 1989 Supplement, 1992, 1993,* and *1995,* tables 2.1, 2.3.

Zealand, and the European Free Trade Association (EFTA) countries—are not reported here but have increased substantially over these years.

Even after allowing for differences between the three major trading regions within the OECD, trade has progressively become more important for economic activity (and in some, but not nearly all, developing countries). If any reversal of global trade growth were to occur, it is believed that it would be more serious for economic performance than in previous decades because trade would fall from a higher base and involve more countries.

Table 2.2 United States, Japan, and the European Community: shares of trade in GDP by major trading region, 1950–93

	Imports as a share of GDP	Exports as a share of GDP
US		
1950	4.0	4.0
1960	4.3	5.0
1970	5.5	5.7
1980	11.0	10.2
1987	10.8	7.4
1988	11.2	8.9
1989	11.2	9.4
1990	11.3	9.8
1991	11.0	10.5
1992	11.0	11.0
1993	12.0	10.0
Japan[a]		
1952	11.0	12.0
1960	10.3	10.8
1970	9.5	10.8
1980	14.9	13.9
1987	7.3	10.5
1988	8.0	10.3
1989	9.3	10.7
1990	10.1	11.0
1991	9.0	10.0
1992	8.0	10.0
1993	7.0	9.0

	Total EC[b] imports as a share of GDP	Extra-EC imports as a share of GDP	Total EC exports as a share of GDP	Extra-EC exports as a share of GDP
EC				
1960	18.9	9.8	19.5	8.7
1970	21.1	8.9	21.5	7.8
1980	28.0	12.4	27.0	9.7
1987	25.6	9.2	27.0	9.0
1988	26.1	9.4	26.9	8.9
1989	27.7	10.1	28.2	9.3
1990	27.3	9.7	28.3	8.7
1991	26.8	9.4	28.1	8.2
1992	26.4	8.9	28.3	8.1
1993	25.7	8.8	28.9	8.7

a. The volatility in imports' shares for Japan between 1970 and 1988 reflects in part the influence of world oil prices.
b. Total EC trade includes all trade between EC countries. Extra-EC trade is trade with non-EC countries.

Sources: Author's calculations based on UNCTAD *Handbook of International Trade and Development Statistics 1979, 1985, 1986 Supplement, 1989 Supplement,* and *1992,* table 6.3; European Commission (1995, tables 38, 41, 42, and 45); OECD, *Historical Statistics, 1960–88.*

This growth in global trade has not been uniform across product categories, regions, or time. This uneven growth pattern in part reflects the quick penetration by the rapidly growing economies (i.e., Japan, Korea, Taiwan) in industrial-country markets in particular sectors and in a short period, generating product-specific trade surges of substantial orders of magnitude.

Table 2.3 shows this unevenness both across product groups and subperiods since 1955. Trade in iron and steel grew rapidly until the mid-1970s; since then trade in this category has been virtually stagnant. Trade growth in textiles and apparel fell with the introduction of the Multi-Fiber Arrangement (MFA) in the early 1970s, but the mid- to late 1980s saw growth rates even higher than they were before the MFA was introduced. Transportation equipment and chemicals show consistently strong trade growth but weaker trade volume growth than for other categories in the mid- to late 1980s. This picture of uneven trade growth extends to other product groups and subcategories within these groups.

An implication of these data is the resilience of world trade growth to trade barriers, whether sector- or instrument-specific. In the textile and apparel area, the trade restrictions introduced in the 1960s aimed to limit the growth of export volumes from developing countries, but the net result seems to have been that exports in these products have continued to grow, and in some cases at higher rates than those set out in the agreements to limit the growth rates of imports (Trela and Whalley 1990; also see Hamilton 1990; Kirmani, Molojani, and Mayer 1984; Mark 1985; Keesing and Wolf 1980). In steel, there was a sharp reduction in trade growth following the onset of trade restrictions in the 1970s, but this was in a period of high oil prices, which resulted in substitution out of steel-intensive products and which reduced steel demand independently of trade barrier effects. Overall, product-specific trade restrictions seem to have had only mild effects on world trade growth, slowing rather than reversing or terminating it.[3]

This raises the question of how big an effect the integration of areas such as textiles, apparel, and voluntary export restraints affecting manufactured goods into the World Trade Organization (WTO) will have on trade growth rates. If the affected sectors achieved reasonable growth under restrictive arrangements—that is, when they were in effect outside the

---

3. While trade-protective measures such as VERs may not have limited trade growth in affected products, there has nonetheless been much debate over their negative consequences. These take the form of economic inefficiencies and distortions, investments induced into countries by protectionist barriers, costs to consumers of the barriers, rent-seeking effects, loss of development opportunities for developing countries, and the general unpredictability they inject into the system (for further discussion, see OECD 1985; Messerlin 1989; UNCTAD, *Handbook of International Trade and Development Statistics, 1985 Supplement*; Kirmani, Molojani, and Mayer 1984; Laird and Yeats 1988).

Table 2.3 Global trade growth by product group, 1955–92
(annual average real growth rates in each subperiod)

Product group	1955–60	1960–65	1965–70	1970–75	1975–80	1980–85	1985–92
Agricultural products and raw materials	3.3	0.9	1.5	−0.4	6.6	−0.7	2.9
Transportation equipment and machinery	11.0	9.5	12.0	7.4	5.8	6.4	7.9
Textiles and apparel	5.3[a]	n.a.	5.4	2.5	6.3	3.9	8.6
Iron and steel	10.5	5.5	9.7	7.0	0.9	1.3	1.9
Chemicals	10.3	9.2	10.0	7.8	7.7	4.7	7.5
Other manufactured goods	7.9	7.8	9.4	5.0	8.5	3.5	11.1

n.a. = not available.
a. For 1953–57.

Sources: Authors' calculations based on UNCTAD, *Handbook of International Trade and Development Statistics 1979*, tables 2.3, A.3, A.6, A.7, A.9, A.10; *1986*, tables A.3, A.6, A.7, A.9, A.10, A.11, 2.3; *1982*, tables 2.3, A.11; *1989 Supplement*, tables 2.3, A.3, A.6, A.7, A.9, A.10, A.11; *1992*, tables 2.3, A.3, A.6, A.7, A.9, A.10, A.11; *1993*, tables 2.3, A.3, A.6, A.7, A.9, A.10, A.11; *1995*.

GATT disciplines—will integrating them into the WTO spark even greater growth, or will countries find other means to restrict the sectors?

Table 2.4 emphasizes the unevenness of global trade growth across regions. Initial postwar trade growth was exceptionally strong, especially in Europe and Japan. Japanese trade growth continued at high levels over the whole period, with a slowing trend through the 1970s and 1980s, while growth in external EC trade also slowed in these decades and closely tracked that of the United States until the last half of the 1980s.

The table reveals another feature of global trade performance: the (on average) higher growth rate for trade between large regions and smaller neighboring trade partners. In 1985–90, growth in trade between Japan and other Pacific Rim countries significantly exceeded that of Japan's total trade. Growth in internal EC trade has often exceeded that of external EC trade. And for the United States, there is a higher growth rate (if by a less pronounced margin) for US and Canadian trade with Mexico than for US trade in general except in the 1970s. Regional trade has thus seemingly been one of the more dynamic elements of world trade.[4]

---

4. GATT reports that on a regional basis, North America, Asia, and Latin America had rates of trade expansion above world average for the second year in a row (*Focus GATT Newsletter* 108, 3). According to UN estimates (1992, 34), intraregional trade in goods in the 1980s

Table 2.4 Trade growth by region, 1955–93 (annual average real growth rates)

	1955–60	1960–65	1965–70	1970–75	1975–80	1980–85	1985–90	1990–93
Exports by major regions to the rest of world								
United States	6.3	5.0	7.1	5.4	5.4[a]	2.3	4.0	6.5
EC[b]	n.a.	4.6	8.3	6.6	5.3	2.2	6.9	−0.5
Japan	16.0	14.7	15.4	8.5	8.3[a]	9.5	2.0	8.9
Exports by major regions to neighboring countries								
US to Canada and Mexico	n.a.	7.4	7.5	5.4	3.4	7.0	4.4	9.3
EC to EFTA[c]	n.a.	15.9	15.1	n.a.	7.2	−0.3	8.0	−2.9
Internal EC trade	n.a.	12.2	11.6	6.5	8.4	1.4	9.8	−3.9
Japan to other Pacific Rim	n.a.	15.2	16.1	8.7	9.0	6.5	10.0	13.0

n.a. = not available.
a. For 1970–80.
b. External EC trade only.
c. Data in this row are affected by changes in the membership of EFTA, most notably in the mid-1970s, when Denmark, Ireland, and the United Kingdom joined the European Community.

Sources: Authors' calculations based on UNCTAD *Handbook of International Trade and Development Statistics 1979, 1986 Supplement, 1989 Supplement, 1993* and *1995,* tables 1.1 and 2.3; IMF, *Direction of Trade Statistics Yearbook,* 1995; OECD, *Monthly Statistics of Foreign Trade,* November 1986, December 1991, and March 1995.

Indeed, regional rather than global partners are either now the largest or rapidly becoming the largest sources of trade for each of the three major traders in the system: EFTA for the European Union (GATT 1993b, table II.27) and Canada for the United States, with Mexico its third-largest partner.[5] Japan's trade with the four large countries of the Association of Southeast Asian Nations (ASEAN)—Thailand, Malaysia, Indonesia, the Philippines—and the four Asian newly industrializing economies—Taiwan, Korea, Singapore, and Hong Kong—has also been growing rapidly since 1986,[6] and these represent export markets as important as the US market.

Beyond the apparent growth in intraregional trade, there has been increasing intraregional foreign direct investment (FDI), much of it going into or coming from the United States, the European Union (EU), and Japan. Intra-EC FDI grew faster than intra-EC trade in the 1980s; the stock of intra-Asian FDI grew faster than intra-Asian trade in the 1980s. The US and Canadian economies have been deeply integrated through investment for some time. Two-thirds of the stock of Canadian outward FDI is in the United States, while Canada represents one-fifth of the stock of total US outward FDI (UN 1992, 34–35). It is expected that NAFTA will increase investment in Mexico by US corporations looking to increase their Mexican production facilities to service the North American market.[7]

In sum, greater integration of regional economies has coincided not only with increased intraregional trade in goods but also with increasing levels of intraregional direct investment, including increasing intrafirm investment by transnationals. Increases in FDI have been both a product of regional arrangements and a significant factor in motivating them.

If some of the most rapid growth in world trade in the postwar years has occurred where countries neighbor one another, one can thus argue that the new regional trade arrangements have contributed to the more dynamic parts of world trade growth. Preferential trade arrangements be-

---

accounted for 61 percent of total EC trade in goods, 41 percent of total trade in goods in Asia, and 35 percent of total trade in goods in North America. Nierop and DeVos (1988) discuss the movement toward regional integration between 1950 and 1980. See Zerby (1990) and Pomfret (1988) for discussion of whether the trading system is moving toward regional trading blocs. According to WTO (1995, 55), there is no statistical support for the view that there is a regionalization of world trade or for the emergence of three trading blocs centered in Asia, Europe, and North America. See also the discussion of these issues in Frankel 1996.

5. In 1994 the United States exported $114.3 billion to Canada, $53.5 billion to Japan, and $50.8 billion to Mexico (IMF, *Direction of Trade Statistics Yearbook*, 1995, 436–38).

6. From $37.8 billion of exports in 1986 to $134.1 billion of exports in 1994 (see IMF, *Direction of Trade Statistics Yearbook*, 1995). This compares with 1994 Japanese exports to the United States of $118.7 billion.

7. There is already a striking amount of intrafirm trade between Mexico and the United States. The United Nations (1992, 2) reports that nearly 40 percent of Mexico's trade with the United States is between affiliates of US transnational corporations (see also Stern and Hummels 1990).

tween neighboring states may violate the GATT principle of nondiscrimination, but they may also have been an important positive factor in postwar growth of trade.

Explaining Strong Trade Growth

No single explanation is widely accepted for the strong trade growth documented above, although its resilience is key to any discussion of the possible impacts of the Uruguay Round. It is often argued that trade grows faster than income because the income elasticity of demand for imports is greater than one in most economies (Houthakker and Magee 1969). But it also follows from this that trade growth should be more volatile than income growth, rising more in expansions and falling more in recessions. But for major postwar recessions, as in 1981–82, such predictions have not been borne out: trade growth did not fall more than proportionally to income.

Rather, recession apparently has affected global trade growth only marginally. Table 2.5 reports growth rates for world trade volumes and growth rates of US GNP, which is often used as a proxy for growth performance in the wider global economy. Interestingly, some of the highest trade volume growth rates have occurred in years when underlying real GNP growth in the world's largest economy has not been that strong (such as in the late 1980s). Even when the US economy has downturned, world trade growth has remained positive; only in the major 1974 and 1981 global recessions did it turn negative.

Another explanation sometimes offered is that rapid internationalization of investment and production has made trade relatively recession-resistant. Today a large percentage of world trade in manufactures is intrafirm,[8] and perhaps more recession resistant, since foreign activities tend to be the more rapidly growing portion of global corporate activity for many North American, European, and Japanese multinationals.

One further argument sometimes offered stresses that the past success of tariff liberalization in the GATT and the concomitant long-term commitment to tariff liberalization has bred expectations of continually expanding world trade under an ever more liberalizing multilateral system. That is, expectations of future liberalization have tended to carry trade growth forward, even in recession, as producers in one country continue to search out new markets abroad for the longer term.

---

8. Julius (1990) discusses the growing importance of intrafirm trade. Data reported by Whitchard (1988) indicate that around 80 percent of US exports of manufactures are internal to the firm, and around 40 percent of imports are within the firm. OECD data indicate that in 1989 over one-third of US merchandise trade was intrafirm (Fujimura 1994, 33).

Table 2.5 Global trade growth and macroeconomic performance, 1950–94

Year	Growth in world trade volume (percentage)	Real GNP growth in the US economy (percentage)
1950–55		4.3
1955–60		2.2
1960–65	7.2	4.5
1963–72[a]	9.2	4.0[a]
1973	10.9	5.8
1974	7.0	−0.6
1975	−3.9	−1.1
1976	11.0	5.4
1977	4.9	5.5
1978	5.9	4.8
1979	6.7	3.2
1980	4.2	−0.2
1981	2.0	2.0
1982	−1.0	−2.5
1983	3.0	3.6
1984	9.6	6.8
1985	3.5	3.4
1986	2.5	2.7
1987	5.8	3.7
1988	7.0	4.5
1989	7.3	2.5
1990	5.4	1.2
1991	2.6	−0.6
1992	4.4	2.3
1993	−1.2	3.1
1994	9.1	4.1

a. Compounded annual rates of change.

Sources: IMF, *World Economic Outlook*, 1982, 1990, 1991, 1995; UNCTAD, *Handbook of International Trade and Development Statistics 1986 Supplement, 1989 Supplement, 1992, 1993, 1995*, table 2.1; OECD (1966, 20).

In the seven GATT negotiating rounds preceding the Uruguay Round, tariffs on manufactured products in most OECD countries have continually been reduced. In the industrialized countries, most of these tariffs have been bound at successively lower levels.[9] The extent of the resulting reductions in US tariffs is summarized in table 2.6. US tariffs had already been cut by 33 percent from the Smoot-Hawley levels of 1930 before the GATT rounds started. By the end of the Tokyo Round, US tariffs were 21 percent of their 1930 levels, with spikes in the tariff profile (such as

---

9. Following the implementation of the Tokyo Round tariff cuts, tariffs on manufactures averaged 6.0 percent in the European Community, 5.4 percent in Japan, and 4.5 percent in the United States (World Bank, *World Development Report 1987*, 135). For evaluations of the impacts of the Tokyo Round tariff reductions, see Cline et al. (1978), Deardorff and Stern (1986), and Whalley (1985).

Table 2.6 US tariff reductions by round, 1934–79 (percent)

GATT round	Dutiable imports subjected to reduction[a]	Cut in reduced tariffs[a]	Cut in all duties[a]	Remaining duties as share of 1930s[b] tariffs
Pre-GATT, bilateral negotiations, 1934–47	63.9	44.0	33.2	66.8
Geneva, 1947	53.6	35.0	21.1	52.7
Annecy, 1949	5.6	35.1	1.9[c]	51.7
Torquay, 1950–51	11.7	26.0	3.0[c]	50.1
Geneva, 1955–56	16.0	15.6[c]	2.5	48.9
Dillon Round, Geneva, 1961–62	20.0	12.0[c]	2.4	47.7
Kennedy Round, 1964–67	79.2[d]	45.5[c]	36.0[e]	30.5
Tokyo Round, 1974–79	n.a.	n.a.	29.6[f]	21.2

n.a. = not available.

a. Weighted averages. Weights used are 1939 imports for rows 1 and 2, 1964 imports for Kennedy Round, 1976 imports for Tokyo Round, and, for the others, the imports of the "latest year available at the time of the Tariff Commission's post-negotiation report" (Evans 1971, 12).

b. This ignores inflation and structural changes in trade. Calculated from the figures in the previous column.

c. Approximations only. These are estimates based on the other two columns. This procedure requires the simplifying assumption that the average initial duty on items which received cuts was equal to that of items which did not receive cuts.

d. Refers to nonagricultural imports from industrial countries only. Mineral fuels are also excluded. The figure for total imports is 64 percent (US Office of the Special Representation for Trade Negotiations 1967, iii).

e. Excludes mineral fuels (i.e., petroleum and petroleum products, basically) and agricultural products. Still, we estimate that this figure is a fairly close estimate of the total percentage cut. Cuts on agricultural products were about 33 percent (Baldwin 1970, 163; almost all of US agricultural imports fit under Baldwin's item 14, for which tariffs fall from 9 percent to 6 percent). As for mineral fuels, there were no duty reductions at all, but their importance in the calculation of the overall average cut would be low because it is a very low tariff item in the first place (2–3 percent in 1964; Baldwin 1970, 163). We have estimated that the weight of mineral fuels in total duty collections would have been less than 3.5 percent in 1964.

f. Excludes petroleum and petroleum products, which were not subjected to reductions, except for some insignificant items. The importance of this omission is relatively insignificant because ad valorem equivalent tariff rates have fallen to about one-fourth of their 1970 level due to rising prices (or to less than 1 percent).

Sources: Lavergne (1983, 32–33); for 1934–47, USTC (1949, 22–23); 1949–51, Evans (1971, 12); 1955–62, first column, Evans (1971, 12); 1955–62, third column, Evans (1971, 13–14); 1964–67, Preeg (1970, 208 and 239); 1974–79, US Congressional Budget Office (July 1979, 9).

apparel) accounting for a large portion of remaining significant trade barriers.

Just how important tariff liberalization has been for trade flows and improved well-being in quantitative terms remains, perhaps surprisingly, a topic of debate. Numerical counterfactual modeling research (Shoven and Whalley 1992) concludes that the economic costs of protection, and hence the benefit of tariff reductions, are relatively small. But in assessing the impacts of tariff liberalization on trade, this sort of research ignores macroeconomic feedback effects on income growth of the type responsible for the large trade declines in the 1930s, and so such results might be discounted. But the relatively small size of the effects remains.

In a general equilibrium study of the effects of tariff retaliation that also ignores macro and growth feedback effects, Hamilton and Whalley (1983) suggested that a full-scale trade war between large trading blocs, such as the United States and the European Community, might involve retaliatory tariffs reaching several hundreds of percent. But in such a case trade flows would only be reduced by one-third to one-half and real incomes by less than 5 percent.[10] These suggest that moving from tariffs much higher than those that prevailed at the end of the 1940s to zero tariffs (lower even than current tariffs) might double world trade but, more importantly, would provide only a smaller stimulus to real income. This suggests that factors other than trade have been key to postwar economic growth but that this growth in income may have been the major force behind the ensuing trade growth.

The fact that both real trade volumes and trade shares in GDP have increased in the postwar years suggests that something besides barrier reduction has been the driving force behind trade growth, especially when one considers that high tariffs remain in a few product areas where trade growth has continued to occur. The feedback effects discussed above could account for this. But it could also be the contribution of a stable system of trade rules in stimulating new market-penetrating efforts from abroad and/or trade-generating foreign direct investment.

While tariff cuts resulting from GATT rounds may not have been the major factor driving the trade expansion, they were nonetheless significant, and they might not have been possible without a General Agreement on Tariffs and Trade. While little room remains for further industrial-country tariff cutting in manufactures, future negotiations building on Uruguay Round commitments to convert agricultural protection to tariffs (albeit at high levels) and on developing-country tariff bindings offer the prospect of further improvement in global economic performance.[11]

---

10. A recent, more empirically based, calculation by Perroni and Whalley (1994) puts this loss at around 6 percent of global product.

11. Prior to the conclusion of the Uruguay Round, Stoeckel, Pearce, and Banks (1990, 10) argued that "tariffs have become largely irrelevant in today's system of protection, which depends on subsidies, bilateral 'voluntary' restraints and 'unfair trade' rules . . . So the GATT has become a victim of its own tariff negotiating success." It remains to be seen if this will remain the case when the Uruguay Round results are implemented. Also, see Laird and Yeats (1987) and Erzan and Karsenty (1989) for discussion of developing-country tariff levels.

System Architecture

We earlier noted the paradox that strong trade growth has coincided with an erosion of the multilateral principles designed to govern and promote world trade. The principles were enshrined in the GATT, which was first negotiated in 1947. At that time, the GATT and the global trading system could be considered one and the same. That is no longer the case.

The term "system" as applied to global trade implies a coordinated and well-organized structure of rules and institutions that oversee and regulate trade. Like other public policy subsystems (i.e., the tax system, the welfare system), the term suggests consistency and forethought in design, a guiding hand to assist in its inner workings, and self-correcting feedback mechanisms helping it change. But to think of the trading system of today, in these terms, is misleading.

Over the postwar years the global trading system has evolved to become less an integrated whole that sets out and enforces rules for world trade and more of a patchwork quilt of overlapping and seemingly inconsistent arrangements (box 2.1).

The global trading system of today consists of four distinct subsystems, each of which interacts with the others:

- The first comprises the multilateral trade rules set out in the GATT in 1947 and now embodied in the charter of the new WTO. It also includes multilateral tariff reductions and additional arrangements negotiated in the various GATT rounds preceding the Uruguay Round.

- The second subsystem captures derogations from GATT rules and principles that are in some way accommodated in the multilateral system but are either formally GATT-incompatible or flagrantly so but never legally established as such. This includes special arrangements covering trade in textiles, agriculture, and other products, as well as the use of special instruments such as voluntary export restraints that are inconsistent with GATT rules.

- The third subsystem captures regional arrangements in the system (both bilateral and plurilateral), set out in various regional free trade area and customs union agreements. Such arrangements are often in open conflict with the nondiscrimination principles embodied in the GATT and has grown sharply in recent years with the North American Free Trade Agreement (NAFTA), the Canada-US Free Trade Agreement, European integration arrangements, and various Latin American and Asian trade arrangements.[12]

---

12. This growth in regionalism is discussed in detail in chapter 6. Between 1990 and 1994, 33 regional integration agreements were notified to the GATT (WTO 1995, 1).

Box 2.1 Key elements in the global trading system

Multilateral trade rules and disciplines limiting country uses of border measures. These are largely reflected in the original General Agreement on Tariffs and Trade (GATT), now in the charter of the World Trade Organization (WTO). There are 38 GATT articles centered on a few key principles: most-favored nation status (MFN), national treatment, transparency of border measures. There have been eight negotiating rounds concluded since 1947—the latest (Uruguay Round) was in effect as of 1 January 1995. The secretariat in Geneva assists in negotiations and in settling trade disputes.

Derogations from GATT rules and disciplines. These include special trade rules for sectors: agriculture (1947, 1955, 1957), textiles (1962), steel (1977, 1984), and computer chips (1986), as well as voluntary export restraints and other gray-area measures that operate in violation of GATT principles. Threatened unilateral actions are also derogations if they would be inconsistent with GATT rules (e.g., section 301).

Regional trade arrangements negotiated separately from GATT arrangements (although most are notified to GATT). These include free trade areas, customs unions, trade preferences for small developing countries, and trade arrangements between developing countries. Examples include EC (1957), EFTA (1959), US-Canada arrangements (1965, 1989), EC-Lomé (1962), CBI (1988), Andean Pact (1962), Australia-New Zealand (1988), Europe–Single Market (1992), US-Mexico (1987, 1989), NAFTA (1994), and the European Union (1994).

Arrangements covering various **issues related to trade.** Most issues go beyond border measures and involve nonconventional negotiating approaches and arrangements. Examples of issues include distribution systems in Japan, ownership concentration (*keiretsu* in Japan, *chaebol* in Korea), and restrictive business practices. Current high-profile issues include trade and environment linkages, competition policy, and trade and human rights linkages. Non-GATT negotiating approaches and arrangements include the US-Japan Structural Impediments Initiative (SII), the Japan-ASEAN Initiative, and bilateral pressure on higher-income developing countries.

■ The fourth subsystem contains what we term nontraditional trade arrangements and covers a number of areas where trade and other policies not covered by the original GATT disciplines interact: domestic distribution systems, competition and antitrust, investment, the environment, and others.

All four subsystems, together with unilateral trade arrangements specified under domestic law, provide the overall framework under which world trade now takes place.

This picture of today's trade policy system is not what was intended when trade and other multilateral institutions were established just after World War II. Indeed, the initial vision was never fully realized: a broad-ranging International Trade Organization (ITO) had been planned that was to set rules governing the use of trade-restricting measures by governments, along with a global institutional structure to oversee them. But the charter for the ITO negotiated in Havana in 1947 was never ratified, and the GATT, a more temporary arrangement seen initially as a stepping-stone to the more permanent arrangement, replaced it. The GATT has instead become the postwar institutional structure for the conduct of world trade.

The original idea behind the GATT was that all signatory countries would agree to broad principles governing the use of trade-restricting measures and on this basis build a system of rights and obligations between the parties to the agreement. Among these principles were nondiscrimination (referred to somewhat counterintuitively as most-favored nation, or MFN, treatment) and national treatment. Set out in GATT Article I, MFN is aimed at preventing discrimination among suppliers at national borders, and national treatment, set out in Article III, is aimed at preventing discrimination against foreign products beyond the national border. These two principles remain today as the cornerstones of the multilateral system of rules.

A further objective of the GATT was the negotiation of global trade liberalization through reciprocal exchanges of concessions (extended more broadly through MFN) and the creation of schedules of tariff rates and any bindings and reductions agreed to by countries in multilateral rounds of trade negotiations. As noted earlier, the seven GATT negotiating rounds before the Uruguay Round successfully reduced and bound tariffs, although they were tariffs largely used by industrial countries and typically used for imports of manufactured products.[13] Thus the multilateral trade subsystem also came to embody the negotiating process, as manifested in the GATT negotiating rounds.

But from 1947 on, the other three subsystems in the wider global trading system grew steadily in importance, reflecting an increasingly inconsistent application of GATT principles (table 2.7). By the launch of the Uruguay Round in 1986, there were a number of derogations in trade arrangements that were clearly inconsistent with nondiscrimination, national treatment, and transparency. Agriculture led the way, with exceptions already in the system in 1947 and since taken further (as in the US waiver of 1955 and Europe's Common Agricultural Policy). Other derogations include special trade rules for textiles, which grew from temporary restrictions in 1961 affecting only a small number of countries into the wider Multi-Fiber Arrangement (MFA), and discriminatory voluntary export restraints (VERs), introduced in the 1970s and 1980s, that at various times restricted trade in steel, autos, footwear, electronics, computer chips, cutlery, and

---

13. Since its formation in 1947, the following rounds of multilateral trade negotiations have taken place under the GATT: Geneva (1947), Annecy (1949), Torquay (1950–51), Geneva (1956), Dillon (1959–61), Kennedy (1964–67), and Tokyo (1973–79). Uruguay (1986–93) was the eighth round. Through these rounds, tariff levels on manufactures fell from approximately 40 percent in the 1940s to about 5 percent in the late 1980s.

Table 2.7 Evolution of the global trading system, 1947–90

Subsystem	1947	1965	1980	1990
Multilateral rules	GATT	Kennedy Round	Tokyo Round	Brussels ministerial, Uruguay Round
Derogations	Agriculture	Agriculture Textiles	Agriculture Textiles VERs	Agriculture Textiles VERs Unilateralism
Regional arrangements		EC-EFTA	EC-EFTA Lomé/CBI US-Canada (Autos) Developing country arrangements	EC-EFTA/1992 NAFTA Lomé/CBI Japan/ASEAN Australia-New Zealand
Nontraditional trade-related arrangements			US-Japan conflicts	Investment Labor mobility Distribution system Competition policy SII Environment/trade Bilateral pressure

other products. And in the late 1980s, a new potential derogation was added to the list in the form of unilateral retaliatory measures, as in the special 301 and super 301 provisions of the 1988 US Trade Act. Economically powerful countries used such potentially GATT-inconsistent measures to get countries to remove or modify specific barriers that the larger powers found to be in restraint of trade or that were otherwise ruled in domestic forums as unacceptable (such as violations of domestic intellectual property protection).

Regional trade arrangements also run counter to the nondiscrimination principle of the GATT, although these arrangements generally have less negative connotations than system derogations. This is because regional trade agreements can create as well as divert trade, and so their overall impact on world economic performance is unclear. Regional arrangements also may interact positively with the multilateral trading system in that liberalization through a regional agreement can apply competitive pressures for similar liberalization in the other, and vice versa. Derogations, in contrast, tend either to prevent liberalization or reintroduce and even tighten protection in areas where barrier reduction had previously occurred.

In 1947 regional arrangements were not envisaged as a central part of the postwar trading system, although provisions were included in the GATT to accommodate them. A multilateral approach to security and other concerns was considered to be the way to proceed. However, from the late 1950s on, regional arrangements grew in importance—through the

Treaty of Rome (establishing the European Community), the European Free Trade Association (EFTA), numerous regional developing country arrangements (in Central America, East Africa, the Andean Pact, and elsewhere), and more recently through the Canada-US agreement, NAFTA, European integration, and many other agreements, especially in Latin America. In addition, each regional arrangement differs substantially in structure and scope from all others.

All these regional arrangements have been legally accommodated within the GATT system through a liberal application of GATT Article XXIV, which allows regional trade groups to form if certain conditions are met, even though they may violate the spirit of MFN. GATT working parties, established to examine each of these arrangements, have consistently avoided making any clear determinations of consistency with Article XXIV.[14] A further complication is that the most recent regional arrangements deal with issues the GATT does not cover, such as labor mobility and financial services. One attraction of such arrangements for the parties involved is that they can be negotiated more quickly than new multilateral arrangements in these areas could be. The net effect has been that consistent application of the key principles of the multilateral system has suffered further. As emphasized above, the implications of this for trade and income growth remain unclear, and in some cases they could be positive.

The inclusion of "nontraditional" issues in the trading system is the most recent development in the system's evolution. This subsystem encompasses nonconventional trade negotiations and treaty arrangements (the US-Japan Structural Impediments Initiative, or SII, for instance); emerging issues not yet under formal multilateral discussion (environmental-trade linkages, competition policy); and a range of non-GATT trade-related issues such as the supposed exclusionary business practices of a number of countries (*keiretsu* in Japan, *chaebol* in Korea), trade-restricting effects of domestic distribution systems (again in Japan), coordination of the regulation of financial institutions (i.e., Europe 1992), investment practices (in the Canada-US arrangement), and temporary entry for businesspersons (again in the Canada-US arrangement). There are no clear multilateral rules in the GATT addressing these instruments, areas, and issues, though all are trade-related. But the political pressures to deal with such aspects have been so strong that small-group negotiations have evolved to discuss them.

---

14. According to Hart (1987), in no case has a working party ruled that a notified free trade area violated Article XXIV. Typical working party reports resulting from consideration of each case have been generally noncommittal, with each participant preferring to "reserve their GATT rights" (329). Furthermore, no ruling on the compatibility of either the European Community or the Common Agricultural Policy with Article XXIV or other GATT articles was made when the working party examined the Treaty of Rome (despite the United Kingdom's strong protests at the time).

As the nontraditional component of the global trade system grows in the latter half of the 1990s, the borders that have defined the trading system will continue to break down. Worker and human rights and the use of trade policy measures to uphold them is one such area. The discussion of "social dumping" is another: that is, low wages and low levels of social programs are argued to have deleterious effects on the importing countries' trade performance that should be offset with trade barriers.

Behind these four subsystems of the global trading system lie domestic legal and administrative structures for collecting tariffs and antidumping and countervailing duties as well as for setting product and safety standards, rules controlling trade in toxic and other waste products, and many other laws and regulations affecting trade.

Together these make up the global trading system; in other words, the system comprises more than just the multilateral rules and disciplines that the GATT (and now the WTO) represent. The postwar years have seen efforts to harmonize some of these other elements in the GATT and elsewhere: common customs nomenclatures, limits on lengthy or overly complex border procedures, and codes on the use of antidumping and subsidies. But despite these efforts, there has been substantial diversity in practice.

Linkages between these subsystems have also grown. As we noted earlier, regional agreements are intertwined with nontraditional issues because smaller forums can deal with these issues much more quickly than a multilateral forum can.[15] The responsiveness of the nontraditional subsystem to emerging issues coincides with increasing inconsistency in the larger global system but also gives it a higher profile. In fact, as the relative rigidity of the multilateral system, with its ever-wider country participation, has increased and it thus becomes more cumbersome to address new issues within it, the multilateral system has helped elevate the profiles of the other three subsystems. The multilateral component of the system no longer dominates it.

System Erosion

We describe the spreading inconsistency in the application of GATT principles as "erosion."[16] But although the word implies something inherently

---

15. Bilateral US-Canada negotiations that concluded agreements in the services and financial services in advance of any GATT accords are an example. The discussions on environment-trade links in the NAFTA negotiations are a further example.

16. Malmgren (1983, 192–99) devotes a substantial section to "Erosion of the GATT system." Camps and Diebold (1986) also discuss erosion. Bergsten and Cline (1983) and Commonwealth Secretariat (1982) have lengthy descriptions of the growth of protectionism in the system and the various sectoral arrangements, VERs, and orderly marketing arrangements of

undesirable, it is not our intent to paint the development in this light. Rather, we mean that the trading system has evolved with a progressively inconsistent application of nondiscrimination, multilateral rather than regional or bilateral negotiations, transparent trade measures (with heaviest reliance on bound tariffs), and national treatment. Erosion is reflected in special bilateral or regional arrangements (including bilateral negotiation under threat of unilateral action); the use of nontransparent measures, typically outside of GATT rules (such as VERs); weak enforcement of GATT rules through dispute settlement and other procedures; and the resort to newer forms of protection over which only lax multilateral disciplines apply (in part, to replace protection surrendered in previous multilateral negotiations).

Erosion in one place leads to accretion in another: though the multilateral system may have lost its preeminent place in the system, regional arrangements and derogations have gained ground. As we indicate above, however, this evolution need not necessarily be adverse for global economic performance. Nor should this erosion be taken as the only noteworthy development in the trading system: we have already pointed out that significant liberalization occurred simultaneously.

How could the multilateral system, designed with such high ambitions, have come to such a pass? Perhaps no international or other rule-based regime could fully deal with all the unforeseen problems and issues with which it might be confronted. Expecting principles written in 1947 to endure for all time has, not surprisingly, proved unrealistic. This is not to say the attempt had no merit, since it may have slowed or weakened the protection that might otherwise have crept in—that is, more and worse things could have happened. But the fact remains that the world has changed, and the wider global trading system has evolved to accommodate the new developments.

But there are other elements in an explanation of the system's evolution. In a multilateral system, all countries have an incentive to announce a strong commitment to agreed system principles, and they hope that everyone else will comply and seek to benefit from the actions of others (under MFN in tariff-cutting negotiations, for example). But countries remain prepared to act pragmatically on their own when necessary. Such a system becomes characterized by strong statements of joint commitment but weaker participant resolve to uphold these commitments.

---

the 1970s—all of which we term erosion. These pieces also refer to the ineffectiveness of the GATT to deal with these developments in the trading system. Even the GATT 1982 ministerial declaration acknowledged this erosion by including statements such as, "they [the Contracting Parties] recognize that the multilateral trading system . . . is seriously endangered," and "disregard of GATT disciplines has increased," and also, "Import restrictions have increased and a growing proportion have been applied outside GATT disciplines" (GATT, *Basic Instruments and Selected Documents*, 29th Supp., 1983, 9).

Another part of the explanation has been the role of security concerns and hegemony within the system in the postwar years. While this is undoubtedly somewhat overstated, the United States filled the role of a hegemonic power in the early postwar years, seeking to solidify a security alliance with Europe against a perceived communist threat and to maintain a US military presence in Europe.[17] The system of trade rules became one way of demonstrating commitment to the alliance and strengthening security arrangements. In such a world, the formation of a jointly agreed rule regime can become more important than its substance, and its evolution away from original system principles may seem of less consequence.

Yet another factor in the system's evolution has been the need to respond to challenges posed by world economic and trade growth. From the 1950s on, Japan has grown rapidly, joined subsequently by the Asian newly industrializing economies and more recently by the ASEAN countries. If strictly upheld, the principle of nondiscrimination in the system would mean that importing countries could not selectively restrain exports from these countries, even in the face of strong political pressures at home resisting adjustment. Put another way, the forms that developments in the global economy have taken in the postwar years have also generated political challenges to key system principles; hence the departures we have seen from these principles are perhaps not that surprising.

As the various parts of the trading system generate policy responses inconsistent with the original GATT principles, one could argue that this is cause for great alarm. For, if the original principles are sound and past attempts to uphold them retarded bad outcomes such as higher or continued protection, then the attempt should continue, even if in the long-run ineffective, in order to achieve short-run gains.

Counterarguments can be made that GATT principles have not kept protectionist impulses at bay, and there is scant empirical evidence to support the contention that but for the GATT, the growing inconsistencies of the postwar years would not otherwise have occurred. Thus, nondiscrimination is thought to be desirable because it prevents trade diversion, but a high set of nondiscriminatory tariffs retards trade more than a low set of discriminatory tariffs. And while multilateral negotiation in the GATT, based on reciprocity, can lower barriers, it can also cause countries to hang on to barriers in order to have something to negotiate.

The growing gap between the trading system as it has evolved and the GATT system that emerged in the 1940s was a major impetus for the Uruguay Round, which was to achieve "system strengthening," raising the question of whether this meant returning the system to GATT prin-

---

17. Keohane (1984) and Ikenberry (1989) discuss the role the United States played in developing institutions after the war. For discussion of the decline of American hegemony, see Calleo (1987) and Whitman (1975).

ciples and making them clearer in their application or whether it implied a strengthening of the more ad hoc system that in reality applied.[18]

This distinction between a system based on principles and rules and a more neutral use of the term "system" as denoting simply a group of accumulated trade agreements is also, in our view, key for the way one thinks about the global trading system and how it may evolve beyond the Uruguay Round. If the global trading system is largely pictured in terms of GATT-based multilateral trade rules, it appears natural for global trade policy to focus on further multilateral negotiations to strengthen and enlarge it. But reexamining the implicit system goals and principles might better serve system performance.

This distinction is especially important if system goals are thought of as reflecting social concerns of a given period that may change as times change. When the GATT was negotiated, multilateralism was linked with the notion of equality among nations and was deemed important for the prevention of future world wars.[19] It was also thought to make country-specific trade retaliation more difficult and hence help prevent a return to 1930s-style retaliatory protectionism. The acceptance of these goals reflected events of the time, the memory of which has since receded.

Multilateralism has changed. Launching and implementing GATT negotiating rounds has become a lengthy process.[20] By the time negotiations are completed, some of the issues put on the agenda at the outset may no longer be of concern, and emerging issues, while agreed to be important, may not be easy to introduce if the agenda has already been set. It can be difficult (and was in the Uruguay Round) to exploit the give-and-take of so many negotiating partners across a wide range of negotiating issues. Also, if individual countries have blocking power in multilateral rule-writing

---

18. According to the ministerial declaration on the Uruguay Round, one of the objectives was to "strengthen the role of GATT, improve the multilateral trading system based on the principles and rules of GATT and bring about a wider coverage of world trade under agreed, effective and enforceable multilateral disciplines" (GATT press release, "News of the Uruguay Round," October 1986, 2).

19. This view was strongly held by US Secretary of State Cordell Hull and other officials. According to Dam (1970, 12), "Hull's philosophy was that free, non-discriminatory trade was essential to world peace." Jackson (1969, 36–40) documents a number of speeches by US officials, including the president, which expressly underscored the need for multilateral institutions to avoid the kind of economic situations that lead to war.

20. After the Tokyo Round was concluded in 1979, the first serious calls for a new round were not made until the 1982 GATT ministerial meeting. It then took until 1986 to gather the necessary support and build political will to launch the Uruguay Round in September 1986. The Uruguay Round was intended only to last four years, but it took seven to complete. The textiles and clothing restrictions are to be phased out over 10 years after the WTO enters into force, resulting in a period of 26 years from the end of the Tokyo Round to the end of the Uruguay Round implementation period.

negotiations, it may mean that subgroups of countries possibly willing and able to take on more obligations might be unable to do so.

While small countries repeatedly reiterate the virtues of nondiscrimination because of the insurance it ought to provide against selective treatment by big countries, the reality is quite different. Throughout the 1980s, many small countries were repeatedly pressured to make concessions bilaterally to larger powers on such matters as intellectual property protection and to agree to VERs. The final stages of the Uruguay Round demonstrated the smaller countries' lack of leverage as it became a two-power negotiation between the United States and the European Union, with results unveiled to the others days before the expiration deadline.

If one views the global trading system as an accumulation of trade arrangements of varying scope and participation, the integrity of the system relative to its organizing principles becomes less of an issue. The system becomes a patchwork quilt of negotiated trade arrangements, handed down through the generations, which within its framework may be altered to pursue specific objectives. It becomes a focal point for countries to pursue common goals. Its contribution is to be evaluated by its outputs (what it has achieved), not its inputs (its organizing principles). Then the system can be recast, based on the answers to the questions, How does the trading system perform relative to its goals and how can its output be improved?

These goals probably cannot be definitively fixed; they may be security-oriented in the aftermath of war or focused on market access when security concerns are no longer paramount (as with the end of the Cold War). Thus, system goals should be periodically reassessed and restated, and the implications for redesign drawn.[21] Refocusing trade policy within the inherited structure may be more important for the post–Uruguay Round trading system than attempts to bolster existing principles such as MFN would be.

---

21. The discussion of the roles of the World Bank and the International Monetary Fund at the G-7 summit in 1994, 50 years after their establishment, confirmed this need for reassessment.

3

The Uruguay Round: Negotiations and Agreements

When the Uruguay Round was launched in 1986, it was seen as the most far-reaching GATT negotiating effort yet undertaken. One of its main aims was to stem the erosion in the multilateral system by dealing with long-standing issues in agriculture and textiles as well as the "new" issues of services, investment, and intellectual property, which had never been addressed in a multilateral forum.[1] The round thus went far beyond the tariff-cutting exercises of earlier rounds, both in the range of issues it tackled and in the much larger number of country participants (there were 117 by the end of the round, of which perhaps 30 to 35 were active in working groups). The round also sought to improve dispute settlement and reexamine key GATT articles.[2]

Initially, the United States focused on services because this was seen as an area of emerging US comparative advantage (and partially equated at the time with US interests in high technology) in which there were no trade rules. The United States subsequently focused its efforts more on agriculture, with a primary focus on Europe's Common Agricultural Pol-

---

1. According to the ministerial declaration, "Negotiations shall aim to (i) bring about further liberalization and expansion of world trade to the benefit of all countries . . . including the improvement of access to markets by the reduction and elimination of tariffs, quantitative restrictions and other non-tariff measures and obstacles" (GATT press release, "News of the Uruguay Round," October 1986, 2).

2. Low (1993, 209–37) discusses the evolution of the Uruguay Round, from the preparatory phase through the Draft Final Act (the Dunkel text). For a detailed examination of the Uruguay Round see Stewart (1993). Schott (1994) also evaluates the Uruguay Round agreements.

icy (CAP). Other agricultural exporters, such as Australia and the Cairns Group, a coalition of developed and developing country agricultural exporters, supported the United States in this endeavor.[3] Larger developing countries (Brazil, India) initially wanted to deal with unresolved backlog issues—such as voluntary export restraints (VERs), agriculture, and textiles—before moving on to new issues such as services. Midsize and smaller countries, influential during the launch of the round, strongly supported system strengthening, particularly in dispute settlement and through a reexamination of the GATT articles. Developing countries generally supported efforts to eliminate textile restrictions, although with varying vigor, depending upon whether they were perceived to be high- or low-cost suppliers, whether they appeared to already have significant allocation of quotas, and whether their quotas were binding. The large array of issues was thought beneficial, as it would allow for crossover bargaining.

The round was scheduled to conclude in 1990 after a promised midterm review in 1988, which was to yield an "early harvest." Little of substance in terms of new market access agreements (including agriculture and textiles and clothing) emerged in 1988,[4] although the review influenced the direction of the rest of the round. The December 1990 ministerial meeting in Brussels, which was supposed to be the last, failed to achieve agreed results, with agriculture being one of the greatest problems. The round continued on toward a final deadline of 15 December 1993, the date on which the negotiating authority granted by the US Congress expired. US-EC differences over agriculture persisted until the final few days of the negotiation, when decisions in nonagricultural areas were adopted, largely as agreed some 18 months earlier in the so-called Dunkel text, along with the final agricultural decisions (*The World Economy*, 1993, 16, no. 2: 237–60).

The negotiations took place against a background of spreading regional trade arrangements involving the larger powers (EC 1992, the European Economic Area, and NAFTA) and in the face of threats of unilateral actions by these same powers (i.e., US section 301 cases and US and EC threats to graduate participants in the Generalized System of Preferences, or GSP, program). It is thus not surprising that participants openly and repeatedly raised the prospect of failure during the negotiations in Geneva.

---

3. The Cairns Group consists of Argentina, Australia, Brazil, Canada, Chile, Colombia, Hungary, Indonesia, Malaysia, New Zealand, the Philippines, Thailand, and Uruguay.

4. In fact, the midterm review decisions had to be held over until a further meeting in April 1989. In hindsight, the midterm review difficulties were a precursor to the difficulties encountered in the Brussels ministerial meeting in 1990 (see appendix B).

The Negotiating Process

The hallmark of the GATT system of rounds has been its multicountry negotiations, conducted within the wider framework of agreed-upon multilateral rules and disciplines. The continuity of this negotiating process and major-power commitment to GATT rules were at stake during the Uruguay Round. In some ways, the process that the round came to represent became almost as important as the round itself.

The Uruguay Round repeatedly encountered difficulties in reaching a conclusion—so much so that there was substantial doubt right up to the final stages about whether a conclusion would be reached at all. (Appendix B outlines the chronology of the round, from the launch at Punta del Este in 1986 to the final ministerial meeting in Marrakesh in April 1994.)

The process raised a number of questions. Will multilateral negotiating rounds continue in the World Trade Organization (WTO) and would such negotiations further global trade liberalization? Did the Uruguay Round reach the outer limits of the number and type of issues and participants that such negotiations could accommodate, and will mini-rounds, more narrowly focused, succeed it? Will permanent negotiation eventually characterize the WTO?

The inability to conclude the Uruguay Round on schedule at the 1990 Brussels ministerial meeting remains as one of the more significant setbacks in the round. Talks stalemated over the level of agricultural support and became discordant over export subsidies and internal border measures; at the time these were represented as the major obstacles to concluding the round. The *Wall Street Journal* characterized the dilemma as EC intransigence pitted against the liberalizing zeal of the United States and the Cairns Group of countries, which were portrayed as relative free traders in agriculture.[5] The European Community, for its part, termed US proposals for major reductions or elimination of subsidies in agriculture "cynical" because the US Congress would not, at the end of the day, be willing to implement them.

A number of factors lay behind these difficulties.[6] From 1947 on, as tariffs fell, successive GATT negotiating rounds de-emphasized tariff cutting and moved more toward rule writing, despite the fact that tariff cutting is easier. This is because countries negotiate bilaterally on continuous variables—that is, tariff rates on different products—and subse-

---

5. "The global talks that were intended to guide the world into a new era of trade and prosperity all but collapsed, and only a major political initiative by President Bush and other world leaders can save them. . . . The talks tumbled over the European Community's refusal to make deep cuts in farm subsidies" (*Wall Street Journal*, 10 December 1990).

6. There were many difficulties in even getting the eighth round off the ground in 1986, and that it happened at all was largely due to the efforts of a group of small and midsize countries (Whalley 1989b, appendix B).

quently extend agreed tariff reductions multilaterally. Rule-writing negotiations are more difficult because agreement on a particular rule is hard to trade against concessions on other rules. And since rule writing is consensual, this change in the focus of successive GATT negotiations has given more leverage to groups that want to block new rules. In the Uruguay Round, only one of the 15 negotiating groups (including services) was devoted to tariff cutting in a major way.[7]

Another factor was the extraordinary breadth of the Uruguay Round agenda. As noted earlier, this breadth was thought to be a strength of the round because of the potential for bargaining across issues and groups. But each of the negotiating groups was in itself so complex that it was extremely difficult to formulate the kind of trades needed to achieve progress. And with 117 participants (though fewer than this number were active delegations), the scope for individual country participation was considerably greater than in previous rounds and thus the complexity of the negotiations was greater.

These elements changed the conduct and character of the negotiations, as well as its outcomes. In early GATT rounds, the focus was on tariff bindings that were concluded in a few months. Representatives of a few governments (23 in the first round) retired to a country retreat for the duration, striking deals and reporting back to their national governments. It was clear to all parties that they each had to give something, in the form of bindings on their own tariffs, and that they would get something that they wanted in return, in the form of bindings on partner tariffs. The Uruguay Round process was very different.

In the Uruguay Round, the representatives of many governments participated in formal meetings in each of the 15 negotiating groups. Most made prepared speeches in which they made demands of the others but usually indicated little in the way of concessions that they would be willing to make. Media coverage turned the meetings into political events. Genuine negotiation of the form that characterized early GATT rounds did not occur until the late stages.

Other developments quite outside the process also impeded progress. One was ambiguity concerning the strength of some participants' commit-

---

7. The objective of the tariff-negotiating group was to obtain overall reductions of approximately 34 percent (the same percentage cut as in the Tokyo Round). Throughout the round, there was disagreement over whether negotiated cuts would be on an across-the-board basis (as favored by the European Community and Japan) or on a request-offer basis (as favored by the United States, which had used the formula approach since 1990). US insistence on a request-offer approach meant that negotiating market access had to be conducted line by line, country by country. Consequently, only a small fraction of tariff cuts had been negotiated at the round's conclusion in 1993, and these under a process that had "added many person years to the process of concluding the Round" (*Financial Times*, 10 December 1993, 5).

ment to the multilateral process,[8] and more specifically concerning whether these players really saw multilateral negotiation as the best chance for liberalizing world trade. Several members of the US Congress, while not advocating outright rejection of the multilateral process, argued that unilateral actions (such as section 301) could serve to accelerate the multilateral process and might in any case be more effective at market opening than traditional GATT rounds.[9] These developments under-scored a drift in the conduct of the round toward negotiation by unilateral pressure.

Nor was the United States the only major player whose commitment was in doubt. The European Community was strongly committed to, if not preoccupied with, further internal integration as part of the Europe 1992 process. Events in Eastern Europe also became a dominant, and perhaps an overriding, EC concern. The lack of Japan's willingness to liberalize in agriculture, most notably in rice, was also taken as an indication of weak commitment.[10]

A particularly important event that occurred in the middle of the round was the passage of the 1988 US Omnibus Trade and Competitiveness Act,[11] which gave the president negotiating authority but also injected threats of unilateral trade measures tied to market opening abroad into the Uruguay Round talks. US trade partners feared that US actions under section 301 would be inconsistent with its GATT obligations and thus provoke confrontation in the GATT. A subsequent 301 action against Brazil that increased US bound tariffs appeared to justify such fears, even though the US action against Brazil was subsequently withdrawn.[12]

---

8. In a meeting in Geneva in September 1991, a member of the US delegation observed: "Multilateralism doesn't work: there's too many countries involved."

9. For instance, Sam Gibbons, chairman of the House Ways and Means Subcommittee on Trade, viewed section 301 as "a trade liberalizing procedure. It is one that we use to open markets, not just for the US but for all the world" (*Financial Times*, 3 December 1990, 6). US Trade Representative Carla Hills noted specific instances in which other countries benefited from market-opening measures resulting from 301 actions: the case of Japan's beef market, whose opening would benefit Australia, and Japan's citrus market, whose opening would benefit Italy. "America is not trying to open markets for itself, but to expand the system," she said (*International Trade Reporter*, 31 May 1989, 685).

10. According to the *Financial Times* (9 December 1990, 6), "The truth is that the Uruguay Round has never been high on the political agenda of many EC governments. Monetary union, single market and eastern Europe have all dwarfed it" (see also "Japanese Keep Their Heads Down as GATT Bullets Fly," *Financial Times*, 6 December 1990, 3).

11. See Low (1993, chapter 3, 62–66) for more discussion of the provisions of the bill and its implications for the multilateral system.

12. In October 1988, the United States announced $39 million in trade sanctions against Brazil over its policies regarding intellectual property. Sanctions included 100 percent tariffs on imports of nonbenzenoid drugs, consumer electronics, and some paper products. Many

Inconsistent negotiating positions also emerged. One such case was services, where the United States had initially been the major demander of a broad-ranging framework agreement. Once the negotiation began to move toward an agreement with sectoral annotations, the United States demanded that certain sectors be taken off the table.[13] This was compounded by inconsistent US positions across service sectors. In broadcast services, the United States argued that the most-favored nation (MFN) principle was needed to deal with European content rules on TV programming, while in telecommunications it was not, so that access abroad could be negotiated bilaterally.

On top of all these developments and toward the final stages of the Uruguay Round, regional trade arrangements accelerated. The fear of a world moving toward trading blocs complicated negotiations. With the fall of the Berlin Wall in 1989, the European Community was discussing new arrangements with Eastern Europe and the former Soviet republics. The United States and Canada enlarged their trade agreement to include Mexico. It thus seemed to many that the major players were now regionally focused—if not as a complete substitute for multilateral progress, then as an insurance policy in case the round failed.

It was argued, by way of partial antidote, that each of these regional developments could spur multilateral progress by pressuring some players to cease their foot dragging in multilateral negotiations and to dissuade others from pursuing a bilateral course. However, these events and the sense that more could follow weakened the collective commitment to conclude the negotiation.

The Uruguay Round negotiation became deadlocked in Brussels over agriculture, with an EC offer that was too minimal for the US administration to take to Congress and a joint US–Cairns Group position that the Community could not accept.[14] In group after group, a range of difficulties were evident after years of negotiation. In services, conflicts involving sectoral coverage and MFN remained unresolved. In antidumping, a conflict over circumvention pitted Japan, Korea, Mexico, and others against both the European Community and the United States. In safeguards, the central issue of selectivity left over from the Tokyo Round remained

---

countries protested this measure in the GATT (USITC 1990, 124; *Focus GATT Newsletter* 66). The tariff increase was removed in 1990 after Brazil agreed to meet US demands. Brazil also dropped its GATT complaint against the United States.

13. In July 1990, the United States asked that banking, telecommunications, civil aviation, and maritime transportation be left out (*The Economist*, 22 September 1990, 75).

14. Before the round was suspended, the European Community proposed reducing farm subsidies by 30 percent over a 10-year period starting in 1986 (15 percent of this reduction had already been achieved). The United States (accompanied by the Cairns Group) stood by its proposal of a 90 percent cut in export subsidies and a 75 percent reduction in internal farm supports over a 5-year period starting in 1991.

unresolved. Even in the supposedly simpler tariff-cutting group, no agreement on tariff cuts had been achieved as the Brussels ministerial meeting concluded.

To the great relief of the participants, the negotiation finally concluded with a draft text in December 1993 that built on the earlier Dunkel text of 1991. This was then upheld at the April 1994 ministerial meeting in Marrakesh. The round concluded mostly because, in the final analysis, no one was prepared to let it fail. The members of the European Union concluded that the system was important enough to supersede narrower political interests in contentious areas such as agriculture and textiles.[15] The United States in turn became resigned to compromise positions far from their stated objectives in areas such as agriculture. And smaller countries, anxious to see a multilateral accord that would weaken the movement toward trading blocs, were eager to adopt any agreement that emerged, confident that it would benefit them.

If there had been no substantive agreement or a shallow compromise with no content, the implications for the global trading system would have been serious. Regional blocs were thought likely to accelerate, trade conflicts were seen as increasing, and an unstable and difficult time was thought to be ahead for the world trading system. It would also have been hard to launch a new round for some considerable time. While the GATT would not have disappeared, it would have been increasingly difficult to enforce GATT disciplines and the GATT could well have fallen into relative disuse, becoming an international pulpit from which countries could address the world on their trade problems with other countries but with little hope of effective remedy.

Concluding the Uruguay Round was not easy, with extensive delays and protracted wrangling. But it did end, and the fact that it ended reduced the risk of collapse of the multilateral system.

So where does this leave us? Commitment to the trading system was shored up. New agreements produced greater market access in such areas as agriculture and textiles and may in the longer run accelerate global trade growth. And new trade rules in areas such as services broadened the system.

But the strength of the effect remains unclear. Especially contentious are implications for the trading system itself. Does the conclusion of the Uruguay Round demonstrate that the bicycle the WTO represents is sufficiently sturdy to hazard another round? Or do the obstacles show that the

---

15. During the final days of Uruguay Round negotiations, the European Union's General Affairs Council was also meeting to gain internal approval of the negotiating package. Unanimous approval was finally achieved only after two conditions were met. First, France insisted that the Union's internal trade policy instruments be strengthened (the United Kingdom and the Netherlands objected to this), and second, an aid package had to be developed to modernize Portugal's textile industry ("Europe," 16 December 1993, 7).

GATT process is rickety and thus that a new approach is needed? Was it strained or strengthened by the range of issues and scope of participation? Or, put simply, is the round system in good shape, because the Uruguay Round concluded, or in bad shape, as evidenced by how close the round came to failing? These questions cannot now be definitively answered; whether the Uruguay Round will be enough to propel the trading system into a new golden age of strengthened discipline and extension of coverage remains to be seen.

The Agreements

The Uruguay Round negotiations produced a final document comprising more than 26,000 pages, including final text, tariff schedules, and other details.[16] This section summarizes some of the key decisions agreed upon at the final ministerial meeting in Marrakesh in April 1994. Appendix A presents the Uruguay Round results in more detail.

Decisions were reached in four main areas:

- improved market access through tariff reductions and in agriculture, textiles, and apparel;

- institutional arrangements covering dispute settlement and creation of the WTO;

- trade rules governing subsidies and countervailing duties, safeguards (VERs), and antidumping;

- new areas of services, investment, and intellectual property.

Market Access

Tariff Reductions

Early in the round, it was agreed that tariffs would be reduced on average by at least a third on industrial products. The resulting tariff cuts, by aggregated product classifications, are listed in table 3.1. These cuts averaged around 35 percent,[17] with larger average cuts in some countries such as Canada and smaller cuts in the developing world (*Focus GATT Newslet-*

---

16. This section is based on GATT, "News of the Uruguay Round 80," *Focus GATT Newsletter* 104, and "Uruguay Round Final Act," 15 April 1994; and IMF, *Survey*, 10 January 1994.

17. Tariffs in some cases are to be reduced by 40 percent. According to data reported in Blackhurst, Enders, and François (1995, 11), developed countries committed to a 40 percent reduction in the average tariff on imports of industrial products.

Table 3.1 Uruguay Round MFN tariff rates and reductions on nonagricultural products (percentages)

Product	Australia and New Zealand			Canada			United States			Japan		
	Old	New	Cut	Old	New	Cut	Old	New	Cut	Old	New	Cut
Fishery products	0.7	0.5	28.6	3.2	2.1	34.4	1.2	0.9	25.0	5.7	4.1	28.1
Forestry products	0.2	0.2	0.0	0.0	0.0	0.0	0.3	0.0	100.0	0.0	0.0	0.0
Mining	1.5	1.1	26.7	2.6	1.3	50.0	1.3	0.8	38.5	1.3	0.6	53.8
Textiles	24.6	14.5	41.1	18.6	11.7	37.1	10.5	7.5	28.6	7.4	6.0	18.9
Clothing	50.5	34.8	31.1	22.9	16.6	27.5	16.7	15.2	9.0	13.0	10.2	21.5
Primary steel	9.7	1.6	83.5	7.4	0.4	94.6	4.5	0.2	95.6	3.9	0.6	84.6
Primary nonferrous metals	11.2	6.4	42.9	4.9	2.7	44.9	2.9	2.6	10.3	4.1	2.4	41.5
Fabricated metal products	17.1	12.7	25.7	9.7	6.0	38.1	4.7	2.8	40.4	3.4	0.9	73.5
Chemicals and rubber	11.9	7.5	37.0	10.3	5.3	48.5	5.0	3.0	40.0	4.1	1.6	61.0
Transport equipment	25.7	19.4	24.5	8.1	5.4	33.3	4.8	4.6	4.2	1.5	0.0	100.0
Other manufactures	11.6	7.6	34.5	6.3	2.9	54.0	3.5	1.5	57.1	2.0	0.9	55.0
Total merchandise trade	14.2	9.5	33.1	7.4	4.2	43.2	4.6	3.2	30.4	4.4	2.7	38.6

Product	European Union			European Free Trade Association			Developing/transitional economies		
	Old	New	Cut	Old	New	Cut	Old	New	Cut
Fishery products	12.9	10.7	17.1	1.7	1.4	17.6	35.2	8.1	77.0
Forestry products	0.0	0.0	0.0	0.2	0.1	50.0	0.1	0.1	0.0
Mining	1.1	0.8	27.3	1.0	0.8	20.0	11.5	9.5	17.4
Textiles	9.0	6.8	24.4	12.2	8.0	34.4	30.3	20.3	33.0
Clothing	12.6	10.9	13.5	17.0	11.4	32.9	14.6	10.8	26.0
Primary steel	5.3	0.5	90.6	4.1	0.6	85.4	8.7	6.1	29.9
Primary nonferrous metals	7.2	5.9	18.1	4.0	2.9	27.5	2.7	2.1	22.2
Fabricated metal products	5.7	3.1	45.6	5.3	3.0	43.4	8.5	6.9	18.8
Chemicals and rubber	7.7	4.2	45.5	5.8	3.0	48.3	19.1	13.2	30.9
Transport equipment	6.9	6.0	13.0	7.5	6.3	16.0	27.2	17.3	36.4
Other manufactures	5.5	2.5	54.5	4.3	2.3	46.5	18.0	13.3	26.1
Total merchandise trade	5.3	3.2	39.6	6.2	3.9	37.1	13.5	9.8	27.4

Source: Based on François, McDonald, and Nordström (1994, table 13).

ter 104). Tariffs in developed countries will be eliminated in some sectors, including in steel, wood and wood products, and pharmaceuticals.

While these cuts will improve access for exporters to these countries, their immediate impacts will likely be modest because tariffs on manufactures in industrial countries were already low (except in the apparel area) and the tariff cuts were concentrated on products with already-low tariffs in order to meet percentage cutting targets. In clothing, for instance, tariff cuts are substantially smaller than average cuts.

African and Caribbean countries expressed strong concerns that the tariff cuts would erode their margins of preference set out in agreements such as the Lomé Convention.[18]

Another issue is the substantial expansion in tariff bindings. François, McDonald, and Nordström (1994, 4) report that developing countries agreed to a large number of bindings, increasing the coverage of tariff bindings on industrial products from 22 percent of tariff lines to 72 percent. As a result, new negotiable tariff instruments were created. In the agricultural area, general-purpose waivers, variable levies, and other unbound protective instruments are effectively gone. While tariff bindings are still at admittedly high levels for some of the key developing countries such as India, the broadened coverage of bindings reflects a remarkable accomplishment.

Agriculture

The agriculture agreement comprises the Agreement on Agriculture; Concessions and Commitments made on market access, domestic support, and export subsidies; the Agreement on Sanitary and Phytosanitary Measures; and the Decision Concerning Least-Developed and Net Food-Importing Developing Countries. The agreements cover the three key areas of export subsidies, domestic supports, and border measures.

More formally, the Agreement on Agriculture brings agricultural trade more in line with the rules and disciplines of the GATT, recognizing that agricultural reform is a long-term process. Members agree to make binding commitments in the areas of market access, domestic support, and export subsidies and to reach agreement on sanitary and phytosanitary measures. Reforms are to be implemented over a period of six years (ten

---

18. Before the end of the Uruguay Round, Christian Aid, a London-based nongovernmental organization (NGO), was advocating that the African, Caribbean, and Pacific (ACP) countries, which have special arrangements with the European Union and are some of the world's poorest, be compensated for their losses during the midterm review of the Lomé Convention (Madden and Madeley 1993, 2). Blackhurst, Enders, and François (1995, 16) report that the Uruguay Round will result in an expansion in the share of African exports subject to duty-free or low tariffs on an MFN basis. Looking at the majority of African exports to the European Union facing tariffs of 0 to 3 percent, they report, "The margin of preference afforded under Lomé is likely to be consumed in large part by associated administrative costs."

for developing countries); the least-developed countries are not required to enter into reduction commitments. All commitments are to be included in members' schedules of agricultural concessions and commitments.

As mentioned in the previous section, the Market Access Agreement converts all nontariff border measures, such as import quotas, to tariffs that provide the same protection. These tariffs, as well as other tariffs on agricultural products, must then be reduced by an average of 36 percent for developed countries and 24 percent for developing countries. Minimum reductions for each tariff line are required. Under the special provisions of annex 5 of the agreement, both Japan and South Korea will address the issue of opening up their rice markets, an area where imports had been previously banned.[19] The agreement also includes a minimum-access tariff quota of 3 percent, which will increase to 5 percent by the end of the implementation period.[20]

Special safeguard provisions have been included for tariffied products that "will allow additional duties to be applied in cases where shipments priced in domestic currencies fall below a certain trigger or in the case of import surges" (GATT 1994a, 46). This introduces the possibility of new protective measures being used in agriculture, a feature that Tangermann (1994) highlights as one of the weaknesses of the agreement. A "special treatment" clause allows for import restrictions to be maintained, under certain conditions, until the end of the implementation period.

In the Agreement on Domestic Support and Export Subsidies, developed countries have committed to reduce domestic agricultural support by cutting their total aggregate measurement of support (total AMS) by 20 percent during the implementation period from its level in the base period of 1986–88. Developing countries are required to reduce their total AMS by 13.3 percent; least-developed countries are again exempted. These reductions apply to all support provided on a product-specific basis or to support that does not otherwise qualify for exemptions.[21]

In export subsidies, developed countries have committed to reducing the value of direct export subsidies by 36 percent of the base-period level

---

19. Under the provisions of annex 5, Japan will allow imports to make up a minimum of 4 percent of domestic consumption, rising to 8 percent by the year 2000 (levels generally higher than required under the minimal access commitment). South Korea agreed to establish a quota of 1 percent, rising to a quota of 4 percent by 2004. At the end of this special transition period, these countries are to comply with tariffication and reduction commitments of the agriculture agreement unless negotiations provide otherwise (Schott 1994, 51).

20. Hathaway and Ingco (1995, 21) note that countries are allowed to include special arrangements in their minimum access commitment and to allocate their minimum access to exporters with special arrangements, as in the case of the European Union and its sugar imports from Lomé countries.

21. See appendix A for details on which policies qualify for exemption from total AMS reduction commitments.

over six years and to reducing the volume of subsidized exports by 21 percent over the same period. The base period for these reductions is 1986–90. Developing countries have committed to reductions of two-thirds those of the developed countries implemented over 10 years; least-developed countries are exempted. Developing countries are exempted from commitments on marketing of agricultural exports or internal transport subsidies.

Provisions in this area also provide for flexibility across years in meeting the export subsidy reduction commitments and aim to prevent the circumvention of the export subsidy commitments. GATT members are also to exercise restraint in applying countervailing duties against products included in the reform process. Criteria for food aid donation and export credits that meet the requirements of the export subsidy disciplines are also included in the agreement. A new Committee on Agriculture is to be established to monitor implementation. Further negotiations to liberalize agriculture will begin in the fifth year of the implementation period—that is, a "mini-round" of future liberalization negotiations, which is for now confined to agriculture.

The Agreement on Sanitary and Phytosanitary Measures covers food safety and animal, plant, and health regulations. While recognizing that governments have the right to use sanitary and phytosanitary measures, the agreement stipulates that these should only be used to the extent necessary to protect human, animal, or plant life or health. Countries are encouraged to base measures on international standards, guidelines, and recommendations; higher standards may only be imposed if there is scientific justification.

Finally, the Decisions on Measures Concerning the Possible Negative Effects of the Reform Program on Least-Developed and Net Food-Importing Developing Countries recognize that such countries may face higher prices for food imports. This ministerial decision sets out objectives for providing food aid and for ensuring that an increasing proportion of basic foodstuffs is provided in full grant form.

In each area, the decisions restrain the trade impacts of the future use of agricultural policies. According to the market access agreement, all non-tariff measures must be converted to tariffs that provide an equal level of protection.[22] This implies that the US use of the agricultural waiver or the variable levy system used in the Common Agricultural Policy would

---

22. According to the agreement, this applies to measures such as "quantitative import restrictions, variable import levies, minimum import prices, discretionary import licensing, non-tariff measures maintained through state-trading enterprises, voluntary export restraints and similar border measures other than ordinary customs duties, whether or not the measures are maintained under country-specific derogations from the provisions of the GATT 1947" (GATT 1994a, 46).

potentially be incompatible with this agreement.[23] Thus, the bindings undertaken in agriculture in converting variable levies and other unbound protective instruments to ad valorem equivalents are as important as the round's immediate barrier reductions.

Despite this, some question remains whether the extent of actual liberalization in agriculture is all that great (Tangermann 1994). The conversion of what were previously quotas into tariffs has not only involved a degree of "dirty tariffication"—that is, the replacement of an existing quota by a higher than warranted ad valorem equivalent[24]—but tariff quotas accompany the change. In the case of the European Union, the key import-restraining region in this area, there are indications that the agreed Uruguay Round liberalization largely coincides with preexisting commitments made as part of internal CAP reform.

The Uruguay Round results in this area divide agriculture importers and exporters. There are positive outcomes for those countries involved in agriculture-related export activities such as Australia, Canada, the United States, Argentina, Brazil, Thailand, Malaysia, and the Philippines, almost all of which are members of the Cairns Group. On the other hand, there are concerns that agricultural net importers, particularly in Africa, may suffer significant losses from the higher prices they will pay for agricultural products.[25] There are also concerns over the uneven product coverage of the decisions, especially the limited new liberalization in sugar and meats. This tends to significantly lower the gains that might accrue to existing exporters such as Argentina (meats) and the Caribbean countries (sugar). Combined with delayed liberalization in such areas as rice for Korea and Japan, the short-run potential for added gains from trade from this key area seems to be less than had been hoped.

---

23. Tangermann (1994) notes that the legality of the use of variable levies is less clear.

24. Hathaway and Ingco (1995, 18) report the tariffication process resulted in levels of protection for many products in many countries as high or higher than under the old system of protection, even after the tariff cuts are applied. For example, in the case of wheat, the EU's estimated tariff equivalent (based on a comparison between the domestic and world price for the base period 1986–88) was 103 percent. However, the tariff equivalent notified under the Uruguay Round schedule was 155.6 percent. Examples of such dirty tariffication can be found in areas, including rice, sugar, beef, pork, poultry, and dairy, and was practiced by both developed and developing countries (table 2b).

25. Madden and Madeley (1993, 10) note that the group of Net Food Importers (Egypt, Jamaica, Mexico, Morocco, Nigeria, and Peru) earlier requested both increased food aid and long-term assistance for agricultural development to compensate for the negative impact of the Uruguay Round agricultural negotiations. See the discussion of this issue in UNCTAD (1990). Harrold (1995, 21) concludes there will be little adverse impact on Africa as a result of the changes in agricultural trade.

Textiles and Apparel

The Uruguay Round decisions covering trade in textiles and apparel involve the phased elimination of the textile restrictions that operate against developing countries under the Multi-Fiber Arrangement (MFA). At the end of the phase-out process, the textile and clothing sectors are expected to be integrated into the GATT. A four-stage phase-out of the MFA over 10 years began 1 January 1995 (see appendix A for details on the MFA phase-out). Growth rates in MFA quotas will be raised in each of the first three stages. At the same time, MFA quota restrictions will cover fewer and fewer products over the period. A new system of temporary selective safeguards will accompany this process. This is a source of concern to some exporters, who fear that this regime could prove restrictive.

The issues here are how quickly the phase-out will occur and whether the eventual elimination of the MFA restrictions will occur cleanly and in a way that removes trade barriers (see the discussion in Trela 1994b). Because a significant number of MFA quotas are nonbinding and the accelerated quota growth rates are low, many fear that much of the effective adjustment is delayed until the tenth year of the phase-out. An additional concern for developing countries is that an eventual removal of the MFA will trigger new antidumping actions in importing countries, removing some of the benefits of MFA elimination.

Model results seem to indicate that the majority of the global gains from the removal of MFA restrictions will accrue to developed countries on the consumption side through lowered consumer prices.[26] While there are developing-country benefits, they tend to be dominated by developed-country consumer side benefits, highlighting the role of developed-country producer interests in maintaining these restrictions.

Trade Rules

Agreement on Antidumping

The antidumping decisions have received a more cynical and skeptical reaction from observers than perhaps any other part of the Uruguay Round agreements.[27] It is widely believed that antidumping became an

---

26. See the model-based calculations in Trela and Whalley (1990). Nguyen, Perroni, and Wigle (1993) produce a similar pattern of results in their analysis of the impacts of the Uruguay Round. According to François, McDonald, and Nordström (1995, 20), elimination of the MFA will lead to significant expansion in textile and clothing production in East and South Asia. Model calculations by Hertel et al. (1995, 22) also show significant increases in apparel output in East Asia.

27. Schott (1994, 85) describes the agreement as a bandage on a "festering sore of trade policy." Hindley (1994, 101) considers the agreement as providing "more grounds for skepticism than optimism." The *Financial Times* reported one dumping negotiator as commenting

all-too-common method of protection in developed countries during the 1980s.[28] In many cases, antidumping cases were dropped after an agreement was reached on a minimum export price or a VER was agreed.[29] Recently, developing countries have also been implementing antidumping legislation and initiating antidumping actions.[30] The changes in the agreement attempt to clarify the method for determining whether a product has been dumped, the criteria for determining whether the dumped imports caused injury to the domestic industry, the procedures to be followed in initiating and conducting antidumping investigations, and the role of dispute settlement panels. The issues in evaluating the antidumping agreement revolve around whether these new rules discipline the use of antidumping duties or simply codify rather than constrain their use.

Procedural Changes   Specific provisions have been added to address such issues as the criteria for allocating costs when the export price is compared with a "constructed" normal value (*Focus GATT Newsletter* 104, 9). The agreement spells out how the importing country can determine the "reasonable amount for administrative, selling, and general costs and profits" that is to be added to the cost of production of the dumped good (GATT 1994a, 145).

This agreement also includes criteria for price averaging (the dumping margin calculated either on a transactions basis or by comparison of home-market, weighted-average normal value to a weighted average of prices of all comparable exports), for allocation of start-up costs, for sales-below-cost tests, and for cumulation. Under the new cumulation provisions, antidumping investigators will be able to add the imports of different countries in determining whether the domestic industry has been

---

that "trying to read this agreement is rather like reading a goat's entrails" (16 December 1993, 5). See also Horlick (1993).

28. According to Messerlin (1990, table 6.1, 110–11), for the years 1979–88, the United States, the European Community, Australia, and Canada combined initiated 1,758 antidumping actions. Low and Yeats (1995, table 5) show that between 1985 and 1992, 1,148 antidumping cases were initiated by signatories to the GATT antidumping code. Again, most cases were initiated by the United States, the European Union, Australia, and Canada, although Mexico is catching up.

29. Finger (1990, annex table 1, 95) shows that for 1980–88, out of a total 774 US antidumping and countervailing cases, 70 percent resulted in a restrictive outcome (including VERs). Staiger and Wolak (1994) discuss the anticompetitive and restrictive consequences of US antidumping investigations. Between 1990 and 1994, the European Union had 151 active antidumping cases, of which 23 were undertakings (European Commission 1995). Tharakan (1993) discusses antidumping action in the United States and the European Union. Finger (1995) discusses the Uruguay Round antidumping agreement.

30. Low and Yeats (1995) report the following countries have recently introduced or reactivated antidumping legislation: Argentina, Bolivia, Chile, China, Colombia, Egypt, Indonesia, Israel, Jamaica, Malaysia, Morocco, Peru, the Philippines, South Africa, Thailand, Trinidad and Tobago, and Venezuela.

injured, as long as the dumping margin of each country exceeds the de minimis level (for detailed discussion see Schott 1994, 80–83; Finger 1995, annex 2; and Stewart 1993 on the agreement's evolution).

Procedures have also been established for the initiation and conduct of antidumping cases. The agreement spells out in greater detail who has "standing," or the legal right, to file antidumping petitions, as well as the conditions to ensure that all interested parties are given the opportunity to present evidence. Importantly, the agreement also makes it clear that unions are eligible to file or support antidumping petitions.

Dispute Settlement While disputes over antidumping investigations are eligible for consideration under the WTO dispute settlement mechanism, the agreement sets out specific guidelines that must be followed. According to the standard of review, the dispute panels could only consider whether the original investigation's establishment of the facts was done properly and whether the evaluation of the facts was unbiased and objective (Schott 1994, 84). This standard of review reflects the US concern that a dispute panel would not be able to overturn a national authority's determination of injury and dumping margins (Stewart 1993, 1536).

While generally procedural and of minor consequence, some antidumping revisions are an improvement. For instance, the de minimis provision requires the immediate termination of antidumping cases involving a dumping margin of less than 2 percent of the export price, a sunset clause requires both antidumping measures and price undertakings to expire after five years, and reviews are required. A number of unresolved issues have been forwarded to the Committee on Antidumping Practices for further deliberation, including anticircumvention rules (Schott 1994, 84).

The antidumping agreement allows national authorities to use substantial discretion in determining dumping and injury, increasing the potential for protecting domestic import-competing industries. Ironically, it also makes exporters in industrial countries vulnerable to antidumping investigations by authorities in the many developing countries that are establishing antidumping regimes.

A particularly worrisome provision is one that allows exporters to escape an antidumping investigation by agreeing to a price undertaking agreement (where the exporter agrees to raise the price of the exported good). While price undertaking agreements can only be negotiated after a preliminary affirmative determination of dumping and injury, the concern remains that price undertakings can be distortive and anticompetitive (Schott 1994, 83).

Agreement on Subsidies and Countervailing Measures

This agreement builds on the Agreement on Interpretation and Application of Articles VI, XVI, and XXIII negotiated during the Tokyo Round (see also Horlick and Clarke 1994; Finger 1995).

One of the main considerations when the round was launched was negotiating the definition of a subsidy. The agreement establishes three categories of subsidies:

- prohibited subsidies, which include those contingent on export performance or the use of domestic over imported goods;

- actionable subsidies, which include those that harm other members, including through "serious prejudice" (see appendix A);

- nonactionable subsidies, which include nonspecific subsidies and specific subsidies for industrial research and precompetitive development and for regional assistance. Assistance for adapting existing facilities to meet new environmental laws or regulations also falls into this category.

Although a step in the right direction, the new definitions are still too broad, and governments will find it all too easy to justify subsidies. This is one of the few places in the Uruguay Round agreements where the environment is directly recognized, but there is a concern that it will provide a "green" loophole through which domestic interests may pressure governments to provide subsidies.

The discussion on countervailing measures sets out disciplines on the initiation of countervailing cases and on investigations by domestic authorities. Disciplines on rules of evidence are also covered to ensure that all interested parties can present evidence and have a say. That countervailing measures were linked to the agreement on subsidies is considered a positive development because in the absence of a definition of subsidy, it had been difficult to determine whether countervailing measures applied. The large number of countervailing duty investigations in the United States during the 1980s led many to believe that further discipline was needed in this area.[31]

Disciplines are also included for the calculation of the amount of a subsidy. A de minimis provision aims to eliminate the harassment effect on small exporters. Timetables for investigations and duration of duties are set out, and special considerations for least-developed and developing countries are also included.

Agreement on Safeguards

Under Article XIX of the GATT, countries are permitted to take safeguard actions to counter an unforeseen increase in imports that causes, or is likely to cause, serious injury to the domestic industry. However, under the terms of the article, the safeguard action must be applied on an MFN basis, and affected countries can request compensation. For these and

---

31. According to Hufbauer (1990, 94), the United States accounted for 90 percent of the CVD cases launched worldwide between 1980 and 1986.

other reasons, GATT members do not frequently employ Article XIX safeguard actions. But there has been a substantial increase in the use of VERs and antidumping actions to curtail increases in imports, especially by developed countries.

Much of the debate during the negotiations was over the issue of selectivity. The agreement upholds the MFN principle, but a provision has been included to allow for departures from nondiscrimination in certain circumstances, after consultations with the Safeguards Committee. The agreement also establishes criteria for determining serious injury and sets out requirements for investigations and time limits for the duration of safeguard measures. A de minimis clause applying to imports from developing countries also applies.

The agreement also prohibits the use of all gray-area measures to shelter domestic industries from imports. Importantly, according to the agreement, "members shall not seek, take or maintain any voluntary export restraints, orderly marketing arrangements or any other similar measures on the export or import side" (GATT 1994a, 278).

All such measures currently in effect must be eliminated or phased out within four years after the WTO enters into force. Each member is allowed to temporarily keep one specific measure in place if agreed with the affected exporter. However, this measure must be phased out by 31 December 1999. All other safeguard measures in place under Article XIX of GATT 1947 must be terminated no later than eight years after first being applied, or five years after the WTO enters into force.

In addition, the agreement provides some relief from the compensation requirement.[32] Compensation to affected exporters is to be decided after consultations. If there is no agreement, the affected exporter may retaliate up to an amount equivalent to the amount of trade affected by the safeguard measure. Under the Uruguay Round agreement, this right is waived for the first three years the safeguard measure is in effect, as long as the measure conforms to the provisions of the agreement.

Although these revisions appear to go a long way toward curbing gray-area measures that lie outside the disciplines of the GATT, it is not clear how nonnotified VERs will actually be eliminated. It is also not clear that the changes to Article XIX will encourage members to use it for relief from imports, since other relief measures, including antidumping, are available.

New Issues

Intellectual property rights and investment were considered two of the key "new" areas on the Uruguay Round agenda. Included at the insistence

---

32. The requirement to provide compensation to affected exporters was often cited as a reason governments chose to pursue alternative methods of import relief such as VERs and other gray-area measures (Hamilton and Whalley 1990).

of the developed countries (and the United States in particular), these two issues were among the areas in which there was a clear North-South divide at the outset (see Stern 1990; Reichman 1993; Braga 1995).[33] During the negotiation, developing countries began to tighten their own intellectual property right protection, largely as the result of bilateral pressure from developed countries. As a result, more progress was made in this area than was originally thought would be possible.

Agreement on Trade-Related Aspects of Intellectual Property Rights

The Agreement on Trade-Related Aspects of Intellectual Property Rights (known as TRIPs) consists of three parts. Part I sets out general provisions and basic principles. These include a national treatment provision and an MFN clause. Part II defines each intellectual property right (IPR) and sets out obligations. In the area of copyrights, for example, members are required to adhere to the substantive provisions of the Berne Convention (1971, in Paris). Computer programs are to be protected as literary works under the Berne Convention. In the area of patents, members have agreed to provide 20-year patent protection for inventions, including both products and processes. The agreement also deals with trademarks and service marks, geographical indications, integrated circuits, and anticompetitive practices in contractual licenses. Part III sets out obligations for members' procedures in domestic law to ensure enforcement of intellectual property rights for both nationals and foreigners. Dispute settlement is to take place within the integrated dispute settlement procedures of the WTO, allowing for possible cross-retaliation on goods for IPR violations.

The developed countries were to have implemented TRIPs by the start of 1996, one year after the WTO went into effect. Developing countries have five years[34] (ten if they must extend product patent protection to previously unprotected technologies); least-developed countries have ten years to implement the agreement.

The intellectual property agreement is thought by many to be one of the most important achievements of the Uruguay Round, given the extent of its coverage, its clearly defined international standards and panel procedures, and the fact that progress in this area has proved elusive for so many years—50 years by some counts.[35] Success in this negotiation was in

---

33. Giunta and Shang (1993–94, 329) discuss the differences between developed- and developing-country views of intellectual property. They conclude that bilateral and private agreements may produce speedier and more effective results.

34. However, many developing countries have been under considerable pressure to implement TRIPs fully after one year.

35. Illustrative of the difficulties is the fact that GATT agreements regarding patent rights on seeds have sparked major protests in India. Lower-income Indian farmers believe the agreement means they will no longer be able to sell or use their seeds after each harvest (*Financial Times*, 7 April 1994, 6; *Ottawa Citizen*, 31 March 1994, G4).

large part due to the developing countries' willingness to fully participate, which in turn was driven largely by bilateral pressure to comply with international standards. These negotiations involved relatively few major concessions on their part, with the exception of a smaller number of developing countries such as India.

It remains to be seen how successful this ground-breaking agreement will be in practice. Both the complexity of the agreements and the fact that the dispute settlement body can allow retaliation on goods trade for IPR violations could be the catalyst for major new conflict within the trading system. And although these arrangements are not explicitly related to trade—except in the name of the agreement—their direct impacts on trade and the performance of the trading system remain uncertain.

Agreement on Trade-Related Investment Measures

This agreement binds members not to apply trade-related investment measures (TRIMs) that are inconsistent with either Article III (on national treatment) or Article XI (on quantitative restrictions). A list of such TRIMs was drawn up that includes local-content and trade-balancing requirements. All TRIMs inconsistent with the agreement must be notified and eliminated within two years. Developing countries have five years to eliminate their inconsistent TRIMs, and the least-developed countries have seven.

While the Uruguay Round results in TRIMs are not all that ambitious, bringing the issue into the GATT allows for potential further progress, perhaps linking such issues as technology transfer and some competition policy matters to trade. For now, trade matters relating to investments are treated narrowly. And while these decisions may have limited impact on developed countries, there may be greater impact on these countries in the future because of the extensive use of TRIMs in developing countries.[36]

Services

The General Agreement on Trade in Services (GATS) contains broad principles covering international trade restrictions affecting services, but there are large sectoral exceptions, and some of the basic GATT principles such as national treatment do not stand as an automatic right. And while the agreement's drafters envisioned specific commitments over market access and national treatment, relatively few such commitments have yet been made, and they have been of seemingly limited consequence. This is one of

---

36. Low and Subramanian (1995) discuss the TRIMs results and how competition policy matters could be dealt with in the GATT/WTO. They also list examples of local-content requirements in developing countries (1995, table 3).

the areas in which the round sets the stage for eventual liberalization, rather than achieving substantive results in its own right.[37]

The decisions affecting trade in services are complex (see summary in appendix A; see also Broadman 1994; Hoekman 1995; Sauvé 1995; *Focus GATT Newsletter* 107, 14–15). Part I sets out a series of general principles meant to govern the use of trade-restricting measures in services. MFN is one of these, adopted from the GATT for trade in goods. Part II discusses obligations and disciplines including transparency of trade measures affecting services, increasing participation of developing countries in world trade, how free trade agreements are to treat services, consultations to end restrictive business practices, and emergency safeguard measures. The fact that the GATS deals only with safeguard measures—and not antidumping or countervailing duties for services—has attracted particular attention (Hoekman 1993).

Perhaps most important to an evaluation of the significance of these general obligations and disciplines are the exemptions, especially the sectoral exceptions set out in the annexes to the agreement. MFN does not apply for notified exceptions in financial services, telecommunications, and, effectively, the air transportation sector, since the whole agreement does not apply to traffic rights. This reduced sectoral coverage undermines the scope of the MFN provision as a general principle, because together these sectors constitute a significant fraction of total trade in services.

In addition, whether the principle of MFN can adequately apply to both negotiations and the conduct of trade in services is questionable in practice, because a simple translation from goods trade is in some cases difficult. As applied to trade in goods, MFN establishes that similar commodities arriving at a national border should not be discriminated against on the basis of country of origin—that is, it is a border-based principle. But MFN has no clear analog in a number of key service categories, because geographical discrimination is inherent to service provision.[38]

In Part III of the agreement, specific commitments covering market access, national treatment, and other areas are set out. As in GATT tariff negotiations, these "commitments" actually are more aptly described as exchanges of concessions on rates and bindings undertaken on an obliga-

---

37. See Hoekman (1993) for discussion of the impacts of decisions in services on developing countries.

38. Thus, for instance, it makes little sense to talk about MFN applied separately to phone calls between Paris and New York, and between London and New York—that is, calls between different and specific geographical locations. In the case of airline transportation, where it is agreed that MFN cannot effectively be applied due to an exception for traffic rights, a similar situation prevails because prevailing bilateral airline treaties specify particular arrangements on bilateral routes.

tions basis. But in services there is more of a concern about the extent of complementarity between such commitments. Hence, a commitment made to market access without a matching commitment to national treatment might be of little value if access is granted to a market in which foreign suppliers are restricted in other ways—say, by limiting the number of branches foreign banks can have when domestic banks face no such limits. Equally, national treatment without market access is of little value. As a result, future bargaining in services will have to take place either on groups of commitments or on commitments that weaken binding restrictions on services trade rather than on nonbinding restrictions.

Part IV of the agreement sets out principles for future liberalization in services through GATT-like rounds, the culmination of which would be a schedule of specific commitments and modifications of past schedules. The fact that many of the restrictions at issue are at the heart of domestic regulatory regimes, which are not so easily modified by mercantilist bargaining as are pure border measures, illustrates the weakness of the round-based approach. Attempting to agree on ranges within which domestic regulatory rules would be harmonized—that is, rules-based talks— might be more appropriate, as might more explicit reliance on bilateral negotiations.

Part V contains institutional provisions involving dispute settlement procedures (much like those in the GATT), the establishment of a Council on Services, and final provisions including entry into force.

There are four annexes to the GATS. Under the annex on the movement of natural persons, governments may negotiate specific commitments that would allow service providers to stay on a temporary basis in another country. The annex on financial services establishes the rights of governments to take prudential measures, including those to protect investors, depositors, and policy holders. The annex on telecommunications applies to measures that affect access to and use of public telecommunication services and networks. It requires that access be given to public telecommunications networks on a nondiscriminatory basis. The annex on all transport services excludes from the GATS traffic rights and directly related activities. However, the GATS will apply to aircraft repair and maintenance services, marketing of air transport services, and computer reservation services.[39]

---

39. When negotiations concluded in December 1993, a work program was drawn up to continue negotiating in the following areas: basic telecommunications (May 1994–April 1996), to develop commitments and a basic set of rules for liberalization; maritime transport (May 1994–June 1996), to improve on commitments already included in schedules on port facilities, auxiliary services, and ocean transport; movement of natural persons (May 1994–July 1995), on temporary entrance and stays of service providers; and financial services (May 1994–28 July 1995) to improve commitments. Negotiations almost broke down when the United States withdrew in June 1995. On 28 July 1995, 29 countries, including the European Union and Canada, agreed to sign the protocol, a temporary MFN-based agreement to last until Decem-

The broad picture is that the GATS is a GATT-like arrangement with some modifications. It is limited in scope and coverage. Its initial liberalization contained few significant initial notifications and specified commitments. And in certain areas progress is hobbled by the attempt to follow GATT principles of nondiscrimination, national treatment, and negotiated concessions when alternatives may be more suited to liberalization of services trade.

Institutional Arrangements

The World Trade Organization and Dispute Settlement

The World Trade Organization (WTO) was created to provide a firmer legal foundation for the management of world trade than was the case under the GATT. It entered into force 1 January 1995. It encompasses the GATT, as modified by the Uruguay Round (GATT 1994a), and all the Uruguay Round agreements and arrangements, including agriculture, textiles, intellectual property, and services, which will be binding on all members. It also covers the four plurilateral trade agreements—on civil aircraft, government procurement, dairy products, and bovine meat—which will be binding only on their signatories.

The WTO will administer the Trade Policy Review Mechanism, cooperate with the International Monetary Fund and the World Bank, and administer the dispute settlement mechanism. A ministerial conference will be held every two years. The WTO will only be open for original membership until January 1997.[40] Significantly, members must sign on to all the Uruguay Round agreements. Unlike the Tokyo Round, in which countries could sign on to different conditional codes, the Uruguay Round and the WTO offer no menu of choices.

Significant changes are expected under the new dispute settlement procedures. Firm time limits now apply to each stage of the dispute settlement process. Importantly, consensus will now be required to reject a panel report rather than to accept it, as was the case before; this could substantially strengthen the process. Along with this come (effectively) automatic rights to a panel. An Appellate Body was also created. Appeals will be

---

ber 1997. Improvements include greater access to markets in ASEAN, Korea, and India. Future negotiating topics in the GATS are to include subsidies, government procurement, safeguards, professional services, qualifications, standards and licensing, services trade, and the environment (*GATT Focus Newsletter* 107, May 1994, 7–8).

40. At the 8 December 1994 meeting of the WTO Implementation Committee, it was agreed that countries would continue to apply the GATT to non-WTO members for 1995 in order to allow extra time for countries to secure their WTO membership (*Focus GATT Newsletter* 113, 1).

limited to issues of law covered in the panel report. Again, timetables for the appeal procedure have been specified.

The dispute settlement mechanism applies to all areas of the Uruguay Round and allows for cross-retaliation under certain circumstances. Several provisions cover considerations to be given to the interests of developing countries and least-developed countries in the event one of them is party to a dispute.[41]

How effective the dispute settlement mechanism will be in strengthening the system will depend on several factors, including the quantity of dispute cases brought forward, the quality of the panel reports, and whether countries actually follow panel decisions. Small countries will now pursue complaints, it is argued, and the system will embody stronger enforcement of the rules. But automatic rights to a panel, with adoption of panel reports automatic barring a consensus vote to the contrary, would seem to create substantial incentives for increased use of panels. This, combined with a complex text from the Uruguay Round, could swamp the Secretariat's ability to deal with the caseload and even lead to a breakdown of the WTO legal process.

Where settlement of contentious issues was delayed under the old system, and subjected to resolution through conciliation, the new, firmer procedures may elevate conflict in the system and make it more open. This could be the case, for instance, with any future US section 301 trade actions. The net result in terms of strengthening of the system is thus perhaps not so clear as it may first seem.

Furthermore, while the changes to dispute settlement procedures are major, we do not see them, in the main, as directly linked to the establishment of the WTO; new procedures would likely have come into being had the old GATT structure remained in place.

Strengthening the trading system—that is, improving the GATT's functioning and decision making—had been an important objective of the Uruguay Round and was one of the issues considered early in the functioning of the GATT System negotiating group. A new world trade organization was suggested midway through the round as a way of achieving this goal, but the idea did not then capture sufficient interest. It was only in the final days of negotiation that the idea of wholesale institutional reform was revisited and accepted.[42]

---

41. Traditionally, developing countries have not made much use of the GATT dispute settlement mechanism (Ching 1992). It is therefore interesting that Singapore made the first request for a panel, over a complaint against Malaysia on restrictions on imports of polyethylene and polypropylene. The request was later dropped.

42. Originally called the Multilateral Trade Organization when it was proposed by the European Community and Canada in 1990, the United States only agreed to accept it a few days before the Uruguay Round ended in December 1993 on the condition that the name be

What the WTO has done is to resolve many of the ambiguities surrounding the implementation of Uruguay Round agreements: how intellectual property rights fit within the GATT system, how to consolidate the complex arrangements from previous rounds and other negotiations, and how to reconcile dispute settlement procedures covering the various agreements and new areas under a single umbrella.

Diverging scenarios can be drawn to illustrate the potential impact of the WTO. On the one hand, the WTO could fulfill the best hopes of its creators, strengthening the global trade system and igniting a new golden age in the trading system, with countries recommitting themselves to global cooperation. Under this scenario, existing agreements are applied with new vigor, and new agreements are arrived at more speedily and with added substance. On the other hand, the WTO could prove to be little different from the GATT regime; an inability to live up to expectations could weaken its credibility and thus hinder rather than promote the trading system. The analytical or empirical basis for favoring one scenario over another seems weak at this juncture, although the degree of government commitment to achieving a strengthened WTO will be a crucial factor.

---

changed to the World Trade Organization (see chapter 7). Stewart (1993, 1942–44) discusses the EC and Canadian MTO proposals.

4

Assessing the Impact of the Uruguay Round

The large array of topics and issues makes it difficult to grasp the content of the Uruguay Round agreements. But quite beyond the agreements themselves, the round's likely quantitative impacts are equally difficult to appraise, in their impacts either on the trading system or the wider global economy. One reason is that not all the components of the round can be readily quantified, and indeed a long list of these components have no quantitative evaluation literature: services, intellectual property, safeguards, countervail/antidumping, dispute settlement, and the replacement of GATT by the World Trade Organization (WTO).

A second reason is that even in the quantifiable areas there are many uncertainties—over the extent of liberalization in areas such as agriculture, over exactly what the preagreement situation was (such as the degree to which quotas under the Multi-Fiber Arrangement were binding or nonbinding), and over which model specification is the most appropriate. Such issues include model form—whether it be dynamic or static, constant returns or increasing returns to scale, competitive or noncompetitive—choice of functional form, and parameter values, many of which have little or no literature for use in evaluative models.

Despite the uncertainties, some attempts at quantitative assessment have been made—both after the agreements were reached and while they were being negotiated. In this chapter, we discuss estimates of impacts from a range of studies, accepting both their relatively narrow focuses and their strong assumptions. Some of the recent studies project short-run economic impacts in terms of incremental trade, welfare, and growth effects that are smaller than those predicted by studies conducted during the negotiations by international agencies such as the OECD and the GATT. This is in large part because actual liberalization in key areas is less substantive than is at first apparent and significantly less substantive than earlier models assumed it would be. In agriculture, this discrepancy can be explained by "dirty" tariffication, combined with tariff quotas, and delayed liberalization, such as with rice in Korea and Japan. And in textiles, it is due to the slow phase-out of the Multi-Fiber Arrangement (MFA), beginning with the initial elimination of nonbinding quotas and the possibility of a replacement regime involving antidumping duties. In addition, the tariff cuts, while meeting consensus percentage reduction targets, are concentrated on already-low tariffs, and the overall effects of these reductions are smaller.

However, we emphasize that these possibly smaller-than-anticipated short-run impacts are also accompanied by new trade-restricting instruments that are negotiable and transparent—through tariffication and bindings in agriculture, a significant extension of tariff bindings by developing countries, and an extension of trade liberalization into new areas such as services and intellectual property. It is these effects that set the stage for a new major reciprocity-based trade negotiation, with the prospect of new liberalization in the medium to longer term.

Model-Based Evaluations

To evaluate the quantitative impacts of the Uruguay Round, models of trade, production, and consumption linkages between major trading areas are needed. A number of studies have been made over the last two or three years, most of which are surveyed by Perroni (1995). The main studies Perroni surveyed are Harrison, Rutherford, and Tarr 1995; Hertel et al. 1995; Nguyen, Perroni, and Wigle 1991, 1993, and 1995; François, McDonald, and Nordström 1995; Goldin, Knudsen, and van der Mensbrugghe 1993; GATT 1993b; Stoeckel, Pearce, and Banks 1990; Deardorff and Stern 1990; DRI 1993; Peterson 1992.

As mentioned above, studies completed before the end of the round generally assumed there would be more liberalization than actually occurred. For instance, later runs with the Nguyen, Perroni, and Wigle (1995) model, which more accurately capture actual negotiated barrier changes, suggest roughly $70 billion in gains using 1986 as a base year, down from their earlier estimate of $212 billion, which was based on barrier changes thought likely when the Dunkel text was released. However, the piece by François, McDonald, and Nordström (1995) provided the basis for the claims by GATT Director General Peter Sutherland in the later stages of the round that there would be *larger* effects than previously thought, due to scale economies and procompetitive effects.[1]

All but two of these analyses use micro-based models, which involve different assumptions and require the specification of key parameters to assess the round's effects. In these studies, the size and distribution of gains among countries depend on the size of trade barrier changes, demand and supply elasticities, market linkages, and other structural characteristics of the economies modeled.

Several of the studies Perroni surveys assume constant returns to scale and perfect competition in their general equilibrium modeling to account for linkages among markets. They also assume imperfect substitutability between domestic and imported goods (the so-called Armington assumption). This latter assumption is commonly made to accommodate "cross-hauling" in trade data—that is, when countries are both exporting and importing a commodity—and to allow for direct calibration of import demand elasticities. The Armington assumption is also believed to lead to strong terms-of-trade effects and relatively weak quantity responses in models analyzing the effects of trade liberalization. Two studies use a different approach and employ a macro-modeling framework.

Despite uncertainties over parameter values and appropriate assumptions, Perroni concludes that these studies, most of which were executed before the round was over, suggest the round will produce global welfare gains of 1.0 to 1.5 percent of world gross product. This translates to global annual gains of $200 billion to $300 billion by early in the next century (the GATT study uses 2005 as a benchmark). These gains correspond to 4 to 7 percent of the present value of world merchandise trade (OECD 1993; Goldin, Knudsen, and van der Mensbrugghe 1993; Nguyen, Perroni, and Wigle 1993).

Using a static, perfect-competition version of their model, the most recent study by François, McDonald, and Nordström (1995) produces an estimate of annual global gains of around 0.35 percent of global product, in percentage terms of GDP, by 2005. This estimate is lower than that of Nguyen, Perroni, and Wigle (1995). When François, McDonald, and Nordström add scale economy and market structure effects, they triple the gains; by then adding dynamic effects, they increase estimates by a further 60 percent, to yield gains by 2005 of 1.3 percent of GDP. These latter two

---

1. In a speech to the annual World Bank/IMF conference in Madrid, Sutherland announced new GATT estimates of $500 billion in annual gains by 2005, up from the previous $275 billion figure. He cited "competition-enhancing effects of trade liberalization and the opportunities that it would offer for spreading fixed costs over larger markets." He also suggested that these gain estimates were on the low side because of excluded effects such as accelerated economic growth, a healthier climate for research and development, and the development of new products ("GATT Says Uruguay Round Worth $500 Billion," *Financial Times*, 4 October 1992).

adjustments are the key to the substantially larger estimate, which under-lay the GATT claim of gains equal to $500 billion per year in 2005—although this estimate is, at the end of the day, within the same range of gains estimates as earlier OECD and other estimates.

The majority of gains are concentrated in agriculture and textiles in most model results, with agriculture the more significant of the two. Most of the gains accrue to developed rather than developing countries and occur on the demand side in textiles and agriculture in developed countries as restrictions are weakened.[2] Impacts across countries are not uniform: while impacts on developing-country groups such as African countries are modest, newly industrializing economies (NIEs) and other agricultural and textile exporters experience significant gains.

The main characteristics of the studies Perroni surveys are listed in table 4.1; estimates of global welfare effects are reported in table 4.2. Nguyen, Perroni, and Wigle (1993) evaluated the Dunkel draft text and obtained an estimate of $212 billion of global gains using 1986 data; this corresponds to about 1.1 percent of gross world product, which was approximately $20 trillion in 1986 prices. This estimate is in line with the $274 billion figure obtained by Goldin, Knudsen, and van der Mensbrugghe (1993) for a 2002 baseline year (projecting world gross product to be approximately $30 trillion in 2002). The earlier GATT (1993b) figure of $230 billion for a 2005 baseline suggests smaller gains than both these studies. The differences in these results reflect differences in data, modeling assumptions, country and commodity disaggregation, and particularly elasticity estimates that provide the parameters for behavioral equations. Assumptions with re-gard to scale economies, market structure, and dynamics are especially key to the larger recent GATT estimates, and these are discussed in more detail below.

Distribution of Gains among Developed and Developing Countries

These studies apparently agree that developed economies will receive the lion's share of the welfare gains generated by trade barrier reductions in agriculture and textiles and that this will occur on the consumption side through lowered prices.

Impacts on individual countries depend on whether they are exporters or importers (especially in agriculture and textiles and clothing), as well as the values used for relevant elasticities. Goldin, Knudsen, and van der Mensbrugghe (1993) find that African countries may lose slightly (−0.3 percent of GDP) from partial multilateral liberalization, while Asian, Latin American, and other low-income countries experience substantial gains (1

---

2. The Goldin, Knudsen, and van der Mensbrugghe (1993) model suggests that only 11 percent of the gains will accrue to developing countries.

to 2 percent of GDP). The possibility that lower-income countries may lose from the round has been especially highlighted by the London-based group, Christian Aid. In its reports, which enjoyed a high profile in Europe, the group argues that certain categories of developing countries—net food importers, countries benefiting from trade preferences, commodity exporters, countries that are too underdeveloped to take advantage of new trading opportunities—will experience losses and face major structural adjustment problems due to the round (Madden and Madeley 1993; Madden 1994). The group argues that if poorer countries do indeed lose, then the decisions from the round are insupportable on income distribution grounds.

In Nguyen, Perroni, and Wigle (1995), the aggregate gain to non-OECD countries is $19 billion, or 27 percent of total gains (whereas their aggregate share in gross world products is 45 percent). Stoeckel, Pearce, and Banks (1990) also find the aggregate gains to developing countries to be small; among them, India gains the most.

According to Nguyen, Perroni, and Wigle (1995), the developing countries that experience the largest welfare gains (relative to GDP size) are middle-income agricultural importers (South Korea, Taiwan, Hong Kong, Singapore), with a 0.6 percent gain, followed by agricultural exporters (Brazil, Argentina, Indonesia, Thailand, Malaysia, the Philippines), with a 0.2 percent gain. The remaining developing countries experience smaller gains (0.1 percent of GDP). As we discuss below, the implicit value of strengthened GATT disciplines could be much more substantial for these countries, although precise quantification of its value is elusive.

In the case of textiles, the elimination of quota rents to exporters is an important factor in explaining the distribution of gains. Essentially, the removal of MFA restrictions transferred these rents from developing to developed countries. Thus, although the removal of trade barriers in these areas may improve developing countries' access to developed countries' markets, the studies indicate that developed economies gain more. Key here is the extent to which MFA quotas are binding, an issue upon which there appears to be some disagreement in the literature (Trela and Whalley 1990).

In agriculture, the round's effect on world food prices is the main determinant of the overall impact on individual countries. Studies indicate that world food prices could rise as a result of liberalization restricted to OECD countries that reduces or eliminates production subsidies; this could entail a loss for the agricultural-importing countries, particularly in the developing world. On the other hand, aggregate impacts will depend crucially upon the extent to which developing countries simultaneously liberalize their agricultural policies to harness resource allocation gains (Brandao and Martin 1993).

Studies either ignore services or use strong assumptions (such as the assumed tariff equivalents of Nguyen, Perroni, and Wigle 1993) to model services trade liberalization, owing to a scarcity of data on trade in services

Table 4.1 Characteristics of models assessing the Uruguay Round's impacts

Study	Key features	Baseline year	Trade liberalization scenarios
Harrison, Rutherford, and Tarr (1995)	General equilibrium structure 24 regions 22 commodity groups Transportation costs Monopolistic competition and increasing returns to scale Full employment of factors Long-run income-investment linkages	1992 and 2005	Uruguay Round agreement
Hertel et al. (1995)	General equilibrium structure 15 regions 10 commodity groups Perfect competition Full employment of factors Transportation costs	2005	Uruguay Round agreement
Goldin and van der Mensbrugghe (1995)	General equilibrum structure	2002	Uruguay Round agreement
Nguyen, Perroni, and Wigle (1991, 1993, 1995)	General equilibrum structure 10 regions 9 commodity groups Direct representation of MFA quotas Full employment of factors	1986	1) Dunkel draft 2) Uruguay Round agreement
François, McDonald, and Nordström (1994, 1995)	General equilibrium structure 9 regions 15 commodity groups Internal and external scale economies Perfect competition Full employment of factors Long-run income-investment linkages	1990 and 2005	Uruguay Round agreement
Page and Davenport (ODI) (1994)	Partial equilibrium calculations of disaggregated trade effects	2005	Uruguay Round agreement
Haaland and Tollefssen (1994)	General equilibrium structure 4 regions 15 products Full employment of factors Increasing returns to scale and imperfect competition	1985	33% tariff cut for manufactures 33% cut in NTBs for manufactures and services
Goldin, Knudsen, and van der Mensbrugghe (OECD) (1993)	General equilibrium structure 22 regions 20 commodity groups Ad valorem representation of MFA quotas Full employment of factors in base case Dynamic structure	2002	36% cut in all tariffs and NTBs

Table 4.1 Characteristics of models assessing the Uruguay Round's impacts (cont.)

Study	Key features	Baseline year	Trade liberalization scenarios
GATT (1993b)	General equilibrium structure 7 regions 10 commodity groups Full employment of factors Dynamic closure	2005	Implementation of Uruguay Round market access offers as of 19 November 1993
DRI (1993)	Macroeconomic structure 12 regions 8 traded goods Dynamic structure with endogenous productivity growth Endogenous unemployment of labor	2000	33% cut in all tariffs and NTBs
Peterson (1992)	Macroeconomic structure 144 regions No sectoral disaggregation	2002	50% cut in all tariffs and NTBs
Stoeckel, Pearce, and Banks (1990)	General equilibrium structure 10 regions 7 commodity groups Transportation costs in trade Endogenous unemployment of labor	1988	1) Cut in tariffs as in Tokyo Round 2) 50% cut in all tariffs and NTBs
Deardorff and Stern (1990)	General equilibrium structure 34 regions 29 commodity groups Ad valorem representation of MFA quotas Full employment of factors in base case Dynamic structure	1987	Complete liberalization by major industrialized countries

NTB = nontariff barrier.

Sources: Deardorff and Stern 1990; DRI 1993; François, McDonald, and Nordström 1994, 1995; GATT 1993b; Goldin, Knudsen, and van der Mensbrugghe 1993; Goldin and van der Mensbrugghe 1995; Haaland and Tollefsen 1994; Harrison, Rutherford, and Tarr 1995; Hertel et al. 1995; Nguyen, Perroni, and Wigle 1991, 1993, and 1995; Page and Davenport 1994; Peterson 1992; Stoeckel, Pearce, and Banks 1990.

and to the difficulty of modeling it. If and when services trade liberalization actually takes place, one could argue that the more regulated economies will experience the largest gains from deregulation and from opening their markets to foreign suppliers and investors.[3] On the other hand,

---

3. See Winston (1993), who estimates that US deregulation in airlines, transportation, and other sectors has resulted in an average price reduction of 9 percent. If matched or more than

Table 4.2 Comparison of global welfare gains estimates

Study	Baseline year	Global annual gain (billions of dollars)	Global gain as share of world product
Harrison, Rutherford, and Tarr (1995)	1992 (short run)	52.6	Not reported
	1992 (long run)	188.1	Not reported
Hertel et al. (1995)	2005	257.8	0.42
Goldin and van der Mensbrugghe (1995)	2002	25.4–235.1	Not reported
Nguyen, Perroni, and Wigle (1995)	1986	69.9	0.4
Nguyen, Perroni, and Wigle (1993)	1986	212.1	1.1
François, McDonald, and Nordstöm (1995)	1992	51–251	0.23–1.1
François, McDonald, and Nordstöm (1994)	1990	65–291	0.31–1.36
	2005	109–510	Not calculated
Page and Davenport (ODI) (1994)	2005	Not reported	Not reported
Haaland and Tollefsen (1994)	1985	Not reported	Not reported
Goldin, Knudsen, and van der Mensbrugghe (1993)	2002	274.1	Not calculated
GATT (1993b)	2005	230	Not calculated
DRI (1993)	2000	Not reported	2.9 (G-7 countries)
Peterson (1992)	2002	Not reported	1.0
Stoeckel, Pearce, and Banks (1990)	1988	95–739	Not calculated
Deardorff and Stern (1990)	1987	Not reported	Not reported

Source: Perroni (1995).

tighter enforcement of intellectual property rights should principally benefit developed countries, which own a large portion of the global stock of intellectual property. None of these impacts are accounted for in current model-based studies, nor are other estimates of impact available.

Based on the Dunkel draft, Nguyen, Perroni, and Wigle (1993) predicted a 20 percent increase in world trade flows from Uruguay Round liberalization. The 1993 GATT study predicted a 12.4 percent increase in the value of world merchandise trade. Again, trade impacts seem to be more modest *ex*

matched in other economies due to services trade liberalization, the gains to the global economy could be substantial.

post: Nguyen, Perroni, and Wigle's 1995 study shows world trade rising by less than 10 percent. On the other hand, compositional effects are more marked; increased specialization leads to a substantial increase in exports of light industrial products (which include textiles and clothing), and to increases of 50 percent for agricultural exporters, 30 percent for agricultural importers, and 35 percent for other countries. Stoeckel, Pearce, and Banks (1990) show a large increase in the volume of exports by ASEAN and middle-income Asian countries ($10 billion to $50 billion) but more modest increases for other developing countries (India's exports increase by only $1 billion to $3 billion).

The studies offer only limited results on growth impacts, sectoral effects, and domestic distributional impacts. None of the studies surveyed discusses adjustment costs. Nguyen, Perroni, and Wigle (1993) find large positive output effects in the textiles and clothing sectors of middle-income developing countries (50 to 100 percent), which are accompanied by a reallocation of workers from other sectors. Liberalization also produces small positive employment effects (1 to 5 percent) in services and in agriculture in low-income developing countries.

Among the studies Perroni surveys, the DRI (1993) study is the first one to incorporate trade impacts on productivity growth, using a methodology based on Baldwin (1989). In his analysis of the potential growth effects of Europe 1992, Baldwin's estimates indicate that European integration could add between one-quarter to a full percentage point to the EC growth rate. This in turn translates into more substantial GDP gains along the growth path (for example, starting from a 2 percent growth rate, a permanent 1 percent increase would generate a 10 percent GDP gain after 10 years and a 21 percent gain after 20 years). The DRI study suggests that the Uruguay Round could generate increases in baseline annual growth rates of between 0.3 and 0.5 percentage points for developed economies, while productivity gains for developing countries would be lower, perhaps only 0.18 percentage points.

In their later study, François, McDonald, and Nordström (1995) use the methodology from a subsequent Baldwin paper (1992) to substantially increase their estimates of gains from the round, by around 60 percent. They assume a fixed saving rate in each region in their model and argue that conventional GDP gains, if permanent, imply a change in the steady-state level of capital in each economy (proportionate under their fixed saving rate assumption). This in turn yields more output, more savings, and a higher capital stock through a multiplier process.

This calculation can mislead in so far as such incremental output gains do not correspond to welfare gains. Productive potential is merely being reallocated over time without changing the discounted present value of potential production from the economy. Moreover, no transition path is specified in such analyses, and so costs along the transitional path are missing. As noted above, after using scale economy and market structure arguments and applying dynamic magnification adjustments, these latest estimates are still 0.5 to 1.5 percent of gross world product, the same range reported by Perroni for earlier studies.

Goldin, Knudsen, and van der Mensbrugghe (1993) examine the effects of trade liberalization on the distribution of value added between urban and rural areas. In all developing countries (except Brazil), urban value added rises, and rural value added rises everywhere except South Africa and Brazil. In general, Uruguay Round trade liberalization leads to a decrease in rural-urban income disparities.

Weaknesses of Studies in Perroni Survey

The studies Perroni surveys all have weaknesses, most of which the studies themselves acknowledge. They do not quantify all of the elements in the round, such as liberalization of trade in services and stronger protection of intellectual property rights, because of data and other modeling problems. Furthermore, outside of the recent study by François, McDonald, and Nordström (1995), they ignore efficiency impacts associated with scale economies, as well as environmental impacts. These model-based estimates also ignore the implications of system strengthening and the strategic value associated with this for particular countries.

As Perroni points out, it is also well known that calculations of the benefits from trade liberalization using assumptions of constant returns to scale and perfect competition yield estimates of gains relative to GDP that are relatively small (typically below 2 percent). Recent theoretical literature on trade liberalization has emphasized the potential importance of scale economies and imperfect competition. In industries in which production exhibits increasing returns to scale and that are characterized by a monopolistically competitive market structure, import barriers can support an inefficient scale of operation by raising the number of domestic firms and reducing their average size. Trade liberalization can force firms to move closer to an optimal scale of operation and encourage exit from the industry, thus generating substantial "rationalization" gains, particularly in small economies (Cox and Harris 1985).

Several model-based studies on the effects of regional integration (i.e., US-Canada, the North American Free Trade Agreement, the European Community) have incorporated such market structure features and have shown that efficiency gains from rationalization of imperfectly competitive industries can potentially dominate gains from trade as traditionally measured. Cox and Harris (1985) estimated gains to Canada from the Canada–United States free trade agreement as high as 8 to 10 percent of GDP. Model-based studies of the effects of Europe 1992 have produced similarly high estimates: the Cecchini report concluded that gains could be on the order of 2.5 to 6.5 percent of EC product. The model-based evaluations of the Uruguay Round that Perroni surveys incorporate assumptions of constant returns to scale and perfect competition, and so these estimates can understate (or overstate) the static welfare gains from Uruguay Round liberalization, particularly for smaller countries.

François, McDonald, and Nordström (1994) incorporate scale economy and market structure features in their model, which also incorporates an Armington structure leading to gains from increased variety of consumption within countries. But because the ratio of average minus marginal cost to average cost is fixed, in their structure the output of each representative firm does not change as trade barriers are varied. As a result, output response in product markets reflects entry or exit of firms rather than adjustment of firm-level production. As such, rationalization and scale economy effects present in other non–Uruguay Round models seem in effect to be absent, as there is no movement along a firm's average-cost schedules. The additional gains using this structure, relative to other structures, would seem to come from variety effects, which could in any case be captured using a constant returns to scale model.

Sectoral and Other Impacts

Other studies than those Perroni surveyed shed light on the potential impacts of the round. Most are studies of quantifiable market-access impacts in given sectors, and more of these focus on agriculture than any other sector; several others concentrate on textiles. There are also data and associated studies on the tariff cuts and bindings. As already noted, quantitative studies are lacking on intellectual property, trade-related investment measures, safeguards, or dispute settlement, and, to all intents and purposes, services, although a small number of tangentially related calculations are sometimes quoted to support various positions.

Agriculture

The agriculture studies have recently been surveyed in Trela (1994a). In a project for the UN Conference on Trade and Development (UNCTAD), Trela surveys 13 model-based studies, most of which were conducted before the full extent of the liberalization in the round was known and hence were subject to the same tendency to overestimate the extent of the liberalization that appears in the studies from the same period discussed in Perroni (1995). Of these 13, a smaller number are full general equilibrium studies, and a further subset are partial equilibrium studies.

Trela notes that most of the studies show that the removal of protection in agriculture, not surprisingly, has a positive effect on developed countries. The elimination of protection in developed countries alone actually raises world food prices by 8 to 15 percent. These results rely on the model-based evaluation that exports of agricultural supplies from developed countries fall with the Uruguay Round liberalization, a conclusion that is dependent on model representation of policies in their ad valorem equivalents rather than as explicit representations (Whalley and Wigle 1991). Whalley and Wigle show that with a voluntary set-aside program, increases in support prices can stimulate production from farmers whose program choice does not change, but if participation rises and the amount of land set aside rises, the net effect on production is unclear.

The models' results vary substantially in the magnitude of the price changes across the products they consider, with the most pronounced variation occurring for products benefiting from the highest levels of protection—primarily wheat, dairy, sugar, and meats in the developed world. Partial equilibrium studies generally show more variation in their reported price effects, but general equilibrium models tend to show more consistency in the price responses.

Interestingly, in all of these model analyses, the simultaneous liberalization of both developed and developing countries seems to significantly dampen world price changes; for some commodities where there are domestic price controls in developing countries, in particular in rice, world prices fall once simultaneous liberalization by developing countries is factored in. Also, most developing countries in these analyses lose from agricultural liberalization if only developed countries liberalize. However, when the developing countries also liberalize, developing-country welfare moves from a loss to a gain.

Some of the models also capture productivity effects, although this is typically done in a somewhat ad hoc manner. The inclusion of price-responsive productivity growth has substantial implications for all of the model results. When liberalization by developed countries alone is examined, model results point to gains for the majority of developing countries. Gains even occur for countries that are net importers of food after liberalization. The only countries that lose are those that are especially heavy net food importers—in North Africa, Bangladesh, or Taiwan. In such analyses, the developing countries are estimated to gain as a group by $16 billion. Furthermore, model results suggest that when developing countries simultaneously liberalize their policies, eventually all the developing countries are better off in a net welfare sense, and only a few incur losses.

The more recent of the studies that Trela examines tend to focus on partial rather than full liberalization and correspond to proposals made at various points in the Uruguay Round. Interestingly, price rises tend to be larger than under full global liberalization because only the positive distortions in the developing countries are removed as a result of developing-country participation in agricultural liberalization. Moreover, when endogenous technological change is incorporated in these analyses, the majority of prices increase slightly more than when that assumption is dropped.

Limitations of Agriculture Studies

Trela emphasizes important limitations in the studies surveyed. Many of the earlier studies only include trade in temperate-zone and subtropical products, leaving a large number of commodities and potential export interests untouched. In addition, as mentioned earlier, agricultural policy interventions in most of the studies are typically only represented in ad valorem equivalent form. As such, they do not adequately address realistic policy representations, and a number of papers argue that a much more realistic representation could even change the sign of the model-based response.

Textiles

Trela (1994b) produced a survey piece of the model-based analyses in textiles as part of the same UNCTAD project. Reviewing these models, Trela emphasizes the dichotomy between the long-run implications of MFA elimination and the adjustment process vis-à-vis the 10-year phase-out of the MFA. She emphasizes that in evaluating the impact of the MFA liberalization there are many factors to weigh, and many of these remain unquantified, such as quality upgrading (substituting into items of higher quality in response to a quota on physical units), quota hopping (relocation of production from quota-restricted to less quota-restricted countries, as, for example, from India to Nepal), and other phenomena.

There are fewer models of the impact of textile liberalization under the round than there are of agricultural liberalization, and most of these are based on data from the mid- to late 1980s, which do not reflect the substantial changes in world trade patterns that have occurred since. For instance, in the 1990s China has become the largest single-country supplier to both the United States and the European Union, and the significance of Hong Kong and South Korea in terms of shares of trade in apparel has declined in recent years.

Like the overall studies in Perroni's survey, the sectoral studies find that the benefits of eliminating MFA accrue largely to developed countries (whose consumers see reduced prices for textiles) in part because developing countries do not receive the rents they enjoyed under quota restrictions. Gains still exist for developing countries, but they are relatively small. Moreover, these small gains will accrue to the majority of developing countries, even the relatively large holders of quotas and higher-cost suppliers, such as South Korea and Taiwan. This reflects the fact that all developing countries are restrained in their potential sales to developed-country markets, and hence the removal of quotas takes market share away from developed countries.

The sectoral studies also analyze the role and size of the rent transfers from developed to developing countries associated with the MFA. They generally project these rent transfers to be smaller than conventionally thought. This is an important feature of the model-based results; most of them assume that full rent transfer occurs, which in turn implies that the importing country is small (i.e., is a price taker in world markets and has an open economy) and the exporting country is large. This is not so in the case of the United States and the European Union, which import textiles from small developing countries. Indeed, in the other extreme—when the exporting country is small and the importing country is large—little or no rent transfer will occur.

Trela also emphasizes complementary work that focuses on other effects from MFA elimination, including internal quota allocation schemes, which are widely used in many exporting countries. Such schemes lock in existing, relatively high-cost sources of supply. Trela cites work showing that these effects dominate the conventional gains to developing countries from elimination of the MFA.

Trela also cites initial results on the phase-out that support the contention that most adjustment will be postponed until the final stage of the 10-year period. In these analyses, the distinction between binding and nonbinding quotas is crucial for the results. However, the data are poor in this area and need improvement. Also, these models do not capture the effects of transitional safeguards, which are part of the phase-out process.

Services

There is relatively little model-based work—and, indeed, little data—on the round's impact on sectors other than agriculture and textiles. This is especially critical in the case of services, whose impact from the round is likely substantial but hard to quantify.

One striking finding in the services area is that potential gains to the United States from eliminating Jones Act restrictions on maritime transportation are of the same order of magnitude as the gains from removing textiles restraints or restraints on automobile dealers in the mid-1980s (François et al. 1996). Cost differentials of domestic and foreign supply of these services, which they show are large, are key to their analysis. More broadly construed, their results suggest that the potential gains from liberalization of services are large, even though the actual effects of the round in this area are relatively small.

Tariff Cuts and Bindings

Finally, data are now available on Uruguay Round tariff cuts and bindings and their coverage. François, McDonald, and Nordström (1995) draw on GATT data on pre- and post-round tariff rates and tariff bindings (tables 4.3a and b). Particularly striking is the change in tariff bindings for devel-

Table 4.3a Tariff cuts in the Uruguay Round[a] (percentages)

Product	United States		European Union		Canada		Developing and transition economies	
	Pre-round	Post-round	Pre-round	Post-round	Pre-round	Post-round	Pre-round	Post-round
Nongrain crops, wool, and livestock	0.0391	0.0314	0.0575	0.0360	0.0401	0.0365	0.1805	0.1391
Coal, oil, gas, and other minerals	0.0130	0.0083	0.0112	0.0082	0.0259	0.0131	0.1151	0.0949
Processed food, beverages, and other manufactured items	0.0358	0.0161	0.0561	0.0264	0.0626	0.0294	0.1800	0.1331
Trade and transport services	0.0000	0.0000	0.0000	0.0000	0.0000	0.0000	0.0000	0.0000
Utilities, construction, and other private and government services	0.0000	0.0000	0.0000	0.0000	0.0000	0.0000	0.0000	0.0000
Forestry products	0.0028	0.0000	0.0001	0.0000	0.0001	0.0001	0.0014	0.0012
Fishery products	0.0118	0.0094	0.1294	0.1069	0.0316	0.0207	0.3522	0.0814
Paddy rice, wheat, and other grains	0.0163	0.0103	0.0421	0.0021	0.0105	0.0069	0.1734	0.1343
Textiles	0.1050	0.0746	0.0901	0.0676	0.1856	0.1173	0.3029	0.2029
Clothing	0.1672	0.1521	0.1260	0.1094	0.2289	0.1655	0.1462	0.1083
Chemicals and rubber	0.0498	0.0300	0.0766	0.0423	0.1027	0.0530	0.1906	0.1321
Primary iron and steel	0.0448	0.0022	0.0530	0.0049	0.0741	0.0036	0.0873	0.605
Primary nonferrous metals	0.0285	0.0264	0.0719	0.0590	0.0488	0.0271	0.0266	0.0211
Fabricated metal products	0.0472	0.0278	0.0570	0.0305	0.0966	0.0601	0.0848	0.0688
Transport equipment	0.0482	0.0460	0.0686	0.0596	0.0813	0.0535	0.2724	0.1728
All mechandise trade	0.0463	0.03231	0.05372	0.03248	0.07412	0.04181	0.1348	0.0978

Table 4.3b Tariff bindings on industrial products[a]
(percentage of tariff line items bound)

Region	Pre-round	Post-round
US, North America	99	100
Western Europe	79	82
Developed countries	78	99
Developing countries	22	72
Economies in transition	73	98

a. Pre-round refers to 1986 base data; post-round refers to the end of the Uruguay Round implementation period.

Source: François, McDonald, and Nordström (1994, table 13 and figure 2).

oping countries—from 22 to 72 percent of tariff line items—and the increase in bindings in developed countries generally and in economies in transition.[4] As a result of the round, the vast majority of tariffs are now bound, some at high levels and significantly above previous levels. In terms of the tariff cuts themselves, they fit within the general target of a 35 percent average tariff cut but, as we noted earlier, tend to concentrate more heavily on small tariffs, so that by the averaging of the percentage reduction figures, though it maintains the target, masks the fact that less substantial cuts were achieved in some sectors with larger initial tariffs.

The Basis for Assessment of Impact from the Round

In the discussion of impacts of the round thus far in the chapter, the basis for assessment is the preceding GATT round. That is, studies cited have judged the trade and consumption effects of incremental changes in barriers and other trade-restricting measures due to the round. The reference point for such evaluations is the status quo. There is, however, another possible reference point: did the trade negotiating round prevent a reversion to some worse outcome, such as a retaliatory Nash equilibrium?

The question of the appropriate reference point is important. Incremental effects of GATT negotiating rounds on trade, welfare, and production tend to be judged as relatively small. But if the alternative in the face of a failure to conclude the round is a full-fledged trade conflict, the contribution of the round would have to be judged as larger by orders of magnitude.

Perroni and Whalley (1994) use a numerical general equilibrium model of the global economy whose primary aim is to evaluate the incentives for smaller countries to negotiate regional trade agreements with large neighboring countries that account for a large fraction of their trade. The study concludes that recent regional trade agreements involving bilateral (or regional) arrangements between larger and smaller countries tend to be insurance-driven. That is, the incentive for smaller countries is safe-haven access to large-country markets in the event of a breakdown in global trade arrangements and a reversion to a tariff-ridden, noncooperative outcome.

Perroni and Whalley use a regional general equilibrium structure calibrated to 1986 data, from which they calculate the welfare implications of global trade conflicts involving complete reversion to a noncooperative outcome. For the world economy as a whole, they compute the real global

---

4. François, McDonald, and Nordström (1994, 4) report that tariff bindings on industrial products for developed countries increased from 78 percent of tariff lines to 99 percent and for transition economies from 73 to 98 percent.

Table 4.4   Regional consequences of a global trade retaliation scenario

Region	Welfare loss or gain from a global trade war as a share of GDP	Tariff level in global trade war (percent)
United States	+1.2	481
Canada	−25.5	117
Mexico	−8.5	181
Japan	−5.2	235
EU	+3.7	1013
Other Western Europe	−32.2	170
Rest of world	−10.6	n.a.
World	−6.0	

Source: Perroni and Whalley (1994, 26).

loss from such a conflict at around 6 percent of global income (relative to 1986 data). But the losses to smaller countries are large, around 30 percent of income, and the gains to large countries (i.e., the European Union and the United States) are significant, indicating both their power in global trade and their relative insulation from global conflicts. As indicated in table 4.4, the tariff levels associated with conflicts of this kind are also very large.

While these calculations are perhaps a little extreme in assuming that a Nash retaliatory trade war would be carried through to its full conclusion, they underline the importance of which basis a study uses for assessment of the round. If the impacts are evaluated relative to the status quo, one set of conclusions is reached. If their impacts are evaluated relative to a Nash equilibrium, the impacts are quite different. We do not mean to suggest that a full-fledged trade conflict is necessarily the appropriate basis for evaluation, but the analyses' sensitivity (or lack thereof) to these assumptions is worth stressing.

Conclusion

All in all, the Uruguay Round represents a substantial change in trading arrangements, great uncertainty as to the quantifiable and nonquantifiable aspects, and some improvement in market access and broadening the system. In the key areas of quantifiable access improvements (tariffs, textiles/apparel, agriculture), we stress on the one hand the more limited liberalization that seems to have been achieved relative to expectations and, on the other hand, the opportunities that have been created for future negotiations because of the bindings and added transparency, particularly in agriculture and to a lesser extent in textiles and apparel.

As with previous GATT rounds, it is also important to underscore that at the end of the day, one of the main impacts of the Uruguay Round has undoubtedly been to underpin the multilateral process. The "bicycle," whose forward momentum so many have emphasized as being crucial to the multilateral process, is still in motion at the end of the round. It heads toward a future negotiation, which, like previous negotiations in the GATT, will likely be fundamentally reciprocity-based negotiations. Our belief is that this negotiation will in part be built upon the Uruguay Round agreements, especially in the key areas of tariff bindings and transparency of barriers.

5

Linkage of Trade Policy to Nontrade Objectives

Toward the end of the round, there was growing interest in potential overlaps between trade and nontrade objectives, especially environmental protection and workers' rights, and thus greater impulse to consider domestic policies in these areas. Dealing with these interactions will be a central challenge for the trading system, even more so in the future than it was during the negotiations.[1] These areas are being considered in the World Trade Organization's Committee on Trade and Environment (CTE) that was established at the Marrakesh meeting.[2]

Clearly, there is a risk of higher trade barriers with this linkage between trade and nontrade policies. The issues are the degree to which a resulting impairment of global economic performance is acceptable in exchange for improved domestic policies, and whether there might not be more suitable instruments for achieving such objectives. Where existing trade treaties and new domestic legislation are inconsistent, the issue of which takes

---

1. This chapter draws in part on material presented in Whalley (1991, 1996).

2. The committee is considering the need for rules to encourage trade and environmental measures for sustainable development, avoidance of protectionist trade measures, and surveillance of trade measures used for environmental purposes (*Inside U.S. Trade*, 3 November 1995, 13–15; *GATT Focus Newsletter* 107, 8; "GATT WTO News," 24 June 1994, 7–9). Schultz (1994) gives a careful analysis of WTO provisions that may affect environmental considerations, including the Agreement on Technical Barriers to Trade, the Sanitary and Phytosanitary Agreement, subsidies, dispute settlement, and public participation. She also makes recommendations to the Committee on Trade and the Environment (Esty 1994).

precedence arises. How will the World Trade Organization (WTO) deal with these issues?[3]

The position one takes on these issues involves inevitable trade-offs. On the one hand, there are clearly legitimate concerns that should be addressed. On the other hand, the measures taken to elicit a desired nontrade outcome may contract trade. On economic efficiency grounds, trade policy may not be the best remedy for nontrade problems. A related concern is policy capture: support for such trade policy interventions may come from those not directly interested in the nontrade policy objective at issue, such as when unions seek improved working conditions abroad as a means of protecting their own members. Because it is impossible to separate policy capture from the appropriate use of trade policy tools, the bias must be weighted toward nonintervention in most cases.

We also comment on the quantitative dimensions of trade-environment and other linkages such as that with competition policy. A number of recent studies suggest that the quantitative implications for overall system performance of the environment-trade linkages identified thus far are relatively small. The resolution of the tuna-dolphin dispute, for instance, will make little difference to the overall performance of the US and Mexican economies, though it will clearly be of great importance to the sectors involved and, indeed, from a symbolic and precedent-setting point of view, is crucial to the environmental and other groups involved (this case is discussed in more detail later in this chapter).

It is true that the debate has focused on a few cases that will be important as precedents rather than hindrances to economic performance. But we suggest that things may be poised to change. We foresee that small, isolated skirmishes of little significance to overall economic performance will escalate into much more wide-ranging policy debates with more pronounced impact on economic activity and trade. The possibility of trade measures being routinely used to offset the effects of wage differentials across economies will have major implications for trade, as will policy interventions to deal with climate change such as carbon taxes, which could hike consumer prices for fossil fuels and have major effects on trade in manufactures.

---

3. The relationship between competition policy and trade policy is also gaining increased recognition. According to Julius (1990, 11) "competition policy has the potential to overtake trade policy as the most contentious area of international economic relations." She also notes the extreme difficulty in negotiating areas of competition policy that require harmonization of domestic regulations. For example, in banking it took 12 years of negotiations before the Cooke Committee achieved agreement on a common set of capital adequacy ratios to be applied in major OECD countries (Julius 1990, 95; Cooke 1989).

Trade and Environment

The clash between environmental and trade policies has a number of origins (Esty 1994, 9–32). One is the higher profile now given to environmental issues in the political arena. Another is the ambiguity over how trade rules relate to environmental issues and the past lack of clear determinations on environmental issues under the GATT (see table 5.1 for case summaries).

These clashes are surfacing in a number of forums and by several means. First come trade measures justified on environmental grounds. These cover such matters as the protection of endangered species, methods used to catch and entrap species, possible threats to rain forests from trade in tropical lumber, trade in hazardous and toxic wastes, and enforcement of environmentally related safety and sanitary standards (typically affecting agricultural products).

In recent years, there have been actions in all these areas and on many fronts. The high-profile GATT panel has been concerned with tuna fishing off the Mexican west coast (*International Trade Reporter*, 12 October 1990, and 20 February 1991; *Focus GATT Newsletter* 78, 2). Tuna were being caught in nets that also caught and killed dolphins.[4] The United States repeatedly asked Mexico to take steps to reduce the number of dolphins killed in these tuna catches and was not satisfied that Mexico had responded. Invoking the US Marine Mammal Protection Act, Earth Island Institute, a California nonprofit group, petitioned for a ban on the importation of canned, frozen, and fresh tuna into the United States from five countries: Mexico, Panama, Venezuela, Ecuador, and Vanuatu.[5] The law also required that canned tuna sold in the United States be labeled so as to certify that the tuna was caught in a dolphin-friendly manner.

The Mexicans requested a GATT panel, arguing that the United States had no right under the GATT to impose such a trade ban. The United States said that under GATT Article XX(g) it could use trade bans to

---

4. Because tuna swim below dolphins in the eastern tropical Pacific Ocean, fishermen could encircle the dolphins with purse seine nets to catch the tuna. In 1986 this caused the death of approximately 133,000 dolphins. Changes in fishing methods reduced these deaths to 27,500. In 1992 an agreement was signed between the major tuna fishing countries that aims to reduce the deaths to dolphins to fewer than 5,000 by 1999 (*International Legal Materials* 33, no. 4 [1994], 886).

5. The Marine Mammal Protection Act also has an "intermediary protection clause," which applied the tuna ban to all countries with whom Mexico and the four other named countries trade. The United States then applied an embargo on tuna imports from another 15 countries, including France, Italy, Spain, and the United Kingdom. The European Community subsequently requested a GATT panel over the US embargo (*Focus GATT Newsletter* 91). The second tuna panel report was issued in June 1994. The panel examined a complaint by the European Community and the Netherlands against the US import restrictions. The panel ruled against the United States and "recommended the Contracting Parties request the United States to bring the measures in question into conformity with GATT obligations" (*Focus GATT Newsletter* 110, 6; report reproduced in *International Legal Materials* 1994).

Table 5.1 Environment-related disputes in the GATT, 1982–96

Year	Countries involved	Issue	Outcome
1982	Canada vs. United States	US prohibition of tuna imports from Canada	Panel ruled the import restrictions could not be justified under Article XX(g) for conservation purposes because the United States had only selective restrictions in place on domestic tuna production and had not restricted domestic tuna consumption.
1987	Canada, European Community, Mexico vs. United States	US taxes on petroleum and certain imported substances (Superfund)	Panel ruled the tax levied on imported petroleum at a higher rate than domestic petroleum was inconsistent with national treatment. However, panel stated it could not rule on the environmental objectives of the taxes and that the GATT had not adopted the OECD polluter pays principle.
1988	United States vs. Canada	Canadian measures on unprocessed herring and salmon	Panel ruled the measures to limit foreign access to certain unprocessed herring and salmon supplies were not justified under Article XX(g) because the measures applied only to selective herring and salmon supplies and did not apply to domestic processors and consumers.
1990	United States vs. Thailand	Thai restrictions of cigarette imports	Panel agreed Article XX(b) could apply to measures taken to reduce the consumption of cigarettes because smoking constituted a serious risk to human health. However, because Thailand did not restrict domestic cigarette production or sales, panel found the discrimination against imported cigarettes was not "necessary" and other nondiscriminatory measures could be found to achieve their health objectives.
1991	Mexico vs. United States	US restrictions of tuna imports under the US Marine Mammal Protection Act and US labeling requirements that tuna products are "dolphin-safe"	Panel upheld the Mexican argument against the tuna embargo on the grounds that national treatment required a comparison of like products between exporting and importing countries and not a comparison of production methods. Panel also found Article XX did not apply in this case because it did not allow a contracting party to take measures to enforce its own laws on animals and natural resources outside its borders. Panel did find in favor of the United States on the labeling issue. Panel report was not formally adopted by the GATT Council, as the United States and Mexico were seeking a bilateral solution.

Table 5.1 Environment-related disputes in the GATT, 1982–96 (Cont.)

Year	Countries involved	Issue	Outcome
1993	European Community, the Netherlands vs. United States	US restrictions on tuna imports on intermediary countries under the US Marine Mammal Protection Act	Panel found that US import restrictions on tuna and tuna products from both primary and intermediary countries were in violation of Article III (national treatment), were against Article XI:I, and were not covered by Article XX. It recommended the Contracting Parties request the United States bring its measures into conformity with its GATT obligations. Panel report remains unadopted. However, the United States has negotiated bilateral agreements with Mexico, Colombia, Costa Rica, Ecuador, Panama, and Venezuela that will commit the Latin American countries to adopt dolphin-friendly fishing practices. US environmental groups recommended (in September 1995) that Congress lift the ban on tuna.
1994	European Union vs. United States	EU challenges several US measures—CAFE Standards, Gas Guzzler Tax, and Luxury Tax—ostensibly designed to encourage higher automobile fuel economy, because they are discriminatory against foreign manufacturers in effect, if not intent	Panel found in favor of the US right to employ such policies, determining that if they were clearly intended to achieve a legitimate environmental purpose, then the "least trade restrictive" obligation did not need to be met. In regard to the method of calculating compliance with its regulations, the panel found partly against the United States. The EU blocked adoption of the report, contending that the approaching US ratification vote on the Uruguay Round had distracted the panel from finding against the United States.
1996	Venezuela and Brazil vs. United States	US requires foreign gasoline producers to use US industry average baseline of contaminants to mark progress toward certain pro-environmental standards	In its first judgment, the new WTO finds the US requirements to be discriminatory against foreign producers. The panel took issue not with the environmental objective, but the de facto discrimination in its implementation. The US EPA itself had earlier testified that the rules used to implement the regulations had been constructed to favor US industry.

Sources: Focus GATT Newsletter 85 and 110; GATT, "Trade and Environment," factual note, 1991; *Financial Times,* 29 September 1995, 4; International Legal Materials (1994).

protect endangered species. But the Mexicans countered that no endangered species were at issue.

The Mexicans also appealed the labeling requirement on the grounds that this violated the marks-of-origin provisions of GATT Article IV, which only requires a mark-of-country origin.

The Mexican panel request marked the first time that a GATT panel had been asked to rule on an environmental issue in this way.[6] Environmental groups went to Geneva both to protest the issue at hand and to decry the perceived anti-environment nature of the GATT.[7]

A related case involved US moves to pressure Japan over trade in sea turtles (*New York Times*, 12 March 1991, A12). The US Commerce Department determined that Japan was contributing to the demise of the hawksbill sea turtle by encouraging domestic trade in eyeglass frames, mirror handles, ornamental combs, and other items made from imported turtle shells. This finding went forward for presidential review and possible imposition of a ban on imports containing turtle shells. The United States declared this particular turtle to be endangered nearly 20 years ago and banned direct imports of turtle shells in 1973, an action that is clearly GATT-legal. The issue was whether the GATT allowed the United States to ban items made from the turtle shells.

On two previous occasions, the United States had determined that Japan was hunting endangered species of whales, but in neither case did the United States apply a trade embargo, in part because it imports very little whale meat. Environmental groups had instead relied on publicity, including that for the associated slaughter of porpoises.

Many other trade actions have been put in place or are under consideration for environmental reasons. Some of these are codified in the 1975 Convention on International Trade in Endangered Species (CITES). One of the better known is the ban on imported ivory, which the World Wildlife Federation helped lobby to bring about in 1987.[8] There has been substantial debate as to the effectiveness of this trade ban; it may have simply increased prices for ivory and hence increased the incentives for poaching and smuggling.

---

6. Interestingly, in an earlier panel report on the US Superfund Act of 1986 sought by Canada, the European Community, and Mexico, the panel said it had no authority to rule on the legitimacy of the environmental objectives behind the fund, only the GATT compatibility of the border tax measures involved (GATT 1991, annex II, 41).

7. In September 1995 US environmental groups recommended that Congress lift the ban on tuna after the United States negotiated commitments by Mexico, Colombia, Costa Rica, Ecuador, Panama, and Venezuela to adopt dolphin-friendly fishing practices (*Financial Times*, 29 September 1995, 4).

8. The ban on trade in elephant and rhinoceros products was extended in March 1992, despite pressure from Zimbabwe and Botswana to allow limited trade in elephant hides and meat. See further discussion of the ivory ban in Barbier et al. (1990).

Trade bans on tropical lumber have also been proposed to deal with threats of rain forest destruction.[9] Some view this course as a relatively ineffective way of dealing with deforestation, since so much lumber cutting in tropical climates is for slash-and-burn purposes (i.e., forest clearing) rather than for export.[10]

There seems to be little doubt that in the majority of these cases, trade bans are a second-best environmental policy (see discussion in Beghin, Roland-Holst, and van der Mensbrugghe 1994). Sometimes this is because the issues are cross-border and affect only small areas within countries, so that use of national policies seems inappropriate; at other times, production controls rather than trade actions would be more effective.

An ancillary issue is whether the forgone gains from trade exceed the environmental costs that trade imposes. Valuing environmental and trade costs and benefits is exceedingly difficult and greatly complicates policy decisions. The value of species reflects potential pharmaceutical benefits from plants and fauna, as well as the "existence value"—that is, the value consumers would place on ensuring the survival of a species or habitat. Samples, Gowen, and Dixon (1986, quoted in Pearce 1991), for instance, put the existence value of the bald eagle at $11 per adult in 1980 dollars, and Pearce (1991) suggests that the current existence value of the Amazon rain forest might be $8 per adult in the countries of the Organization for Economic Cooperation and Development (seemingly undervalued at about $3 billion). Such estimates are at best conjectural, but economists' estimates of gains from trade are also conjectural, with large ranges typical.

The relevant legal issues address the rights of GATT members to use bans to control imports under Article XX(b) of GATT.[11] In the case of bans of transshipment of hazardous or toxic substances, GATT disciplines are relatively clear. There have been numerous cases of bans being applied to international trade in nuclear waste, spent fuels, PCBs, and other hazardous materials. In no case has the importing country's GATT right to employ such a ban been contested.

But in the agricultural area, environmental issues become intertwined with issues of health and safety, greatly complicating matters. The Eu-

---

9. In 1991 the Netherlands called for a ban on all imports of tropical timber that is not "sustainably" produced (Barbier et al. 1991). See also the discussion of alternative economic approaches to slowing forest clearing in Pearce (1991).

10. According to Anderson (1992, 164–65), "Eighty percent of all wood produced in developing countries is not for industrial use but simply for fuel." Forests were a particularly contentious issue at the Earth Summit in 1992, where developing countries blocked developed-country import bans of unsustainable forest products.

11. Petersmann (1993) discusses legal questions surrounding environment and trade disputes in the GATT and how the environment question was handled during the Uruguay Round negotiations.

ropean Union justified trade restrictions based on its detection of residual growth hormones in US cattle.[12] The United States took issue with the restrictions, claiming the hormones did not pose a health risk. This case escalated into a major US-EC trade conflict during the Uruguay Round.

Interactions between trade and environmental policies, however, go further than trade bans. The trade effects of domestic environmental policies are also an issue. A high-profile case in this area involved regulations in Denmark requiring the use of reusable containers for soft drinks and beer (*The Economist*, 14 October 1989). The rules were challenged in the European Court of Justice by the European Commission on the grounds that similar regulations did not exist in other European countries and that they forced non-Danish companies wishing to sell in Denmark to use separate production facilities at great cost. Danish companies selling into the rest of Europe, it was alleged, faced no such disadvantage. As such, the regulations were alleged to be a trade impediment in violation of the Treaty of Rome. The European court first found in favor of the Commission and required Denmark to suspend their reusable bottle regulation, drawing the ire of environmental groups. In September 1988 the court found in favor of Denmark.

This case became for environmentalists a clear example of how trade interests can dominate environmental interests[13] and how international treaties could contravene the rights of EU member states to pursue domestic environmental policies. They also saw it as a herald of further conflicts between environmental objectives and trade treaties. The environmental advocacy community henceforth pointed to GATT regulations as inappropriate constraints on the application of domestic environmental laws.

Consequently, many of these groups called for amendments to the GATT that would allow for domestic environmental actions even if they violate other GATT provisions. One such group, the Canadian Environmental Law Association, suggested that Article XX of the GATT be amended to contain a new environmental protection provision (Shrybman 1989). According to this provision, nothing in the GATT should be construed as preventing any party from taking any action deemed necessary to protect the environment, including the establishment of import or export restrictions or the use of subsidies, nor prevent any remedy of adverse environmental effects or those affecting conservation of natural resources.

The group defined actions considered necessary to preserve the environment and suggested that in any dispute that may arise under the GATT regarding actions, domestic or otherwise, taken to protect the environ-

---

12. See appendix C for details of this dispute. Already, disputes have been taken to the WTO based on the Sanitary and Phytosanitary Agreement, including a dispute between the United States and South Korea over inspection requirements for imported fruits and vegetables.

13. The unwillingness of the GATT panel to rule on the appropriateness of US policies on environmental grounds in the Superfund case was another.

ment, the onus should be on the complainant to prove that the measure was not taken in good faith and that it was unreasonable. The broad sweep of this proposed amendment further illustrates the growing conflict between domestic environmental policies and international trade obligations created in a preenvironmental era.

The North American Agreement on Environmental Cooperation

This issue is likely to be even more contentious in the 1990s. It already arose in bilateral US-Mexico trade discussions as part of the North American Free Trade Agreement (NAFTA) negotiations because of the strong perception in the United States of relatively lax Mexican standards.[14] The pressure from US interest groups to recognize environmental issues in the trade agreement was so great that a side agreement on the environment had to be added before the NAFTA could be submitted to the US Congress for ratification.

The environment side agreement reinforces the commitment of each country to enforce its own domestic environmental laws and policies, creates a Commission for Environmental Cooperation, and establishes a cooperative work program (Canada 1993b). Priorities include establishing limits for specific air and water pollutants, performing environmental assessments of projects that cross borders, and providing reciprocal legal recourse for damage or injury caused by transborder pollution.

In the event that consultations fail to resolve a dispute over a country's failure to enforce its environment laws, an arbitral panel may impose a fine of up to $20 million for the first year. In Canada, the fine would be handled through the domestic courts, but in the case of the United States and Mexico, failure to pay the fine could result in trade sanctions.

Trade and Global Environmental Problems

That trade policies may need to take account of *global* environmental challenges is a further potential element of trade-environment conflict that has been little considered in debates on policy. But it is a long-term concern among trade policy practitioners.[15] It has commonly been assumed

---

14. Leonard and Christensen (1991) quote a 16 December 1990 *Christian Science Monitor* report that the entire Mexican federal budget for enforcement of environmental regulations is only $3.15 million (see also "Just South of the Border, Down Pollution Way," *Financial Times*, 17 May 1991, 5). However, there is some evidence that NAFTA and the expansion in trade and growth could have environmental benefits. Grossman and Krueger (1991) found that once a country's per capita income reached $4,000 to $5,000, pollution problems were alleviated as political pressures for environmental protection increased. In addition, trade liberalization could lead to specialization in sectors that cause less environmental damage. That greater environmental degradation does occur prior to such stages of development is, of course, indisputable.

15. See the discussion of possible levies on "dirty trade" within the UN Environmental Program (*The Economist*, 8–14 September 1990, 24–25).

that what is necessary to deal with global warming, chlorofluorocarbons (CFCs), and other environmental matters is an international treaty binding all signatories to reductions in levels of harmful emissions or production of which they are a byproduct. Such treaties typically rely on their signatories' commitment to abide by treaty provisions rather than specifying explicit enforcement procedures.

Such an approach neglects key interactions between environmental and other policies. Typically, global environmental policy involves a significant public-good element, since one country's actions may confer benefits on all others. To use a GATT approach to enforcement and rely on a withdrawal of concessions within the environmental area as the enforcement device simply does not seem practicable. In theory, global treaties on carbon emission reduction could specify penalty systems that would allow countries to deviate from the target levels if other countries did not meet their commitments. But this would not yield a withdrawal of equivalent concessions, as in the GATT. What seems more likely is that large countries would use threats of actions in other nonenvironmental policy areas to enforce environmental treaty commitments.

Trade sanctions have been proposed as such an instrument. Thus, environmental commitments agreed upon either globally or by a subset of larger developed countries could conceivably be in part policed through trade threats or actual retaliatory measures pending compliance, as judged from an industrial-country viewpoint.[16]

Also, if growth continues in China through the late 1990s and into the next century, given current emission levels in China, trade policies in OECD countries could be linked to China's adoption of more energy-efficient technologies and could be used to encourage China to reduce coal burning and move to oil, gas, or even nuclear power.

Even for localized problems such as US-Mexican transborder pollution or acid rain in Europe, trade threats could be part of the interaction of policies linking enforcement to environmental objectives. This possible threat of cross-retaliation onto trade in goods triggered by nonfulfillment of environmental norms and standards almost exactly parallels the debate on intellectual property enforcement in the Uruguay Round.[17]

The present system of multilateral rules has little to say about environmental policies and their impact on trade (though it may eventually under the influence of the Committee on Trade and the Environment), and further erosion of trading rules already weakened through such uses of trade actions may by itself impede global economic performance in the 1990s. Even after

---

16. There is a large North-South element in this potential conflict area. Some of the issues are discussed more broadly in Pearce et al. (1992).

17. We are grateful to Patrick Low for this observation. Japan recently began to tie environmental guidelines to aid-funded projects (*South*, February 1991, 12).

the Uruguay Round, all that countries are entitled to do under the WTO is ban imports of hazardous or toxic substances on health and safety grounds and take measures to protect endangered species. Any use of trade threats to achieve environmental objectives would run full-square into the disciplines contained in the general agreement. Environmentally motivated trade measures executed in a WTO-incompatible manner generate complaints to a WTO panel, with a dispute settlement procedure ultimately sanctifying retaliatory measures. To be WTOcompatible, any increases in barriers would have to take the form of increases in WTO bound tariffs.

In reality, environmentally motivated trade threats from larger countries would, in all probability, involve unilateral actions or threats of antidumping or other contingent trade-restricting measures. The severity of these would likely increase with escalating concerns over environmental issues. Such developments may put pressures on the trading system in the late 1990s. As the severity of such threats increases, wider problems for the global trading system will also rise to the surface. Attempts will be made to introduce environmental considerations into future WTO rounds or other trade negotiating forums.[18] And the vocabulary within which trade policy is debated could well swing more toward discussion of "green" versus "dirty" trade.

Trade and Environment in the Uruguay Round

The Uruguay Round agreement did relatively little to address the trade-environment issue because it was not part of the negotiating mandate.[19] But because of its higher profile later on in the negotiations, the issue proved important to developments running parallel to the negotiations themselves, and in particular in defining the WTO work program.[20] Environmental groups made much of the fact that the word "environment" did not even appear in the draft final act (the Dunkel text). Also, the failure to set out environmental objectives for the trading system was seen as a chance squandered to centrally address the issue and set out broad principles for the WTO.

This is not to say that the Uruguay Round's decisions are free of environmental implications.[21] For instance, they discipline the trade-restricting

---

18. Ever since the December 1990 ministerial meeting in Brussels, trade-related environment issues have been widely agreed to be on the agenda for any future rounds of talks. The work program agreed in Marrakesh is a further indication of this.

19. This section draws on the discussion in Uimonen (1994).

20. Many events helped raise the profile of trade and environment (virtually unheard of at Punta del Este in 1986) during the Uruguay Round: the tuna-dolphin dispute, the Earth Summit at Rio de Janeiro in June 1992, the vocal opposition of environmentalists to the NAFTA, and their efforts to block US adoption of NAFTA and the Uruguay Round.

21. For a summary of the Uruguay Round agreements and the environment, see GATT (1994b) and Schultz (1994).

effects of standards and regulations. The agreements on subsidies, countervailing duties, and intellectual property rights all have implications for environmental issues.

Publication of the GATT tuna-dolphin panel report in August 1991 was a defining moment for the round in this regard. It sparked a debate on GATT's authority over environmentally motivated trade restrictions, including national measures to protect environmental resources, as well as trade restrictions required in cases of noncompliance by international environmental agreements such as the Montreal Protocol and the Basel Convention on hazardous waste.[22] The tuna-dolphin panel also raised issues of the interpretation of Article XX of GATT.

In 1992 the GATT Secretariat published *International Trade 1990–91* (vol. 1), which also elevated the debate; it contained an entire chapter devoted to trade and the environment. In it, the Secretariat asserted that Article XX exceptions permitted import restrictions, but only if the environmental damage was generated by a product, not if it originated from the production process or method (PPM) that had been used to generate the product. This issue of PPMs was raised in several subsequent guises in the later stages of the round.

In the round itself, the sanitary and phytosanitary (SPS) measures and technical barriers to trade (TBT) agreements address problems raised by a number of contentious cases, including the Canadian beer can case, involving an environmental levy on beer packaged in cans.[23] The objective of these agreements is to minimize the negative effects of standards and regulations on trade and their ability to act as disguised trade barriers, while allowing GATT members to maintain standards necessary for the protection of human, plant, and animal life and health. In the TBT agreement, measures include those for environmental protection as well as those regulations which apply to PPMs.

Each agreement defines a national-treatment obligation and a necessity test, much like those in Article XX. There are loose harmonization agreements in each of the two, but the TBT agreement could become a focal point for environmental trade disputes. European countries, for instance, have been playing a leading role in developing new regulations covering waste production and recycling, which include schemes that require producers to either take back their packaging waste for disposal or recycling or pay fees to local authorities to accomplish the same objective. Because

---

22. Both the Montreal Protocol and the Basel Convention allow members to apply restrictive trade measures against nonmembers. The compatibility of these provisions with GATT Article XX has not yet been determined (GATT, *International Trade 1990–91*, vol. 1, 25).

23. In its annual budget, the Province of Ontario on 30 April 1992 introduced an "environmental levy" of 10 cents per can. The tax did not apply to soft drink cans. As most US beer exported to Canada is in cans, the United States believed the tax was protectionist (USITC 1993, 55; *GATT Activities in 1992*, 45–46; Mander and Perkins 1994).

the Uruguay Round disciplines in this area seemingly restrict domestic policies rather than border measures, they promise to be a source of ongoing conflict.

The Subsidies Agreement makes several changes to earlier rules, with potentially significant implications for environmental issues. The agreement defines a subsidy, which the GATT had not previously done, and applies to "specific" subsidies, classified in three categories.[24] Accordingly, the imposition of countervailing duties to punish lax standards would not be justifiable. The Uruguay Round agreement also sets out general subsidies, characterized by governmental financial contributions, as nonspecific subsidies and therefore nonactionable; thus nonspecific environmental subsidies are now permitted.

In the intellectual property area, the debate has been over whether the Uruguay Round agreements tighten or weaken intellectual property protection and has focused on whether developing-country access to new environmentally related technology has been improved.

On other environmentally related matters, the Uruguay Round negotiations generated varying degrees of ambiguity. In the area of standards, the thrust of agreements is to discipline trade barriers while allowing for differences in nonborder measures. Exactly how much discipline will be exerted on national regulations, especially in a case of SPS standards, and what will constitute sufficient scientific justification for high standards remain unclear.

The subsidies agreement yields clearer, albeit somewhat arbitrary, results. The use of countervailing measures to deal with unfair trade practices in the form of lax environmental standards will not be permitted. But the agreement will allow subsidies that, for example, take the form of forgone revenue for environmental taxes.

The decisions in the Uruguay Round, therefore, touch tangentially on trade and the environment and leave most of the central issues in this area for future resolution.[25]

Quantitative Dimensions

Recent studies portray a picture of limited consequences for global system performance from several of the proposed environmentally motivated

---

24. A specific subsidy is one considered only available to "an enterprise or industry or group of enterprises or industries within the jurisdiction of the authority granting the subsidy" (GATT 1994a, 230). The definition of a subsidy rests on whether there is a financial contribution by a government or other public body.

25. The Committee on Trade and Environment is to report to the first ministerial meeting of the WTO in 1996 on issues under its mandate to consider. At that time, the work and terms of reference of the committee will be reviewed.

trade actions, such as those designed to offset advantages accruing to exporters from countries with relatively lax environmental standards or the trade implications of sectorally focused trade actions, as in some of the species-related cases.[26] On the other hand, researchers have neglected some areas of environmentally motivated policy, such as carbon taxes,[27] that could have dramatic consequences for world trade, since large taxes affecting a major portion of aggregate global economic activity are involved.

These cases, in the main, require general equilibrium exercises that calibrate models to various benchmark or base-case data sets, followed by counterfactual analysis around base cases. A few such models have been constructed, and they have added an important dimension to the debate. One recent example is Perroni and Wigle (1994), who calibrate their model to a 1986 global data set covering three major groups—North America, other developed countries, and low- and middle-income countries—and a variety of pollutant activities.[28] Emissions generated through productive processes interact with various specified natural and geographical processes, including absorption and transmission of particulants through the atmosphere and oceans. In the model, these emissions contravene global environmental standards and hence worsen environmental quality for consumers.

The model covers six goods and sectors, chosen to span high and low levels of industry emissions and also to separate higher technology from lower technology industries. Having calibrated their model to a 1986 benchmark data set, they then analyze the effects of increased trade on environmental characteristics through a set of alternative trade policy scenarios, including removal of all global trade barriers.

Another recent model-based analysis looks at the effects on trade of possible US trade barriers raised to countervail perceived lax standards in key trading partners including Mexico (Low 1992). The study looks at

---

26. This section draws on the discussion in Whalley (1996).

27. Carbon taxes have already been levied in Denmark, Finland, Norway, Sweden, and the Netherlands. They are generally imposed in addition to existing taxes on fossil fuels (OECD 1994, 169). A recent OECD review of policy trends indicates there is a good deal of interest in excise taxes on goods such as energy to take more account of environmental considerations. It reports that some countries (Denmark, Sweden, Norway, and the Netherlands) are shifting from income taxation toward indirect taxes, which may include environmental taxes. Other countries (Austria, Finland, Germany, Belgium, and France) are increasing the use of specific environmental taxes (OECD Letter 417, August–September 1995, 7).

28. Perroni and Wigle directly capture the welfare effects of changes in environmental standards in explicit utility evaluations in their model, embodied in the form of damage functions.

pollution abatement costs by type of expenditure and by sector for the United States and explores what might happen to Mexican exports to the United States if the United States were to levy a special import tax to offset pollution abatement control costs incurred by US domestic industries, under the assumption that such costs in Mexico are either zero or unmeasured.

Low identifies pollution-intensive or "dirty" industries as those with the highest pollution abatement or control expenditures. He examines these industries' contribution to Mexican exports and simulates the effects of the tax on these exports using a partial equilibrium structure, which captures relevant demand-supply elasticities. Impacts on the level of trade in the original base-period data can then be evaluated.

Low has attracted substantial attention for his conclusion that the trade impacts in this case are small.[29] His study shows that US industries' pollution control expenditures represent only a small component of total costs, with only 18 of 123 industries paying more than 1 percent of the value of their output. The highest such expenditure is one industry with 3 percent; the weighted average is approximately 0.5 percent. On this basis alone, the impact of a special import tax, while still dependent on assumed elasticity values, would likely be small.

Using a simple elasticity-based approach and 1986 data, Low calculates that the imposition of such a tax would reduce Mexico's exports by less than 2 percent. In light of the approximate real doubling of Mexican trade with the United States between 1985 and 1992, the agonizing over potential application of environmentally based trade measures would appear unwarranted because of their small effect on direct trade flows.

Further model analyses capture international trade effects of policies to reduce carbon emissions (Whalley and Wigle 1991; Piggott, Whalley, and Wigle 1992). These studies analyze policies designed to deal with global warming, such as a carbon tax. The goal of the proposed tax is to stabilize global carbon emissions at early 1990s levels (the so-called 'Toronto call,' after the 1989 global scientific conference in Toronto, at which the objective was first stated).

---

29. These data, in turn, are linked to the data on abatement costs, which show the relatively small costs involved. Low's conclusion is consistent with that reached by Tobey (1990), who uses an econometric approach to test the significance of pollution effects in a Heckscher-Ohlin-Vanek model. A commodity's relative pollution intensities are defined in terms of pollution abatement costs incurred in the production using similar US data, with endowment data from Leamer (1984) and trade data from UN trade statistics. Tobey's conclusion is that stringent environmental regulations imposed on industries in the late 1960s and early 1970s by most industrial countries have not affected trade patterns to any measurable extent in the most heavily polluting industries. A more recent piece by Levinson (1994) concludes that differing environmental regulations across the US states have little effect on location decisions, in part because the cost shares involved are small.

Whalley and Wigle (1991) evaluate possible international impacts of various carbon tax options. The primary factors in their production functions are divided into energy and nonenergy inputs, with the former being subdivided into greenhouse (fossil fuels) and nongreenhouse energy. The model captures production of energy-intensive and nonenergy intensive products, as well as the international trade in these goods.

Piggott, Whalley, and Wigle (1992) examine subregional and unilateral reductions in carbon emissions that would be optimal, using a model that incorporates parameters to represent preferences toward climate change. Results are preliminary, and the trade component of results is in some cases a byproduct of analyses primarily directed toward other issues. But given the relative absence of such quantification thus far, these results provide important input to the current debate.

Initial results of Perroni and Wigle (1994) suggest that increased international trade generally has little impact on environmental quality. They also conclude that the magnitude of welfare effects of environmental policy changes are not significantly affected by simultaneous changes in trade policies. Environmental policy also has negligible effects on the size and regional distribution of the gains in trade liberalization. The tentative conclusion reached is that the extent of trade and environment interactions may be smaller than the intensity of recent debate would suggest.

In contrast to Perroni and Wigle's results, Whalley and Wigle (1991) and Piggott, Whalley, and Wigle (1992) show potentially large effects on international trade flows from a carbon tax.[30] They do not directly report trade impacts, since this was not their major focus, but in the presence of large carbon taxes, which apply to a significant input component for manufacturing (and where the tax rates that are required range as high as 800 percent in order to stabilize carbon emissions at 1990 levels), the cost component feeding through to manufactures is large. The result is a potentially major impact on international trade in manufactures and changes in trade patterns. Global consumption of energy-intensive manufactures falls sharply, and with it global trade.

Some scenarios suggest that a tax at such high levels could have consequences for global trade as major as any other economic development in the postwar years. Whalley and Wigle (1991), for example, project major changes for key regions in net trade patterns between energy-intensive goods and other goods arising from such a tax. In this scenario, Japan changes from a net exporter of energy-intensive manufactures to a net importer, as does the European Union. Other Europe, including Eastern Europe, changes from a net importer to a net exporter. In Piggott, Whalley, and Wigle (1992), there are further incidental analyses of trade impacts

---

30. The OECD has focused much attention on the economic effects of carbon taxes as well as other economic instruments for environmental purposes (OECD 1992, 1994).

from carbon taxes, and some of their unpublished results also suggest large trade impacts of a major global carbon tax.

Thus preliminary indications from model-based quantitative analyses are that the trade-environment conflicts that have been the subject of most of the debate in the GATT and other forums, including those associated with relatively lax standards, may have only limited consequences for overall global economic performance. While there are still only a few quantitative results for broader environmental actions, logic would suggest that this would hold true for any attempt to apply environmentally based trade measures to narrow sectoral issues such as the tuna-dolphin dispute.

On the other hand, the trade consequences of major environmental interventions that have not figured as prominently in the debate, such as a possible global carbon tax, could be considerably more substantial. In an extreme case, they might even reverse the growth in world trade in manufactures that we have seen in the last four decades of GATT-based trade liberalization. No doubt this quantitative picture will be further refined in the years ahead.

Competition Policy

The linkage of trade policy to domestic competition (antitrust) policies has been touted as a possible central component of a future round (Feketekuty 1993; Hoekman and Mavroidis 1994; Low and Subramanian 1995). Indeed, there are many elements that could be addressed.

First are the direct effects on trade following from a lack of internationally coordinated competition policies (Graham and Richardson 1996). To our knowledge, there are no quantitative studies to give even orders of magnitude of these effects. The most obvious conflicts involve anticompetitive practices originating outside a country's borders. Thus, suppliers from countries A and B may collude in joint activities in country C, perhaps through market-sharing agreements. Or there may be informal agreements under which the two suppliers agree to fix prices in country C or contractual arrangements involving tying purchases to various selling conditions or to the purchase of other products or services.

This situation occurs in its most extreme form when all suppliers to a market are outside the country, but similar situations can prevail if domestic suppliers service only a small portion of the market. Because of the strong presence of multinational companies in many of their domestic markets, developing countries, especially smaller ones, are most affected. But the problem also arises in midsize OECD countries where foreign suppliers serve significant portions of the market for a range of manufactured products.

The central issue is the lack of extraterritorial reach of the importing country's domestic competition policy. Advocates of an international negotiation on competition policy, therefore, suggest that measures be adopted to make it possible for countries to control collusive behavior of foreign firms on their soil. Such measures would generally lead both to freer trade and to larger international gains from specialization where the collusive practices restrict trade.

The approach generally suggested is to allow affected groups in importing countries to issue complaints for review and perhaps action before antitrust agencies in the countries from which the suppliers originate. Several problems with such an approach are widely acknowledged. One is the likely asymmetry of the number of such cases across countries; another is the information-sharing requirements involved between agencies.

Further, there have been strong objections from some quarters to an international negotiation on competition policy on the grounds that the trading system has traditionally focused on government-to-government negotiations and arrangements, not rules constraining private-sector behavior. Extending international trading rules to deal with private-sector behavior is argued to be unworkable since it would require governments to share or at least discuss proprietary commercial information, whose confidentially would be difficult to secure.[31]

The counterargument is that the WTO already encompasses private-sector actions (even if to a small degree) through, for instance, the antidumping code, which specifies arrangements under which petitions for antidumping relief by private parties may proceed. A second element of linkage between competition policy and trade focuses on lack of harmonization. The lack of both extraterritoriality and harmonization of competition policies is said to lead to pressures for trade remedies, particularly antidumping remedies in the case of price predation.

Antidumping laws are needed, it is claimed, because national antitrust authorities cannot easily determine foreign suppliers' actions, pricing, or cost structures and thus antitrust laws cannot effectively constrain predation by these suppliers.[32] The growth in the use of antidumping duties in the 1980s occurred in part because of these limits on the reach of national competition policies.[33]

---

31. The US-EU bilateral agreement on competition policy does not provide for the exchange of confidential information, but there are efforts under way to ease the restrictions.

32. See the discussion of EU antidumping practices in GATT (1993b) and European Commission (1995). Vermulst and Waer (1995) discuss Europe's post–Uruguay Round antidumping regime. Trebilcock and York (1990) cover a more wide-ranging discussion of practices in North America, Europe, and other regions.

33. According to USITC (1995, 3.1), from 1980 through 1993, 682 antidumping cases were filed in the United States, with 39.4 percent of these cases resulting in affirmative final determination.

To make competition policy international in reach, courts would need jurisdiction over more than national transactions. This would not only represent a major change in transnational legal structures and the operation of national court systems, it would also involve a surrender of jurisdiction by national legislatures to supranational bodies. The willingness of legislatures to agree to such changes is thus a major impediment. In all probability, any approach to this issue would have to be incremental rather than discrete.

The case of the European Union is often cited to demonstrate what could be feasible elsewhere.[34] There are no antidumping cases between its members because Articles 85 and 86 of the Treaty of Rome cover competition policy, backed by the enforcement powers of the European Court of Justice. Consequently, proponents of making competition policy a central part of future global trade negotiations point to the European case.[35]

Because firms in individual EU member states cannot initiate antidumping actions against those from other member states, antidumping actions are limited to trade matters outside the European Union, with the associated benefit of increased trade flows between members. In addition, the European Court of Justice is empowered to make rulings, levy fines on both firms and national governments, and enforce competition statutes. The European court represents an accumulation of 30 years of jurisprudence, and national governments are willing to both accept and comply with court rulings. This in part reflects the depth of the wider commitment to European integration and suggests that attempts to achieve similar results quickly elsewhere would probably prove difficult.

A more recent example of how limits can be applied to antidumping duties, with corresponding implications for competition laws, is the bilateral Australia–New Zealand Closer Economic Relations (CER) trade agreement. Under it, both countries have renounced use of antidumping and countervailing duties against each other, though they rarely applied such measures bilaterally in the past.[36] The two governments have empowered a body to investigate transnational violations of antitrust practices. It does not go as far as Europe in seeking to harmonize competition law; there is, for example, no unified superior court.

---

34. For more discussion of how EU competition policy works, see European Community (1989, 13–21) and GATT, *International Trade 1990–91*. For an overview of competition policy issues and review of antitrust policies in 10 countries and the European Community, see Boner and Krueger (1991) and Faull (1993).

35. In a draft report from the European Parliament, it was suggested policymakers should consider "a global competition policy to replace dumping measures" (*Financial Times*, 22 November 1990, 8).

36. When Australia enacted its implementing legislation (the Trade Practices Act of 1990), there was only one antidumping action against New Zealand (on frozen peas). It was revoked (GATT 1994c, 59).

Other observers question both how to remove antidumping laws as impediments to trade and whether their removal is necessary. For instance, it has been argued that an expansion of the national-treatment principle, currently applying to trade in goods under GATT Article III, to encompass both investment practices and competition law should be sufficient. If national treatment were to apply, then all suppliers in a market would have to abide by the same laws, including laws of the host country as they relate to anticompetitive practices in the supplying country.

Under such a literal interpretation, an extension of national treatment to competition policy would make it possible for a government in, say, country C to prosecute firms for colluding in countries A and B on the basis of their behavior in C. There are some, however, who would argue that such extended national treatment is impractical because the extraterritoriality implied would be impossible to administer; they instead advocate harmonization as a more practical approach.

A further difficulty with such harmonization efforts is that competition laws differ sharply across countries. For instance, following 1986 reforms to the competition laws (Canada 1993a), Canada has relied more heavily than before on private actions to enforce competition statutes. Thus the law gives private parties rights to sue for damages for infringements of competition law. Other countries, however, continue to use international bureaus and tribunals more heavily to oversee the activities of key corporate actors, intervening, regulating, and prosecuting as necessary. The difficulty of harmonization is thus also reflected in the problems of meshing alternative approaches to domestic law.

A third area where competition law and trade policies impinge, albeit more indirectly, is in the extraterritorial application of domestic competition laws, in particular regarding investment, mergers, and acquisitions.[37] Investment restrictions under competition laws of source countries, for instance, may still apply as companies enter other markets and as mergers and acquisitions take place. There have, for instance, been cases in which a merger between the two parent companies in country A was ruled as inadmissible by competition agencies in country B because of the implications for the two subsidiary companies in country B.[38] The concern is

---

37. In October 1994 the US government released draft guidelines for antitrust enforcement abroad. These guidelines confirm that actions can be taken against foreign anticompetitive behavior that affects US exporters and consumers. The guidelines also allow the United States to take action against a foreign cartel that colludes to raise prices if the cartel members make substantial US sales (*Financial Times*, 19 October 1994, 6, and 25 October 1994, 25; Griffin 1994).

38. For example, Julius (1990, 99) cites the case of a New York state court blocking the takeover of a UK-owned mining company by a South African–controlled firm. Since the UK-owned firm had assets in the United States, the New York court was able to block the takeover.

that some of these conflicts over extraterritorial application of domestic laws may spill over to the trade arena and elevate tensions.

Multilateral arrangements would have to be changed to deal with such problems. GATT Article III, addressing only trade-related issues beyond the national border, embodies the principle of national treatment. Its objective is to limit trade-restricting measures to transparent border measures and ultimately to make them all tariff-based. It in no way attempts to deal with competition policy. Companies that wish to bring actions against foreign competitors can only do so on the basis of these companies' actions within borders, not abroad.

Several recent attempts to synchronize competition laws are typically bilateral rather than pluri- or multilateral and may well become more common, especially if initiating a new round with competition policy as a major element proves difficult.

One of the more prominent of these has been the establishment of binational dispute panels under chapter 19 of the Canada-US Free Trade Agreement to review decisions—dumping, subsidy, or injury determinations—made by domestic agencies in either country.[39] These panels are empowered to determine whether national decisions are consistent with the domestic law and practice of the country involved. Decisions ruled inconsistent can then be remanded back to the appropriate domestic agencies for a further determination. While such panels in no way represent full cross-border harmonization,[40] they do demonstrate how incremental coordination can weaken the trade-restricting effects of measures designed to deal with trade issues arising beyond national borders that are not dealt with by existing GATT disciplines.[41]

These competition policy issues illustrate the search for new mechanisms through which countries can confront trade impediments between them that result from a lack of harmonization of domestic laws. The

---

39. Anderson and Rugman (1989) evaluate this process, both procedurally and substantively. See also Boddez and Trebilcock (1993).

40. Efforts by the NAFTA members to harmonize antidumping and subsidy rules by the end of 1995 were scrapped. Talks continue.

41. There are ongoing efforts to achieve coordination of competition policies. In September 1991 the United States and the European Community signed an agreement to improve coordination and cooperation of antitrust enforcement. This agreement was ruled void by the European Court of Justice in August 1994 because it should have been negotiated by the Council of Ministers and not the Commission (Commission of the European Communities, press release, 23 September 1991; "News and Events," The World Economy 17, no. 5, 791). In October 1994 the European Commission submitted a proposal to the Council for a new antitrust agreement with the United States. The terms of the new agreement would be the same as the original agreement. Other bilateral agreements that have been signed include United States–Australia, Australia–New Zealand, United States–Canada, and Germany–United States. There is some recognition of competition policy issues in the Uruguay Round agreements, including in TRIMs, TRIPs, and the GATS (Report of the Group of Experts 1995, 10).

central issues are how far short of full integration one can go and still achieve benefits, and how this can be done without infringing upon national autonomy in ways that are politically unacceptable.[42]

Other Linkages

While the main focus of cross-policy linkages has been the environment, and to a lesser extent competition policy, trade policy both has been and continues to be proposed as a means of achieving other non–trade policy objectives. If these other linkages intensify in the 1990s, the approach to dealing with trade and environment issues could serve as a precedent for responding to other concerns.

Labor Standards

Using trade policies to promote workers' rights and fair labor standards has received increased attention. These issues arose as part of the US debate over whether to grant fast-track authority for negotiations for a free trade agreement with Mexico[43] and then again before the signing of the Uruguay Round agreements in Marrakesh, when the United States and several other developed countries attempted to include workers' rights on the agenda of the WTO work program. This attempt failed because developing and newly industrialized countries opposed it. But the issue was raised again during the renewed debate on fast-track negotiating authority, which the Clinton administration sought to include in the Uruguay Round implementing legislation.[44]

---

42. The many impediments to harmonizing competition policies internationally make it seem unlikely a global, multilateral competition policy agreement could be reached. According to the Report of the Group of Experts (1995, 14–16) to the European Commission, an international competition code superimposed on national laws is not a realistic short- or medium-term option. They recommend developing a plurilateral agreement with a dispute settlement mechanism. They stress the importance of including countries in Asia, especially Japan, and certain Latin American countries.

43. See *Financial Times*, 25 March 1991. In an "action plan" submitted to Congress on 1 May 1991 to generate support for fast-track authority, the Bush administration pledged to negotiate a joint action plan with Mexico concerning labor issues. It was to cover improved working conditions, child labor laws, and health and safety measures (*Financial Times*, 2 May 1991, 6). Under President Clinton, the United States negotiated side agreements to NAFTA over the environment and labor.

44. Interestingly, provisions concerning environment and labor issues had to be dropped from the fast-track negotiating authority due to lack of support, especially from the business community (*Financial Times*, 24 August 1994, 1). Congress did, however, direct the president to seek a working party on labor standards in the WTO. President Clinton approved legislation making observance of workers' rights a condition of the international lending institutions (*Financial Times*, 16 August 1994, 1). Anderson (1995) discusses the implications of linking both environment and labor standards issues to trade policy.

The debates in the 1990s have precursors in the 1983 Caribbean Basin Initiative (CBI) and the 1984 extension of the Generalized System of Preferences (GSP) and can be traced as far back as the International Labor Conference in Berne in 1906 and the Havana Charter for the ITO in 1947.[45]

Under the CBI, potential beneficiary countries are evaluated according to a number of criteria, including whether workers are given "reasonable workplace conditions and enjoy the right to organize and bargain collectively" (Charnovitz 1986, 61).[46] While this is a discretionary criterion, many Caribbean countries have taken it seriously, which has led to commitments to improve workers' conditions in Haiti, Honduras, the Dominican Republic, and El Salvador (Charnovitz 1986, 66).

As part of the renewal of GSP in 1984, the US Congress added a fair labor standard to the mandatory criteria for country eligibility. Under the 1984 act, beneficiaries can be denied preferential treatment if they are not providing internationally recognized workers' rights. These rights generally include "the right of association, the right to organize and bargain collectively, a prohibition against forced labor, a minimum age for child labor and 'acceptable' conditions of work" (Charnovitz 1986, 67).

This provision has often been used to reevaluate, and in some cases deny, beneficiary status. Both Romania and Nicaragua have been denied beneficiary status as a result of a review of labor standards, and in 1987 Chile was removed from eligibility for preferential treatment. Subsequent annual reviews have led to either the reexamination of eligibility, or the suspension of benefits for Myanmar (Burma), the Central African Republic, Israel, Malaysia, Haiti, Liberia, Syria, and Indonesia.[47]

The United States has attempted to include the fair labor standards issue in discussions at the multilateral level, both during the Tokyo Round and in the post–Tokyo Round work program but could not generate enough support for wider involvement. Currently there are no articles or codes in the GATT or the WTO that apply to workers' rights specifically, although members can protect against the products of prison labor under Article XX(e) (GATT press release, "News of the Uruguay Round," 38).[48]

---

45. For the history of international fair labor standards, see Charnovitz (1986, 1992), and of the ITO, see Wilcox (1949).

46. This criterion was also included in the 1989 CBI-II legislation to extend and expand the CBI preferences.

47. Under the 1990 review, the Office of the US Trade Representative designated Namibia, Chile, Paraguay, and the Central African Republic as eligible for duty-free status, while under the 1992 review, Syria was suspended for "not taking steps to afford internationally recognized workers' rights" (USITC 1993, 98).

48. Had the Havana Charter been implemented, Article 7 on Fair Labor Standards would have applied. Under this vaguely worded article, members were to recognize the importance of fair labor standards and their mutual interest in improving working conditions. Each member was to take steps to eliminate such unfair conditions.

The North American Agreement on Labor Cooperation

Workers' rights and labor issues gained a high profile during the debate to launch the NAFTA negotiations and maintained it throughout the negotiations.[49] Thus, when President Clinton took office in January 1993, after the conclusion of the NAFTA negotiations, the administration announced that NAFTA would not be submitted to Congress for ratification until a separate side agreement on labor was negotiated.

The labor side agreement reiterates the commitment in the NAFTA preamble to "improve working conditions and living standards" in all three countries and "to protect, enhance and enforce basic workers' rights." Each country is committed to enforce its own labor laws. Cooperation on labor issues will be achieved through a Commission for Labor Cooperation and the establishment of a cooperative work program.

If a country is found to persistently fail to enforce its labor law, an arbitral panel may impose a severe fine.[50] In Canada, the fine would be enforced through the domestic courts, but in the cases of Mexico and the United States, failure to pay the fine could lead to trade sanctions. US and Mexican labor organizations recently filed the first complaint under the side agreement, accusing Sony of obstructing free association of Mexican workers (*Financial Times*, 17 August 1994, 5).

Foreign Policy

Trade policies have also been used to support foreign policy objectives.[51] These measures often take the form of trade embargoes, either against all trade with the target country or against specific products. The latter are used to exploit a country's weakness or to deprive the country of access to needed technology on national security grounds. In some cases, trade sanctions are a substitute for military confrontation, as in the case of UN-backed economic sanctions against Iraq in the fall of 1990.[52]

In other cases, trade measures are used to protest human rights abuses, as in South Africa. Once the offending policy of apartheid had been dismantled, trade sanctions were dropped. Trade sanctions are used to de-

---

49. Vocal opposition to the negotiations came from a coalition of workers' rights groups, environmental groups, organized labor, and consumer groups. The Bush administration's action plan, submitted to Congress 1 May 1991, aimed to address the concerns of these groups and generate support for the negotiations (*Financial Times*, 30 January 1991, 4; *Congressional Quarterly* 49, no. 18 [4 May 1991]).

50. The panel may impose a fine of up to $20 million for the first year (Canada 1993b, 94).

51. Hufbauer, Schott, and Elliott (1990) document 116 cases in which economic sanctions have been used since World War I, most of them since World War II.

52. In this case, it was an unsuccessful substitute, as military confrontation followed in early 1991. The United Nations currently has economic sanctions in place against Iraq and Libya.

stabilize political regimes, as a method to control nuclear proliferation, and in an effort to curb international terrorism.

These trade restrictions can often be justified under GATT Article XXI (security exceptions), which allows trade measures to protect a country's security interests. But when the United States decided to restrict imports of Nicaraguan sugar in 1983 by dividing its sugar quota among other Central American countries, Nicaragua took its case to a GATT panel. In March 1984, the GATT Council adopted the panel report, which argued that the United States had violated its GATT obligations. When the United States imposed a total trade embargo on Nicaragua in 1985, Nicaragua again requested a GATT panel. In 1986, GATT ruled the US embargo was justified under Article XXI and not in violation of GATT rules, but the action was considered contrary to the GATT's basic objectives.[53] The United States maintained the trade embargo until 1990.

The United States has also revoked a country's most-favored nation (MFN) status as a trade policy measure, as it did with Poland between 1982 and 1987. Until recently, China's MFN status was reviewed each June and had been hotly debated, mainly over human rights issues.[54]

While the use of trade policy restrictions to further foreign policy is not new, its effectiveness has generally proved disappointing. According to Hufbauer, Schott, and Elliott (1990), sanctions in and of themselves are usually inadequate to generate the desired response. In many cases, sanctions lose force because not all partners have upheld them. Other times, sanctions can hurt a sanction-imposing country's own companies and economy, thus undermining political support for maintaining them.

The experience with trade sanctions used for foreign policy objectives has important implications for other nontrade issues. Beyond the potential trade diversion and market distortions that such measures create, there is increased potential for major political conflicts. By hoisting trade barriers under a "green" flag, a workers' rights banner, or even a national security cloak, against which the targeted country has no defense, the country imposing such barriers adds to the risk of erosion of the multilateral system.

---

53. However, the GATT panel was not authorized to examine the validity of Article XXI itself, as it is considered to be up to each individual country to determine its national security interests. Thus the panel could not really rule on whether the United States had breached its GATT obligations. The panel report did recommend that in future cases the council consider the possibility that Article XXI could be invoked excessively or for other purposes if the interpretation of the article is left entirely up to the GATT member invoking it (GATT Activities in 1985, 58; Hufbauer, Schott, and Elliott 1990, 180).

54. In 1991, for instance, there was much discussion of China's record on human rights and even some discussion that China was exporting goods produced by prison labor, which the United States does not allow. In 1994, President Clinton reinstated China's MFN status and removed the link to human rights.

Dealing with Nontrade Objectives in Trade Policy

Perhaps the central issue in designing responses to pressures to use trade policy for nontrade objectives is finding the appropriate trade-off between, on the one hand, the concern to improve social or other conditions, including the environment, and, on the other hand, the risk of a closing or a partial closing of the trading system. As we have noted above, the growing profile of these issues and their spread into wider sets of arrangements suggests that trade policymakers will more frequently confront this trade-off. Indeed, the WTO Committee on Trade and Environment has an explicit mandate to examine the appropriateness of such interventions.

Two key elements should weight the policy emphasis toward openness in the trade regime. One is the risk of policy capture—that is, the support and use of nontrade objectives as a way of introducing or supporting protection that benefits special groups. Thus, to counter competition from low-wage countries, unions support the introduction of protection ostensibly in response to working conditions in other countries. Separating out genuine concerns from the narrower interests is clearly difficult. In addition, it is not clear in many cases what policy response is best. In many cases, alternative domestic measures can discipline environmental policies, although in some cases foreign governments are unwilling to impose them.

The late 1990s may well see the clash between nontrade objectives and trade policies become even more prominent, and in ways that were little anticipated at the birth of environmental movements in the 1960s. If global policy responses to such issues as global warming are indeed enacted, the consequences for both regional imbalances and patterns of trade between regions will likely be severe. In addition, attempts to use trade policy as an instrument to enforce global environmental policies would create further pressures on the trading system and would accentuate a sharp divergence in environmental standards across countries. Conversely, if effective responses to legitimately threatening global environmental threats are not crafted, the very foundations of trade may collapse.

Global trade institutions (especially the GATT/WTO) have evolved largely as if there were no such linkages to trade, and recent environmental arrangements (such as the Montreal Protocol on CFCs) seem, from a trade policy viewpoint, to have given only limited thought to implementation and enforcement among signatories. Global institutional evolution to reflect these linkages seems to be in its infancy, and the 1990s is likely to see heightened trade/nontrade conflict, followed by institutional adaptation to accommodate these pressures.

6

Regionalism and Trade Blocs after the Round

The fear that the world was dividing into three competing trade blocs centered around the United States, the European Union, and East Asia not only contributed to the conclusion of the Uruguay Round, it was a major preoccupation during the negotiations and has been since. If the round had failed, it was believed that the stampede of countries seeking to join at least one trade bloc would accelerate. But the round's successful conclusion, it was believed, would slow the momentum for regional integration and weaken the desire of smaller countries to align themselves with blocs. Since the conclusion of the round, the Asia Pacific Economic Cooperation forum, or APEC, became the focus of smaller countries' concerns that there were now just two competing blocs—Europe and APEC—and their effect on the World Trade Organization (WTO) and the larger trading system.[1]

Smaller countries' fears of exclusion from the blocs led a few to place as much, if not more, importance on being inside a regional bloc as on achieving a conclusion to the multilateral round. Larger countries, in turn,

1. At the APEC summit held on 14–16 November 1994, the members agreed to accelerate liberalization of trade and investment measures. Developed countries in the group, including Canada, the United States, Japan, and Australia, were to begin eliminating tariff and other barriers to trade and investment in the year 2000, achieving an open market by 2010. The developing-country members have until 2020. Subsequently, the APEC developed-country members at the Osaka summit moved their start date to 1997. APEC liberalization is to be done in a GATT-consistent manner and is meant not only to support the multilateral system but to help stimulate further multilateral liberalization. Indeed, it is cited as a factor in bringing the Uruguay Round to a close (APEC 1994; *Financial Times*, 16 November 1994, 5; *Globe and Mail*, 15 November 1994, B4).

used the threat of active regional negotiation more intensively during the Uruguay Round than in earlier rounds to pressure other large countries to participate multilaterally. Exclusionary trade deals raise the prospect of trade diversion (as first discussed in Viner 1950),[2] and with it fears of a global gravitation toward large trading blocs locked in mortal trade conflict.

Regional arrangements have been a significant element of the trading system since the early 1960s. However, it is the recent negotiations that have fueled trade bloc fears. The bilateral negotiation of the Canada-US Free Trade Agreement, held as the round was being launched, was the first of these negotiations, followed by negotiation on its enlargement to include Mexico in the North American Free Trade Agreement (NAFTA) toward the end of the round. At the Miami summit held in December 1994, 34 countries from North, Central, and South America and the Caribbean jointly agreed to negotiate a Free Trade Area of the Americas by 2005. European commitment to expanded regional integration could be seen in the negotiations between the European Union and the European Free Trade Association to form a European Economic Area, in EU association negotiations with former Eastern European countries, and in subsequent accession negotiations with Austria, Finland, and Sweden. The Association of Southeast Asian Nations created the ASEAN Free Trade Agreement (AFTA)[3] and Australian and New Zealand formed a Closer Economic Relations (CER) pact. Latin American countries are pursuing both NAFTA accession and new regional arrangements such as Mercosur.[4]

Little in the Uruguay Round agreements responds directly either to the spread of regionalism or to weaknesses in GATT rules and disciplines in restraining it.[5] But the new Understanding on Article XXIV does make clarifications. For example, it specifies methods for comparing the overall level of tariffs before and after a customs union is formed. Negotiations on compensation must begin before the common external tariff is implemented to minimize the short-term trade diversion effects. To increase

---

2. Viner's classic discussion of the benefits and costs of customs unions and free trade areas was framed in terms of trade creation and trade diversion.

3. AFTA members agreed in September 1994 to accelerate the implementation period of their free trade area from 15 years to 10, making 2003 the deadline for the regional free trade area. In September 1995, economic ministers again accelerated the implementation period, making 2000 the deadline. The aim of AFTA is to reduce tariffs on trade within ASEAN to 0 to 5 percent.

4. deMelo and Panagariya (1993) cover most of these regional arrangements. Appendix C provides information on many of the regional and bilateral trade arrangements, and the WTO (1995, appendix table 1) provides details on the regional integration agreements notified to the GATT and the WTO.

5. Jackson (1993) presents some ideas for changes in GATT procedures, linked to an enlarged role for the trade policy review mechanism. WTO (1995, 63–64) discusses the difficulties of Article XXIV and the working parties and offers suggestions for future improvement.

transparency, all agreements must be notified to the WTO under Article XXIV and be examined by a working party. However, the negotiations failed to arrive at a consensus on the Article XXIV requirement that such regional pacts must cover substantially all trade, which has been at the heart of most concerns involving regional arrangements.

While concerns have focused on the negative consequences of a movement to regional trade blocs, there have been active academic debates about whether regionalism is really bad since losses from higher postretaliation barriers between blocs are offset by gains from freer trade within larger blocs (Krugman 1991; Haveman 1992) and about whether initial movements away from multilateralism and toward regionalism are reversible since, in a dynamic game with enforced penalties for deviation from multilateral rules, multilateral cooperation can reassert itself (Bagwell and Staiger 1993).[6]

Indeed, further regional trade deals can be a useful source of momentum toward new trade liberalization when the multilateral system is perceived as yielding little new liberalization or, worse, as creating new inefficiencies in global trade. Regionalism can be either good or bad for system performance. It can lower barriers between regional partners and stimulate trade; it can exclude other countries from liberalization which could be globally inefficient. It can make multilateral negotiations either more or less difficult to conclude. No general rules seem to apply.[7]

Despite this ambiguity, too much may have been made of the threat of new regionalism. The world was headed toward regional trading blocs before the round concluded. And unlike the older regionalism of the 1960s and 1970s (such as EC formation and enlargement), which was fundamentally trade-creating, what marks much of the new regionalism is smaller countries approaching larger countries with whom they extensively trade already. Typically, the larger country undertakes little new liberalization. Only the smaller country liberalizes, but a premium or side payment is made that benefits the large country. In return, the larger country ensures continued market access for the smaller country.

This type of regionalism tends to be redistributive toward larger countries, through the side payments, and to the degree that barriers remain little changed, is not especially disruptive of trade. Competitive pressures

---

6. Largely absent from the literature, however, is the view that small countries enter regional arrangements driven by insurance, or safe-haven, concerns rather than by the desire to improve market access (Perroni and Whalley 1994). Also see discussion in next section.

7. One of the main visions of the Eminent Persons Group, which advised leaders during APEC's formation, is that APEC would attempt to achieve agreement on areas not yet resolved at the global level. Liberalization achieved at the regional level would be available to interested nonmembers, who would be willing to accept the obligations. This "competitive liberalization" is seen as a way of "ratcheting up" trade liberalization to promote "open regionalism" (Bergsten 1994, 20).

between countries seeking such arrangements will also spur regional trade liberalization and thus improve regional economic performance.

In this chapter, we argue that small countries will continue to seek safe haven–driven arrangements, even while bloc consolidation and deepening continues (most notably in the Asia Pacific with the move toward APEC).

We suggest further that the Uruguay Round, with its successful conclusion, has been a factor in reducing the incentive to launch new regional agreements. During the round, large countries put multilateral pressure on other large countries by threatening to launch such agreements. Small countries offered large powers the prospect of regional negotiations so as to increase their leverage in the regional talks. With the end of the round, these sources of pressure subsided, as did smaller countries' fears that there would be no successful multilateral outcome.

We also discuss the risks of a consolidation of trade blocs leading to eventual conflict in which interbloc trade barriers rise. We emphasize that such barrier increases are as likely to be triggered by external shocks or macroeconomic disturbances as they are by the formation of blocs per se.

In our view, blocs based on current regional arrangements cannot be seen as cohesive units pitted against other blocs. We highlight how large-power trade conflicts in the 1990s between Europe and the United States spread outside of GATT disciplines and became the subject of bilateral intermediation and implicit conventions to contain threats of retaliation. For these reasons, we argue that the threat of interbloc trade retaliation leading to widespread closing of the trading system has been exaggerated, even if it cannot be entirely dismissed.

We finally argue that in the evolving two-tier system there is a role for more leadership by the large powers to reduce stresses on the system. We outline a series of WTO-compatible steps the larger powers could take to demonstrate their joint commitment to the multilateral system and to help dampen fears of interbloc trade conflict. While smaller countries would undoubtedly fear that such initiatives constituted large-power collusion, we would argue the initiative could nonetheless strengthen the world trading system.

Older and Newer Regional Arrangements

Regional trade arrangements have long been present, not only in the postwar global economy but also in the interwar and prewar periods. Indeed, in most economic systems, key players have typically sought accommodation among their competing interests, frequently as an exclusionary device. This was true of the colonial trading systems, it remained true of the large power–dominated trading systems of the late 19th century, and it continued into the early years of the 20th century. Regionalism is not new.[8]

Appendix C documents some of the key elements of postwar regionalism, particularly agreements involving Europe and the United States (i.e., the European Economic Community in 1957 and the nearly simultaneous formation of the European Free Trade Association [EFTA], the Canada-US Auto Pact of 1965 and the 1988 Free Trade Agreement, EC enlargement, EC-EFTA, and NAFTA).

Other arrangements usually attract less attention because the trade they have covered has been relatively small (i.e., the Latin American Free Trade Association of 1960, the Central American Common Market of 1960, the contemporaneous East African Common Market, the Chile-Mexico Bilateral Trade Agreement concluded in 1991, and the 1992 Chile-Venezuela bilateral arrangement). Negotiations on trade preferences among developing countries, the Generalized System of Trade Preferences (GSTP), continue under the auspices of the UN Conference on Trade and Development (UNCTAD).[9]

While many (or most) of these small-country arrangements subsequently broke down, they emphasize the point that postwar regional arrangements have been the rule rather than the exception. Indeed, putting the prospects for an eventual APEC arrangement on one side, Japan, Hong Kong, and China remain as the only major economies that are not participants in some form of explicit regional free trade arrangement.

GATT Article XXIV sets out the conditions under which its members can establish free trade areas with other members, and these have been liberally interpreted.[10] Of the over 60 preferential trade agreements referred to GATT working parties since 1947, none has been ruled in violation of GATT, though individual-country objections have been common and ardent (such as the United Kingdom's objections to the EC's Common Agricultural Policy in 1957).[11]

---

8. Regional trade arrangements have been discussed in Anderson and Blackhurst (1993) and deMelo and Panagariya (1993).

9. But see the cautionary discussion of the GSTP scheme in Hudec (1989), who argues that negotiating preferences in a regime of unbound tariffs (as most developing-country tariffs were prior to the conclusion of the Uruguay Round) is virtually doomed to failure. More details on the GSTP scheme can be found in Hamza (1987).

10. The APEC Eminent Persons Group recommended that GATT Article XXIV be amended or reinterpreted to require all regional trade arrangements to commit to reducing barriers to nonmember countries. (APEC 1994, 30–31). The WTO (1995, 68–69) also suggests that individual agreements should be examined regularly within a common forum. Another approach would be for an annual assessment of whether regional initiatives are weakening the trading system or contributing to barrier reduction.

11. See the discussion of Article XXIV consultations in Hart (1987). According to the WTO (1995, 3), only 6 working parties out of the 69 that had completed their examinations of

More recent regional trade agreements such as NAFTA, APEC, and EU-EFTA contrast with the older regional arrangements not only in country coverage but also in underlying objectives.[12] A most striking feature of some of the recent regionalism is that seemingly small countries with little negotiating power have initiated and successfully concluded trade negotiations with larger countries.

This has been in large part because their concern has primarily been security of access to their largest markets rather than a desire to improve access through conventional reciprocal exchange of trade concessions.[13] Thus, the large countries have had substantially more negotiating leverage than the smaller countries and have been able to extract a payment for access guarantees through smaller countries' trade and nontrade concessions, and the smaller countries have been willing to pay the required premium.

An examination of the Canada-US and NAFTA agreements reveals that it has been the smaller acceding country that has made the majority of the concessions (table 6.1). These include restraints on their domestic policies affecting royalties, pricing, and security of supply arrangements, as well as explicit trade concessions.[14] Along with formal concessions, smaller countries have assented to domestic policy changes sought by the larger country, which while not explicitly part of the treaty arrangement become implicitly so.[15] While previous authors have noted the largely one-sided nature of recent agreements (Whalley 1993; Wonnacott 1993; Winters 1993b), the observation has been generally absent in policy debates on their merits or effects.

Thus, Canada's request for a bilateral negotiation in 1985 stemmed from its desire to avoid being "sideswiped" by US trade actions,[16] a concern that

---

regional agreements by 1994 reached consensus on conformity of the agreement with Article XXIV. This is likely because the Understanding of Article XXIV, though it clarified many aspects, left many difficult issues untouched.

12. Whalley (1993) and Hufbauer and Schott (1992) review the Canada-US agreements and NAFTA, Winters (1993a, 1993b) reviews the EU association agreements, Bollard and Mayes (1992) summarize agreements in the Pacific.

13. A Toronto newspaper reported then-President Carlos Salinas of Mexico as saying early in the NAFTA negotiating process, "What we want is closer commercial ties with Canada and the United States, especially in a world in which big regional markets are being created. We don't want to be left out of any of those regional markets, especially not out of the Canadian and American markets" (Globe and Mail, 10 April 1990, B1).

14. The word "concession" here is used in a negotiating sense and covers policy and other changes that may benefit domestic consumers as well as foreigners.

15. These have included changes in patent protection for foreign pharmaceuticals in Canada and commitments of funds to environmental programs in Mexico.

16. See the Report of the MacDonald Commission, the Canadian federal body that recommended Canada negotiate a bilateral trade agreement with the United States (Canada 1985).

Table 6.1 Asymmetric concessions in recent regional agreements

Agreement	Key features	Asymmetric concessions
US-Canada FTA	Phased bilateral tariff elimination over 10 years New bilateral dispute settlement procedures	Exclusions (textiles/apparel, shipping) Security of supply provisions in energy Domestic policy restraints over energy pricing Limits on investment screening Changes in patent/intellectual property arrangements (not formally in agreement) Changes in domestic arrangements in wines and spirits
NAFTA	Phased trilateral tariff elimination over 15 years Dispute settlement procedures as in US-Canada FTA	Asymmetric liberalization in agriculture (corn/beans in Mexico, little in agriculture in US-Canada) Domestic policy restraints on energy pricing in Mexico Limits on investment screening Sugar protection in Mexico raised to match US levels Mexico adopts auto content rules along lines of US-Canada FTA (with revised numbers) Mexico finances border environmental cleanup (not formally in agreement) Mexico strengthens intellectual property protection (not formally in agreement)
EC agreements with Hungary, Poland, and Czech and Slovak Republics	Liberalization to EC exports and investment in returns for phased reciprocal elimination of EC duties in "sensitive" products	Protection for EC investment in Hungary, Poland, and Czech and Slovak Republics Guarantees of competition policy (antitrust) reform in Hungary, Poland, and Czech and Slovak Republics

Source: Perroni and Whalley (1994).

led it to seek special treatment under US trade remedy laws. Similar concerns in part motivated Mexico's 1990 request for a bilateral negotiation with the United States (subsequently incorporated in the NAFTA negotiation), although Mexican policymakers' desire to lock in domestic policy reform via the agreement was also important, if not dominant. The subsequent interest in acceding to NAFTA expressed by Chile, Colombia, Costa Rica, New Zealand, Venezuela, and other countries reflects similar insurance-driven objectives.

Likewise, the EFTA countries, Eastern European countries, Turkey, and North African countries have sought negotiations with the European Union to achieve safe-haven agreements, particularly containment and eventual removal of explicit sectoral protection in key export industries (garments, footwear, steel, and agriculture). Agreements in Asia have fewer of these elements (i.e., the 1985 Australia–New Zealand CER is more like the older agreements).

The resulting imbalance of concessions is apparent. In the Canada-US case, tariffs were already low before the agreement, and save in apparel, petrochemicals, and a few other areas, their bilateral elimination meant relatively little.[17] But in apparel, a remaining tariff quota restrains entry to US markets for Canadian producers at trade levels above the preagreement situation; in maritime transportation, the United States' restrictive Jones Act is preserved; in energy, differential domestic/foreign pricing in Canada is outlawed and security of supply provisions are granted to US purchases of energy products; in investment, screening procedures are relaxed in Canada; and (although not in the agreement, but occurring simultaneously) significant Canadian changes were made in patent protection, including patents affecting foreign pharmaceuticals.

In the case of NAFTA, tariff elimination is asymmetric because of higher initial levels in Mexico:[18] Mexico liberalizes substantially in corn and beans with little significant US or Canadian agricultural liberalization, raises sugar protection to match US levels, eliminates the Mexican auto decree, adopts auto content provisions as in the Canada-US Agreement, agrees to and partially finances environmental cleanup, and commits not to differentially price domestic and foreign energy products.

The EU association agreements with Eastern Europe guarantee competition policy reform in the former state-controlled countries, along with protection for EU foreign direct investment and liberalization for EU products in return for the European Union merely phasing a reciprocal elimination in "sensitive" products (Winters 1993b, 122).

In negotiations sparked by a small country's desires for a safe haven, the incentives for the larger countries to join such negotiations are also clear: namely, to take advantage of an opportunity to deal with nontrade issues with the smaller country, to elevate—even if only incrementally—their bargaining power with other large countries, and to use the threat of proceeding to regional arrangements to pressure recalcitrant multilateral negotiating partners of similar size.[19]

---

17. As noted by Whalley (1993, 335), before the agreement came into force, the average tariff on Canadian exports to the United States was approximately 1 percent, and nearly 80 percent of Canadian trade with the United States was already duty-free.

18. Weintraub (1991, 57) reports an average Mexican tariff of 9 percent; Hart (1991, 94) puts trade-weighted Mexican tariffs at 8 percent. This is in contrast to GATT-bound Mexican tariffs of 50 percent and average Mexican tariffs before 1985 of around 45 percent.

19. Then-Senator Lloyd Bentsen, chairman of the Senate Finance Committee, is quoted by Dymond (1989, 14) in the debate on the Canada-US Free Trade Agreement as saying, "The FTA with Canada means that the United States can say in Geneva, 'If you won't work with us to open up world trade, then we can negotiate trade agreements with other countries on a bilateral basis, and those countries will have the advantage of it and you won't be sharing in it.'"

Our contention is that some of the more prominent new large country–small country trade arrangements are fundamentally safe haven–driven rather than reciprocity-driven. Under these arrangements, large countries grant more secure access to small countries in exchange for side payments and nontrade concessions. The large country reduces its bargaining power vis-à-vis other large countries in the case of a free trade area (because other large countries can export through the FTA partners) but enhancing it in the case of a customs union. In both cases, the larger country forgoes the opportunity to play strategically against the smaller countries.[20] Small countries obtain protected and preferential access to the larger country's market,[21] and, in customs unions, see their retaliatory power against third countries increased.[22]

Overall, these arrangements have less impact on trading system performance than more conventional regional arrangements because their direct impact on trade flows is relatively small, but they may have a marked redistributive impact in favor of larger countries. The issue is thus less whether these arrangements are good or bad in the classical Vinerian sense of impacts on trade than whether they should (or even can) be disciplined multilaterally—to some degree on redistributive as well as on other grounds.

The Risk of Interbloc Conflicts

The regionalism of recent years has heightened speculation that the trading system might move further toward more clearly defined regional trade blocs in the late 1990s and resultant conflicts. The scenario painted before the end of the round was that, if multilateral negotiations broke down, the multilateral system would progressively erode as dispute settlement weakened and GATT rules were violated with greater frequency. In frustration, it was believed, the European Union, the United States, and Japan would each beef up existing networks of regional arrangements as well as enter into new and more extensive arrangements. At some point, these regional arrangements would become so important and the multilateral system so weak that trade blocs would dominate the global trading sys-

---

20. Relative to an unconstrained trade war, the net effect of the formation of a free trade area is thus to raise global welfare, whereas the global welfare effect of a customs union is ambiguous (Kennan and Riezman 1990).

21. In the event of a trade war, trade between blocs will fall, but intrabloc trade will rise.

22. And if large countries calculate that, with the side payments, the formation of regional blocs is to their advantage, multilateral arrangements may become less attractive to large countries than a two-tier system of multilateral-type rules among the larger countries with safe-haven regional arrangements with smaller satellites.

tem. The successful conclusion of the round has lessened the probability of this scenario coming to pass.[23]

Nonetheless, concerns about the impact of regionalism remain. In one scenario, the forces propelling regional arrangements continue in the 1990s, despite the successful conclusion of the round, and smaller countries become even more dependent on trade with their larger neighbors, which oblige by negotiating bilateral arrangements. What Wonnacott (1990) has termed a "hub and spoke" structure may emerge, with an increased potential for trade tensions between the major powers.[24]

In this situation, both large and small countries increasingly see their interests as lying in negotiating new regional rather than multilateral trade arrangements. If countries believe themselves driven to this course by a weakened multilateral system, that system could become destabilized. Alternatively, competition between the multilateral and regional arrangements might produce more liberalization than would have happened if there had been no regional negotiations.

Current concerns over global fragmentation also stem from a perceived change in focus in large-country trade policies, particularly those of the United States.[25] For instance, US trade policy over the last 10 or so years has moved from a near-exclusive focus on multilateral rules and disciplines to unilateral measures and threats—via section 301, threats of Generalized System of Preferences (GSP) graduation,[26] and antidumping or countervailing duty undertakings—which the United States has viewed as "creating a level playing field" and as essential to gaining increased access for US goods and services, protecting the US market from unfair trade, or pursuing intellectual property rights. These efforts were initially targeted chiefly at Japan and subsequently at the Asian newly industrializing economies and the ASEAN countries. These policies have been

---

23. Former GATT Director General Peter Sutherland saw no threat to trade from blocs (*Financial Times*, 3 July 1994, 4). A further report by the WTO (1995) concluded that while there had been rapid growth in regional groupings, there was no evidence that discriminatory trade blocs were emerging.

24. Also see the more recent discussion of potential hub-and-spoke systems in Europe in Enders and Wonnacott (1994).

25. In the early 1980s, there was still a strong US emphasis on the multilateral system, but policymakers began to think in terms of "negotiating with like-minded countries." By the mid-1980s, the United States made it quite clear that without progress on a multilateral basis it was willing to negotiate on a "bilateral or plurilateral basis with like-minded countries." Negotiations for free trade areas were opened with Israel and then Canada (USITC 1984, 1986). For more recent commentary see "Trinidad and Chile Top List for US Links," *Financial Times*, 7 July 1994, 7).

26. The renewal of the US GSP scheme in 1985 required beneficiaries to meet a number of requirements, including on workers' rights and protection of intellectual property. Asian NIEs graduated from US GSP in the late 1980s included Korea, Hong Kong, Singapore, and Taiwan.

widely regarded as successful from a US viewpoint, since targeted countries have generally complied with the stated US goals. Except in the case of Japan, this approach is generally credited with obtaining the desired market opening, and more quickly than would have been the case under the multilateral process.[27]

The United States' bilateral negotiating focus generally has reflected hemispheric rather than global concerns. Canada and Mexico (and to a lesser extent the Caribbean) have been the principal theaters for the US bilateral focus, despite the fact that these countries were the initial *demandeurs* of regional trade agreements. In the Canada-US talks, NAFTA, and the Caribbean Basin Initiative, the United States initially responded cautiously to overtures from smaller countries and then moved proactively to substantive negotiations when the benefits of such negotiations became clear. Its strong interest in subglobal negotiation continues in the form of APEC.[28]

US trade partners' have taken these developments to indicate a growing US regional focus arising from its disenchantment with the multilateral process and a belief in the efficacy of regional talks in pressuring other partners to finish multilateral negotiations. Although the broad direction of US policy is similar in each regional arrangement, the content of each varies. This highlights a further attraction of bilateral negotiation—the ability to tailor agreements to fit circumstances.

Did the Uruguay Round accelerate the division of the world into regional blocs? We think not. One key reason, noted earlier, is that much of the new regionalism has only limited effects on trade and does not constitute cohesive trade blocs in pursuit of common trade policies toward third countries. In addition, we also noted earlier that the round itself fostered some of the new regionalism, the incentives for which diminished with the round's conclusion. Small and large countries alike no longer need regional talks as leverage in the round or as a hedge against its failure.

Other factors may dampen trade bloc concerns. In its 1994 report, the APEC Eminent Persons Group detailed an ambitious regional liberalization effort that could help promote global free trade in conformity with GATT principles.[29] According to C. Fred Bergsten, who chaired the Emi-

---

27. Finger (1990) discusses the success rate of US antidumping and countervailing duty actions in the 1980s in leading to negotiated export restraint agreements.

28. US efforts in APEC have also been directed at ensuring that an Asian regional trade group does not exclude the United States and does include Japan. The Malaysian government had been working toward establishing an East Asian Economic Caucus, which would exclude the United States, but this effort has been unsuccessful. With the November 1994 APEC agreement to accelerate trade and investment liberalization, APEC members lessened the chances for EAEC success and reinforced US influence in the area.

29. In August 1995 the EPG released a report calling for APEC members to accelerate the liberalization timetable agreed to in the Uruguay Round by 50 percent. This would involve implementing tariff reductions in two years rather than four, reducing farm subsidies in three

nent Persons Group, there are large gains to be had from eliminating the substantial barriers remaining in the region, in the greater potential for dealing effectively with regional trade conflicts, and from APEC's ability to reinforce the GATT and the multilateral system and maintain European interest in the multilateral system (*Financial Times* editorial, 2 September 1994, 15; letters to the editor, 8 September 1994, 10; APEC 1994). While there are concerns over a weak global trading system and other regional arrangements, as well as security concerns in the region, further liberalization in the Asia Pacific would undoubtedly help stem protectionism. Also, the EPG proposals conform to, or even go beyond, GATT obligations and would thus be a force for global trade progress.

Despite all these arguments, concerns persist among some policymakers and academics that spreading and deepening trade blocs, combined with shocks to the global economy and lowered expectations of the system's ability to deal with them, will erode remaining joint commitment to an open system. This could produce a degree of system closing, despite the commitments made in the round and despite the best efforts of the WTO, that would reduce income and trade. This is the replaying of the 1930s scenario, which, while unlikely, provokes strong feelings.

Perhaps the most plausible scenario is that a number of adverse developments, each of seemingly limited consequence, prove cumulatively deleterious to the trading system. These might include mounting sectoral derogations to accommodate the new regional arrangements, threats of new barriers emerging from large-power conflicts, new mechanisms for the application of barriers on a contingent basis, escalation and emulation of unilateral measures,[30] and the trade-depressing and protection-enhancing effects of a drawn-out recession in the 1990s.

Under such a scenario, each factor reinforces the system-closing tendencies of others. Recession increases the risk and severity of sectoral derogations, which in turn make recovery from recession more difficult. Threats of unilateralism fuel concerns over major-power conflict, which in turn more strongly legitimize threatened unilateral actions. The resulting downturn in trade puts more pressure on firms to seek remedy from contingent protection, which deepens recession and bolsters unilateralism.

---

years rather than six, and accelerating the liberalization of textiles and apparel trade (*Financial Times*, 31 August 1995, 3).

30. An example is European emulation of US section 301 through regulation 2641/84, which dates back to 1984 (Arnold and Bronckers 1988). Under the regulation, a complaint can be filed with the EC Commission when an EC industry is "injured as a result of an illicit commercial practice of a foreign government that is 'incompatible with international law or generally accepted rules' " (Brand 1990, 14). If the Commission accepts the complaint, it must pursue dispute settlement procedures in the GATT. Once the GATT mechanism is complete, the Commission must decide whether to propose retaliatory measures against the foreign government. For discussion of the EC dispute against US section 337, see Brand (1990) and Bayard and Elliott (1994).

While one can perhaps overplay both the risks and the potential barrier increases, the fact remains that trade in the late 1990s faces an uncertain future, one in which the major powers are reevaluating their trading relationships.

The worst-case scenario would be an outbreak of new retaliatory trade conflict between large trading blocs, independent of growth in new regional arrangements. Perhaps the European Union imposes measures against the United States, which retaliates, which sparks counterretaliation, and so on, the severity of which would depend on the breadth of the products covered by the retaliatory measures.[31] Japan-US trade frictions could also be a spark for such a scenario.

In the 1980s, EC-US trade conflicts over EC enlargement, for example, or in the citrus-pasta war involved retaliation that was largely contained to narrow product groups and usually involved only a single round of retaliatory trade actions before bilateral conciliation occurred. Though limited, retaliation in the 1980s was more confrontational than in the 1970s, and the concern in the late 1990s is that with no new multilateral round in prospect and with more bilateral conflict in the offing (i.e., possible agriculture-based disputes, more US-Japan bilateral conflicts,[32] and conflicts from further EU enlargement), trade conflicts will accelerate, culminating in more retaliatory episodes with significant impact.

Ten or even twenty years ago, such a scenario would be dismissed as far-fetched. It cannot be today, although in its extreme form it remains implausible. The European Union and the United States have in the past recognized a joint interest in mediating their trade disputes and will no doubt continue to do so.

A less extreme scenario focuses on the economically harmful consequences of the threat that barriers will increase rather than that they do actually increase. This encompasses threats of introducing new barriers as well as the activity of existing systems of administered protection, whose introduction is conditional upon various criteria (i.e., dumping, subsidy, injury; see discussion in Anderson and Rugman 1989).

---

31. Retaliation through across-the-board import surcharges under Article 12 of the GATT would constitute such a serious outcome. Another example is the US suspension of the Bretton Woods system in 1971, which was accompanied by a 10 percent surcharge.

32. US-Japan bilateral trade tensions over the Japanese car and parts markets again resulted in the United States threatening retaliation in May 1995. The United States had been negotiating unsuccessfully for two years for improved access to the Japanese network of car dealerships as well as deregulation of the Japanese replacement parts markets. When the United States announced it would impose 100 percent tariffs on Japanese luxury cars, Japan requested consultations under the WTO dispute settlement procedures. The consultations resulted in a bilateral agreement 28 June. Japan indicated the market-opening measures would be extended to all trade partners (see WTO, *Focus Newsletter*, no. 3, 1995). The agreement will be monitored by the European Union.

The prospect of future trade barriers can have effects similar to actual barrier increases because producers in exporting countries become more reluctant to invest and trade. Indeed, uncertainty over the size of future barriers can be even more damaging to trade if exporters come to view investment in export businesses as a no-win and risky proposition—that is, they face barriers if they are successful and no barriers if they are unsuccessful.

Administered (or contingent) trade barriers result from legal processes (process protection) that allow domestic producers to request barriers based on alleged harm to them. Tribunals investigate these allegations, making decisions and perhaps imposing remedies.[33] Frivolous petitions may be initiated to harass foreign competition. This uncertainty as to the outcome from petitions for remedy amplifies the threat to exporters.[34]

Furthermore, interim duties may be imposed pending a final decision, with no compensation paid to the importer when a complaint is not upheld. Again, exporters become less willing to explore new trading patterns, and trade growth falters. As discussed earlier, the Uruguay Round agreements have attempted to lessen the harassment effect of administered protection as well as to make the procedures more transparent. However, it is fully expected that the revised rules (on antidumping and countervailing duties) will be used to their fullest extent to provide relief from perceived unfair trade.

Thus, this scenario for interbloc conflict in the system in the 1990s focuses on threats of new barriers, with corresponding implications for new investment activity. New, visible trade barriers could emerge from new large-power trade conflicts and serve to partially close the system, or the threat of new barriers could erode the commitment of exporters.

Avoiding Bloc Conflict

In all the scenarios painted above of increasing regionalism, the Uruguay Round does not hasten interbloc conflict, but neither does it fully contain it. It remains an issue beyond the round.

In assessing the extent of risk of heightened interbloc trade conflicts, it may be useful to examine why some of the bleak scenarios laid out earlier have not already transpired. First, the trading system generated strong trade growth through the 1970s and 1980s, especially following the 1981–82 recession, and while there was erosion in multilateral disciplines, the

---

33. USITC (1995) describes the sequence and time limits of US procedures. Grinols (1989) and Low (1993) also discuss the various US trade remedy procedures.

34. Messerlin (1989, 573) reports that even the threat of initiating antidumping actions reduced exports to the European Community.

overall trading system remained fairly open. And even today, unilateral measures have yet to be widely used by any country, including the United States. And the coverage of antidumping and countervail actions by the larger OECD countries, while significant, remains small in terms of the fraction of trade that existing duties affect.[35]

Few instances of retaliation took place outside the GATT process during this period. A party first took a trade dispute to a GATT panel, and if an adverse ruling was adopted or implemented in the panel report, only then did the dispute move outside GATT channels for possible retaliatory action. Fears that conflicts would escalate were consequently muted, and the risk of major system closing was not seen as all that credible.

What happened in some of the US-EC disputes in the 1980s is documented in appendix D. One case was a dispute over Community enlargement (to include Spain and Portugal), when the Community raised tariffs against third countries on various products. It sparked another dispute by introducing discriminatory tariff preferences on citrus products toward (mainly) North African countries, which led to the "citrus-pasta" war with the United States. A third was a dispute over EC canned fruit subsidies under the Common Agriculture Policy. In each case, the United States took the initial retaliatory step and met with EC counterretaliation. Conciliation followed with a lag.

These retaliatory episodes did not lead to wider trade conflict. Rather, retaliation was confined to the broader product categories within which the dispute originally occurred—within agriculture, in the case of the citrus-pasta war. Furthermore, implicit conventions seem to have evolved among the protagonists, further limiting retaliatory actions before serious efforts at conciliation occurred (in the case of the citrus-pasta war, one retaliation per protagonist).[36]

This relatively successful record of containment in the 1970s and 1980s, and the implication for the late 1990s, can be read in different ways. One interpretation is that the GATT was relatively unimportant for containing trade disputes; the parties conciliated bilaterally because of their strong joint interest to do so.[37] The joint cost of an even more hostile trade war would damage both and outweighs their perceived loss from a less-than-advantageous settlement. Trying to set formal rules to dictate how this

---

35. These numbers, such as those quoted by Nam (1987), are deceptive, since in the case of antidumping actions they do not include cases where actions have been withdrawn due to price undertakings.

36. At one point in the EC enlargement dispute, the United States stated it would implement proposed retaliatory restrictions on EC goods in a way that would not cause damage to EC exporters, on the condition the Community did the same, in order to buy more time for conciliation (*International Trade Reporter*, 23 April 1986, 534).

37. The analogy is to the behavior of firms and unions during strikes, where the large majority of strikes are settled in the first few days.

conciliation might take place may do more harm than good, as they may reduce the scope for conciliation. Thus, one lesson for the 1990s that could be drawn from trade conflicts in the 1980s is that narrow trade conflicts do not mushroom into across-the-board, tit-for-tat trade retaliation. The joint incentive to resolve these conflicts proves too strong.

An alternative interpretation is that the GATT did indeed help restrain retaliation in the 1970s and 1980s, despite the fact that there was large-power retaliation outside GATT rules. The protagonists believe the benefits in the wider cooperation and commitment that the GATT/WTO represents are too great to risk fatally weakening it by retaliatory acts. Thus, trade hostilities that move beyond the WTO are settled relatively quickly.

Under this interpretation of the experience of the 1980s, each successive episode of retaliation becomes more dangerous because it demonstrates the protagonists' weakening commitment to the multilateral rules and their inclination to test their rivals by pressing more conflicts of greater scope and holding out longer for advantageous settlements.

Under this analysis, the threat of major trade retaliation was kept at bay in the 1980s only because it was in its early stages, postwar alliances still linked trading partners, and joint commitment to the system was still strong enough to impel reconciliation of trade conflicts.

But this environment has changed (as we note in more detail in chapter 7). The trading system of the late 1990s will likely differ from that of previous decades in a number of important ways: the move from unipolarity (i.e., the hegemonic status of the United States) toward a three-power (the European Union, the United States, and Japan), two-trading bloc (APEC and Europe) world; the effective end of the Cold War and the removal of the strategic underpinnings of the trading system; a progressive weakening of the WTO as a focal point, eroding the perceived joint benefits of collaborative activity; and the increasing rapidity of change in the system and the potentially larger adjustment problems associated with this. There is a danger that increasingly severe trade conflict involving the major powers will weaken the trading system. The 1995 US-Japan dispute over auto parts raised just such an alarm.[38]

The Uruguay Round was supposed to strengthen the multilateral system. Thus, reform of the system's institutional structure was seen as a key element of the talks. It was to reverse existing derogations, strengthen

---

38. The bilateral dispute between the United States and Japan over autos was the first test of major-power commitment to the WTO and the multilateral system since the WTO came into effect. The US announcement that it would unilaterally impose 100 percent tariffs on Japanese luxury cars gave many the impression that the United States was not strongly committed to the system. Had the measures gone into effect and the dispute gone to a panel that had then ruled against the United States, the credibility of the WTO's dispute settlement capabilities and the multilateral system would have suffered a serious blow. However, consultations at the WTO led to a resolution of the dispute, and it provided a much-needed show of support for the institution (WTO, *Focus Newsletter*, no. 3, 1995).

existing rules and extend them to new areas, such as services, provide more effective enforcement, and thereby to reverse erosion in the multilateral system and maintain its openness. If it could do all this, the need for regional arrangements would diminish.

While many countries have acknowledged the potential benefits from the creation of the WTO, it is not clear whether they can muster sufficient political commitment to deal with major-power conflict that could emerge suddenly in response to future shocks to the system.

For this reason, we believe it would be prudent to explore approaches complementary to the WTO to mitigate both the risks and the effects of major-power conflicts. We prefer to focus on new trilateral arrangements between the three major trading powers to encourage stronger joint commitments on trade.[39] More active leadership on their part could go some way toward improving system functioning, although endorsement of this approach by other WTO members would be desirable.

The outcome of such an arrangement should be WTO-consistent trade disciplines capable of strengthening both multilateral disciplines and the larger global trading system. Instead of waiting for a new round, which, once launched, could take more than a decade to complete, the three major powers could begin to develop a trilateral framework for trade immediately and put in place mechanisms to help defuse trade conflicts. Simply because such an approach does not fit directly within the current multilateral framework does not, in our view, preclude pursuing it.

This trilateral approach could involve a gradation of measures. One possibility might be to enlarge the scope of the Trade Policy Review Mechanism, agreed to in the Uruguay Round, as it applies to the three large powers. They could, for instance, support an effort to continuously monitor their bilateral trade flows, their barriers against each other, as well as emerging conflicts and market situations—acting, in effect, as an early warning system on large-power trade disputes.[40] This could perhaps be accomplished by committing more resources to the WTO Secretariat to enhance its investigative capabilities.

---

39. See Jones (1989), who recommends the negotiation of a formal agreement between, at a minimum, the United States, the European Union, and Japan to eliminate the use of discriminatory trade restrictions against each other. Ludlow (1989) recognizes a new international political environment that should not be kept separate from international trade policy discussions and recommends establishment of an institution to encourage dialogue on both. Such a mechanism could alternatively involve separate bilateral arrangements among the three.

40. The United States and the European Union did agree to set up an "early warning system" to identify potential bilateral trade disputes (*Financial Times*, 4 February 1994, 5). Such an agreement could be expanded to include Japan. The European Union also has an agreement to monitor the bilateral discussions between the United States and Japan to ensure that agreements do not exclude third countries (*Europe*, 21–22 November 1994, 6). Perhaps these bilateral agreements could become trilateral and be made transparent for the entire WTO membership.

A subsequent step might be agreements to limit retaliation. These rules could explicitly apply to trade disputes that spill out beyond the GATT process. The three could, for example, confine any retaliation to the broad product category involved in the dispute (such as agriculture). They might agree to place an upper bound on all retaliation of the value of trade affected by the dispute. They might stipulate that after one round of retaliation each, they automatically move to some form of conciliation. They might also agree on a cooling-off period—say, six months—between successive rounds of retaliation and counterretaliation. The idea would be to contain the potential for wider damage to the trading system through unconstrained retaliation.[41]

Yet another step might be for joint trilateral commitments either to forgo certain GATT rights (such as Article XII balance of payments measures in response to import surges from each other) or, if this were regarded as too extreme a step, to agree to a cooling-off period on use of such measures. A year, pending notification of intent, could, in some cases, allow sufficient time for underlying macroeconomic imbalances to right themselves and for exploration of other approaches to outstanding trade problems.

Oil price shocks or a further worsening of the US trade deficit could provoke the major powers' use of trade-restricting escape-clause measures under GATT Article XII. Although it has been little used in recent years, if Europe or the United States were to impose a temporary across-the-board import surcharge of, say, 25 percent because of sharp and rapid deepening of their trade deficits, global turmoil and countermeasures would likely result.[42] Trilateral agreements in this area could help defuse such threats.

Trilateral talks could make progress on other fronts as well. For instance, in the late 1980s the three regions sometimes pressured a smaller trading region to make a concession in areas outside of GATT (such as intellectual property). When these concessions were discriminatory, the other large powers would request the same concession be extended to them, generating further conflict.

One such case involved US threats to graduate Korea from the GSP in the late 1980s unless Korea changed its intellectual property arrangements

---

41. Abbott (1985, 525–30) illustrates the consequences of bilateral disputes involving a series of retaliation and counterretaliation measures using a game theoretic framework. See also Conybeare (1987).

42. In response to the mounting bilateral imbalances that the United States faced in the early 1980s, a number of surcharge bills were introduced in the US Congress in 1985 (Rousslang and Suomela 1985). Whether one of the industrialized countries would actually resort to Article XII measures is difficult to anticipate. During the Uruguay Round, the United States questioned whether changes in the international monetary system did not make this article and Article XVIII unnecessary. In 1990, the negotiating group could not even agree whether these should be subject to negotiation (Stewart 1993, 1872). However, some modifications to the articles were included in the Uruguay Round final act, including time schedules, transparency, and clarifications to consultation procedures (GATT 1994a, 29–32).

away from process to product patents (to reduce the number of filings necessary for a given invention). Korean concessions applied only to the United States. Consequently, the European Community also threatened Korea with GSP graduation unless these benefits were fully extended to the Community. When Korea refused, the Community in 1988 made good its threat.[43]

Thus, one further avenue for a large-power trade agreement might be to limit bilateral negotiation by the three with their smaller trading partners to only incorporate those nondiscriminatory concessions, whose benefits could be fully extended to all other trading partners.

The three large powers should also contemplate implementing arrangements that would freeze problem situations. They could, for instance, commit themselves to no new bilateral negotiations for an agreed period, pending developments in the WTO and on other fronts. This would help relieve further pressures in the system: suspicion in the United States of exclusion from European enlargement and integration, concerns in Japan and Europe over their exclusion from NAFTA or Free Trade Agreement of the Americas (FTAA), and possible confusion in the United States and Europe over the directions emerging in subregional agreements in the Pacific.

The goal of all these concrete measures would be to encourage the large powers to act in a cooperative and transparent manner so as to strengthen the system (for further discussion, see Bergsten, Davignon, and Miyazaki 1986). Such a framework could coexist alongside G-7 discussions on international financial issues—exchange rates, debt issues, and interest rates—where major-power leadership has been accepted for a longer period, as in the Plaza Agreement of 1985 and the Louvre Accord of 1987 (for further discussion, see Bergsten 1990; Funabashi 1988). Factoring in trade aspects of the wider relationship between the three major powers in the late 1990s would be a step toward building the long-sought integrated financial-trade approach to international economic policymaking.

The obvious weakness of the trilateral approach is that it might appear to other countries as a vehicle for facilitating collusion among the large trading powers.[44] It might further fragment the trading system into three

---

43. For further discussion and examples of bilateral pressures, see Whalley (1989a). However, in September 1991 the EC and Korea finalized a patent accord that provided EC products with retroactive patent protection in Korea.

44. Bryant and Hodgkinson (1989, 7) note: "In practice a judgment has to be made about which is the greater danger: that in the absence of cooperation between governments, international interaction will work to the detriment of public policy . . . or, alternatively, that collusion between governments will work against the public interest." In their view, "cooperation between governments, particularly democratic governments, can be plausibly expected to further the collective interests of their people."

large trading areas, with satellite, or client, trading partners attached to each of the three.[45]

These concerns do not in our view rule out exploration of the trilateral option. Indeed, it ought to be seriously considered, because a single multilateral framework likely will fail to fend off major trade conflicts in the 1990s.

Pursuit of this approach could strengthen the multilateral system by generating new WTO-consistent arrangements that extend the large powers' existing multilateral obligations. WTO compatibility is therefore an important ingredient in this approach.[46]

---

45. It is unclear what the best arrangements are for smaller countries. They could actually benefit if large countries engaged in retaliatory trade wars with one another because, if they were not subject to the retaliation, they would gain from the trade diversion. On the other hand, a collapse in trade among the major powers could generate a global recession of major consequence, one in which smaller countries would suffer more than proportionately, as they are more trade-dependent. Perroni and Whalley (1994), for instance, report general equilibrium calculations in which smaller countries suffer a 25 percent income reduction in the event of an all-out global trade war.

46. The involvement of other parties is a possibility, but not a necessity. Such involvement would tend to weaken and slow down the three-country process we advocate, but perhaps an observer, jointly nominated by the WTO members, could facilitate information sharing.

7

The WTO's Role in Strengthening the System

There is no doubt that the creation of the World Trade Organization (WTO), which supersedes the General Agreement on Tariffs and Trade (GATT), represented the most dramatic institutional change in global trade arrangements since the GATT was founded. It is a permanent arrangement where GATT was only temporary, a consolidated and integrated whole where GATT was disparate and disorganized, and it is the repository for dispute settlement procedures stronger than those under the GATT (see chapter 3 and box 7.1 for more description of the WTO's features). Great hopes are pinned on its ability to generate an elevated joint commitment to a strengthened focal point for the system with stronger enforcement of system rules, to weaken those forces that have eroded the system, to lessen the risk of trade wars, and generally to lead to yet stronger global economic performance.

Others have a less rosy view, seeing the WTO largely as a shell into which the Uruguay Round and previous GATT agreements have been placed. No new arrangements, structures, or major changes in function are involved. And a new dispute settlement mechanism would have occurred anyway, as the terms for it were largely negotiated before creation of the WTO was added to the agenda.

The WTO has been criticized for not defining clear principles at its inception in such new areas as trade and the environment. In the United States and also in India, concerns have been raised about potential loss of national sovereignty to the WTO, particularly with regard to dispute

---

Box 7.1   Key features of the World Trade Organization (WTO)

- The WTO is a single institutional framework encompassing the GATT (as modified by the Uruguay Round), all agreements and arrangements concluded under it, and the complete results of the Uruguay Round.
- It is to be headed by a ministerial conference meeting once every two years.
- A General Council is to oversee operations of the organization and its ministerial decisions and to act as a dispute settlement body and a trade policy review mechanism.
- The General Council is to establish subsidiary bodies: a Goods Council, a Services Council, and a TRIPs Council.
- The framework ensures a single undertaking approach to results from the Uruguay Round; that is, WTO members must accept all the results of the round.
- Plurilateral agreements cover civil aircraft, government procurement, dairy products, and bovine meat. Membership in these is optional.

---

settlement procedures.[1] Others have expressed concerns over the integration of disciplines covering goods, services, and intellectual property, which, under the new dispute settlement procedures, could facilitate cross-retaliation in the goods area—for example, for infractions of intellectual property norms—and could raise barriers to trade.[2]

WTO as System Strengthening

So, are the WTO's proponents or its detractors right? There are several underlying issues: the problems the WTO was created to solve, the degree to which the WTO represents a substantial change in the system, and the degree to which it may later evolve into a system-strengthening institution, as well as how to define "system strengthening."

The WTO was created in part in response to the increasingly cumbersome, complex, and ever more inconsistent nature of the GATT. This became particularly apparent as Uruguay Round negotiators tried to determine the appropriate location for new codes in areas such as intellectual

---

1. The perceived threat to US sovereignty was raised by many opponents to the GATT deal in the run-up to the vote in the US Congress. In order to generate enough support to pass the Uruguay Round agreements, President Bill Clinton agreed to an initiative by Senator Robert Dole to set up a WTO Dispute Settlement Review Commission, comprising five judges, who will review all final WTO dispute panels that find against the United States to determine if the WTO panel exceeded its authority or acted outside the agreement. After three such determinations in a five-year period, a process for US withdrawal from the WTO can be started (*Economic Report of the President* 1995, 213; Rubin 1994, 3405).

2. Although others argue that if firmer intellectual property protection results with no barrier increases, this is a good thing, not bad.

property and services, given inconsistencies of past GATT rounds. The impermanence of the GATT has already been mentioned as a source of discontent with the system.

That the GATT was a provisional body is without doubt, and the cumbersome nature of the arrangements within the GATT is also clear. Certainly, the WTO is in many respects a major step toward building a solid foundation from which to manage the multilateral trading system. With a status comparable to that of the World Bank and the International Monetary Fund (IMF), the WTO is likely to enhance linkages between trade and finance and improve cooperation between the three institutions.[3]

The consolidation of all the agreements and arrangements under a single umbrella represents a major simplification in the structure of global trade arrangements. If combined with greater resource commitments, the total package could strengthen institutional authority considerably.

The creation of the WTO, therefore, should be welcomed. But it is now essentially a shell into which previous GATT arrangements have been placed, and hence it is an organization that has yet to be tested.

How may the WTO evolve?[4] One potentially important feature of the new arrangements is the ministerial conference meeting to be held every two years, at which implementation of the Uruguay Round agreements can be reviewed. These conferences can be seen as a first move toward permanent negotiation and better global trade policy management.[5]

Whether the ministerial conference will eventually embody permanent negotiations has been widely discussed. Our view is that these conferences are an unlikely vehicle for substantive reciprocity negotiations along the lines of GATT rounds of the past. They may help mediate conflicts and reduce tensions, but without clear agendas and timetables agreed in advance, major negotiations will probably not occur.

Most GATT negotiations initially focused on unresolved business from previous rounds, and subsequently integrated this old agenda with an agenda of newer issues. This trend will likely continue in the aftermath of the Uruguay Round as well, and perhaps over the 10-year implementation period for the agriculture and textiles agreements. The round process was slow and incremental; the WTO is likely to continue in a similar vein, and the ministerial conferences are unlikely to effect much change in this.

---

3. Agreement has already been reached between the WTO and the IMF on guidelines for strengthening cooperation. Improvements include granting each institution observer status and providing access to documentation and data bases (WTO, *Focus Newsletter* no. 3, 3).

4. Schott (1994, 35–36) provides a timetable for further WTO negotiations.

5. According to former GATT Director General Peter Sutherland, the institutional change will mean an end to ad hoc negotiating rounds and thus multilateral trade negotiations "will become a permanent event" (*Focus GATT Newsletter* 105, 6).

Whether the WTO comes to be seen as the primary vehicle for trade liberalization and dispute resolution will depend very much on how members, especially the major players, implement and adhere to the agreements.[6] For instance, if there is minimal liberalization in industrial-country agriculture and textile markets, if bilateral trade disputes are resolved outside of the WTO dispute system, or panel decisions are ignored, the credibility of the WTO will suffer significantly. In this case, the overall global trading system could continue to perform well, but that performance might may be more the result of events in other areas of the global trading system, such as the regional arrangements.

The viability of the WTO will also depend on how it deals with emerging issues. This not only includes trade and the environment, trade and competition policy, and human and labor rights issues but also other issues related to economies in transition that are joining the WTO, as well as ongoing issues related to trade in services.

What is meant when the WTO is touted as a major component of a strengthening of the multilateral system? We touched on this in chapter 2, in which we discussed how the erosion of the multilateral system of the 1970s and 1980s led to what we described as a system gap (discussed also in Whalley 1995), which was filled by regional arrangements, derogations, and the accommodation of nontraditional issues. The development of the World Trade Organization is a clear effort to stem the erosion and shrink the gap between the multilateral system and the overall global trading system and thus to strengthen the multilateral system.

System strengthening, however, remains an ambiguous term somewhat, and its application to the WTO is not free of interpretive problems. We focus here on four interpretations. One view of system strengthening is that it involves the establishment of trade rules that are more consistent with the underlying principles of the trading system. A second view takes system strengthening to mean stronger enforcement of existing trade rules through firmer dispute settlement and tougher penalties. A third interpretation is it is a system that better resists pressures for new protectionist measures. Finally, a fourth focuses on the widening of the multilateral trading system to cover more areas and trade-restricting measures. All of these views of system strengthening

---

6. For the purposes of determining what the creation of the WTO means for the future of the trading system, we set aside an evaluation of the new dispute settlement procedures, because they would likely have been incorporated into the GATT even without the WTO. This separation is by no means clean, since the possibility of cross-retaliation is a feature of the WTO that would likely not have been present under any revised GATT dispute settlement procedures, because of the separate nature of the different decisions. Thus it is true that by integrating them within a single umbrella framework the WTO has strengthened dispute settlement procedures. For a detailed account of dispute settlement reform, see Stewart (1993, 2669–870).

are reflected in arguments that the WTO has achieved a strengthening of the multilateral system.[7]

System strengthening, in the sense of stronger and more consistent application of agreed GATT principles, usually focuses on nondiscrimination (MFN), national treatment, and transparency. Indeed, these were the focus at the launch of the Uruguay Round because of the ongoing erosion of GATT principles, especially MFN. Moving to a permanent international trade body with a charter, a larger support staff, stronger powers, and a broader and a more clearly articulated mandate for negotiating trade and other rules, it was hoped, would refocus the system on these principles.

The Roots of Institutional Reform

The first WTO advocates were in part looking back to the stillborn International Trade Organization (ITO), which was negotiated in 1947 but not ratified by the US Congress in 1951, partly on the grounds that it contained too many compromises of free trade principles (Diebold 1952; Wilcox 1949; Bronz 1956; Jackson 1969; Brown 1950). The ITO is perhaps best understood as the GATT at the point of negotiation in 1947—but placed in a broader legal framework and with additional chapters covering restrictive business practices, commodities, and labor practices (see appendix D). The ITO made no reference to linkages between real and financial arrangements, one of the points of departure in calls from Italy and the European Community for an initiative in this area during the Uruguay Round (*Financial Times*, 30 March 1990, 4; 6 April 1990, 8).

One of the strongest proponents of institutional redesign has been Jackson (1969), especially in his later work (1989, 1990a), which set out proposals for restructuring the GATT institution. His approach proved close to the actual WTO structure agreed to in the Uruguay Round. It incorporated a new charter without many substantive obligations, which he saw as continuing to be expressed in the GATT, albeit on a definitive rather than a provisional basis. There would be a number of other codes or agreements, all of which would be facilitated or served by a WTO structure.

The major benefit Jackson saw in such an arrangement was the coherence that such an organization would embody through its charter, its clear

---

7. There is also the key issue of exactly what it is that is being strengthened and why. Thus, the text of the Punta del Este declaration that launched the round stated that one of its objectives was to "strengthen the role of GATT, improve the multilateral trading system based on the principles and rules of the GATT, and bring about a wider coverage of world trade under agreed, effective, and enforceable multilateral disciplines." The chairman of the Contracting Parties at the end of the round referred to Uruguay Round results that "must serve as a vehicle for strong economic growth" (*Focus GATT Newsletter* 105, 1); others refer to strengthened disciplines (on dispute settlement, antidumping, subsidies, countervail) rather than a strengthened system.

mandate, and its orderly rules for the Secretariat—that is, in its form rather than its substantive content. By moving from the provisionally applied GATT to a WTO, trade arrangements would be placed on a clearer legal basis.[8]

Variants on this approach can also be found in other writings.[9] For instance, Camps (in collaboration with Gwin, 1981) set out the main elements of a world production and trade organization that would supersede both the GATT and the UN Conference on Trade and Development (UNCTAD) and take over some of the functions of both. Most of the national governments' contractual obligations in the GATT framework would thus remain in force.[10] It was to deal with trade and industrial policy questions, and its mandate was also to extend to service industries. There was to be a rule-making facility, and surveillance and consultation functions with respect to foreign direct investment (FDI) and business practices. They also included trade-related aspects of agriculture and commodity agreements affecting conditions of trade (excluding arrangements dealing with energy).

The umbrella organization was to be global and open-ended, with a plenary body for the organization directed by consensus. All subsidiary bodies were to operate transparently, and they proposed several such bodies: a Trade Policy Review Board with functions similar to the executive boards of the World Bank and the International Monetary Fund, a tariff and trade code that would remain under the GATT, a developing-country trade committee, an advisory council on the global economy, a council on FDI, and a commodities board.

These proposals addressed the difficulties facing the trading system through a change of organizational form to make its legal basis clearer. There was substantial overlap in the various approaches, as the arrangements were largely an extension of those already in the GATT. However, many of the operations such bodies were to undertake, including questions of coverage and strengthened dispute settlement, could all be discussed within the GATT. The issue, therefore, was the same as it is today: does changing the institutional form of the GATT make a substantive contribution to strengthening the multilateral system? We now turn to an

---

8. Jackson emphasizes the need for the trading system to be governed on a "rules basis" and not on a "power basis." See the discussion in Jackson (1989, 1990a) on rule- or power-oriented diplomacy. Jackson also wrote (for a World Trade and Commerce Organization) on the need for a new constitution (1969, 789–93).

9. Other proposals to redesign the GATT include the Organization for Trade Cooperation suggested by GATT members in 1955 (Jackson 1969, 51), the GATT-Plus by the Atlantic Council of the United States (1976), and the OECD Free Trade and Investment Area by Hufbauer (1989).

10. The contractual commitments made in GATT must remain if the liberalization achievements are to be preserved, according to Camps and Gwin (1981, 150–87), who also note the danger of eroding past progress if attempts are made to rewrite the system from scratch.

examination of how the WTO is to address the four elements of system strengthening discussed above: establishing rules to stem the erosion in basic trade principles, more strictly enforcing existing rules, combating protectionism, and broadening the issues that the system covers.

Shoring Up Trade Principles and Stronger Enforcement

The WTO has indeed emphasized MFN and national treatment, even attempting to extend these principles to the services trade. It seeks greater transparency through the trade policy review mechanism (TPRM) and by allowing some increased rights to information for third parties in dispute settlement cases. Overall, the thrust is to adhere to the basic principles of the GATT and the multilateral system.

Beyond a more consistent application of existing trading system principles is a further view of system strengthening as the more vigorous enforcement of existing trade disciplines. The WTO is widely credited with achieving system strengthening in this sense, primarily through its dispute settlement procedures, but the penalties accompanying determinations of a violation are also important.

Before the Uruguay Round, violations of trade rules had gone unchallenged: either complaints were not brought forward, or ambiguous interpretations of GATT rules slowed or diluted their translation into operational significance, or the penalty arrangements were not strong enough to ensure compliance.[11] For example, there had been some 60 regional trade agreements notified to the GATT before the Uruguay Round was launched and for which GATT working parties had been established, and yet in no case had any clear determination been made as to GATT incompatibility under Article XXIV, including in the cases of the original European Community and the Common Agricultural Policy (Hart 1987; WTO 1995).

Dispute settlement procedures have been strengthened, it is widely agreed.[12] There used to be several opportunities for the protagonists in a trade dispute to block the implementation of dispute settlement procedures, including the formation of a panel, the adoption of a panel report, or agreement as to rights to retaliate. Indeed, only once were rights to retaliate granted: to the Netherlands in a celebrated 1953 agricultural case with the United States, which in part led to a US request for an open-ended waiver for use of agricultural protection.[13]

---

11. Hudec, Kennedy, and Sgarbossa (1993) set out a detailed discussion and quantitative analysis of postwar GATT dispute settlement cases (see also Bliss 1987; Jackson 1989).

12. Jackson (1994) sets out his sense of both weaknesses and improvements from the Uruguay Round.

13. The Netherlands was authorized to restrict imports of US wheat flour as retaliation for a US failure to comply with a panel finding against its import restrictions on Dutch dairy products (GATT, *Basic Instruments and Selected Documents,* 1st supp., 1953; Hudec 1992).

While a fair degree of system strengthening has been achieved in these dimensions, elements of system weakening also accompany these changes. One is that new dispute settlement procedures may not be strong enough to restrain countries from taking actions that fall outside the system rules, and hence the net effect may simply be to create more conflict. The United States' continued use of section 301 measures, for instance, may generate more open conflict within the system than there was previously and weaken it.[14]

Another potential weakness could become apparent if the dispute settlement case load grows quickly (perhaps due to new disputes arising from complex text in the Uruguay Round Final Act), overwhelming the WTO Secretariat and thus undermining the credibility of the process.[15] In addition, penalties remain weak (a withdrawal of equivalent concessions) and must be agreed to by a consensus decision of the council.

It is naive to think that countries have refrained from using dispute settlement procedures merely because of difficulties with process. Other factors inevitably influence events. Mexico, for instance, soft-pedaled their tuna-dolphin dispute with the United States in part because of the potential adverse impact a GATT panel report might have had on the NAFTA negotiations. Thus, while the dispute settlement changes are an important element of a strengthened system, it is impossible to project how large an effect these measures will have, especially in terms of how the major players in the system follow and implement future dispute recommendations.

Resistance to Protectionism

The third interpretation of system strengthening is that it should enhance the ability to resist new elements of protection. Claims for the WTO on this

---

14. On March 1994, President Clinton signed an executive order to reinstate the super 301 provision of US trade law. Under it, the administration is required to list what it determines to be "unfair" traders and negotiate an acceptable solution or impose sanctions (see Low 1993, 87–88, for analysis of previous US experience with super 301). Bayard and Elliott (1994) report the results of a statistical analysis of 72 regular, special, and super 301 cases completed between 1975 and 1992. They conclude that section 301 had been reasonably successful in opening foreign markets, especially after 1985. However, more recently, section 301 has been used less and has been less successful. The authors note that the actual trade gains to the United States from applying 301 were not large. Jackson (1995, 23) discusses the relationship of 301 to the WTO.

15. Jackson (1994) also stresses this point. In particular, the deadlines raise concerns. While generally considered a positive development, especially for developing and small countries, deadlines may slip if there are many simultaneous proceedings involving many technicalities. This could reduce the WTO's credibility and weaken the system. For thorough discussion of the WTO dispute settlement mechanism, see Vermulst and Driessen (1995) and Komuro (1995).

score have been more restrained. These elements of protec
both intercountry trade conflict—especially of the type often a.
with the events the 1930s—and within-country pressures for prot
including growing use of contingent protection (antidumping and co
tervailing duties).

Little in the round directly addressed this notion of system strengthen-ing. In antidumping, there is little of substance; if anything, the changes make it easier to administer protection through antidumping measures. If the developing countries that have recently implemented antidumping legislation were to file cases, there would be a danger of system weaken-ing.

In subsidies and countervailing duties, a definition and new classifica-tions of subsidies were the main contributions. There is nothing to address how countries are to behave toward each other in the event of a trade conflict outside WTO disciplines: how frequently they might retaliate, against which goods or services, and how nonprotagonists are to be treated.

Uruguay Round bindings (i.e., in agriculture or with developing-country tariffs) represent a clear restraint on domestic protectionist pres-sures. But to achieve tariffication and other liberalization in agriculture, new safeguard arrangements have been created that may introduce new trade-restricting measures. One can also argue that pressures will grow for instrument substitution—for example, antidumping duties in place of Multi-Fiber Arrangement (MFA) quotas or as an accompaniment to re-duced tariffs.

But at the end of the day, many countries, particularly the smaller countries most affected by large-country protectionist measures, claimed that the conclusion of the round, including creation of the WTO, could promote resistance to protectionist measures best by reinforcing the coop-eration achieved in the seven previous GATT negotiating rounds.[16] This belief is reflected in the "bicycle" theory of multilateralism—namely, to preserve what you have, you have to keep moving forward on the GATT bicycle or else fall off.[17]

The counterargument is that there are many ways of achieving coopera-tion on trade policy; the WTO is merely one such way. In the 1980s there

---

16. It is worth noting that modern game theory has no well-developed theory of how cooperation in small-group situations either emerges or works. There are some simple-minded notions of cooperation-preserving mechanisms, such as Rubinstein's (1982) folk theorem, which stresses penalty systems strong enough to enforce any outcome, but beyond this there is little, and what there is cannot be directly applied to the WTO process.

17. This view is often associated with Bergsten (1975, 209–24; see also Destler 1986), though it is reflected elsewhere as well. According to the GATT director general, "The new agree-ments, the new rules and structures it sets up—all mean a commitment to a continuing process of cooperation and reform" (*Focus GATT Newsletter* 105, 5).

were three instances of bilateral trade retaliation between the United States and the European Community, all relating to matters concerning the Common Agricultural Policy, the United States, and EC enlargement. A retaliatory trade process broke out in each case but was confined to agriculture by mutual agreement and with implicit limits placed on the size of each retaliation. Each outbreak was eventually mediated bilaterally. Thus, while instances of tit-for-tat retaliation outside the formal multilateral channels are seen as system weaknesses, the fact remains that such cases have been resolved using non-GATT mechanisms that may have been quicker and more effective.

Greater Breadth of Coverage

Finally, system strengthening in the sense of broader coverage of areas and trade-restricting measures has also been claimed for the WTO. The Uruguay Round brought three new areas—services, investment, and intellectual property—within the WTO framework.[18] This is a clear signal that the WTO and the multilateral system can embrace nontraditional areas, thus closing the system gap. If these new areas were left to regional arrangements, many countries, especially developing countries, would be excluded. A distinct two-tier system would emerge.

Strengthening has also been achieved, it is argued, through wider coverage of trade-restricting measures. Indeed, one of the central arguments made in the initial discussions on services liberalization was that use of new protective trade measures affecting services would be unconstrained in the absence of any multilateral agreement, which in turn could erode wider performance from the global economy.

But greater breadth could weaken the system in other senses. As noted in chapter 5, violations in the intellectual property area, for instance, could now meet with retaliation in the form of higher trade barriers on goods—that is, the gains from trade could be forgone to achieve nontrade objectives and a weaker trade system would result. Similar trade-offs could arise in trade and environment, and in worker and human rights.

Restricting Major Trade Conflicts

The ability to consistently defuse trade conflicts has been an important characteristic of a strong postwar global trading system, and the WTO is often claimed as strengthening this capability.

---

18. See Hoekman and Sauvé (1994) and Sauvé (1995) for a broad overview of liberalizing trade in services, including the Uruguay Round results. Hoekman (1993) also discusses how the Uruguay Round decisions in services will affect developing countries.

As noted earlier, however, the number of retaliatory episodes before the Uruguay Round's completion was already surprisingly small.[19] Occasionally, implementations of panel rulings have been delayed for a time. But, as noted earlier, where retaliation has threatened to erupt beyond the conventional GATT process, the wider trading system (including bilateral mediation) has been surprisingly successful in containing any disruption of trade. Thus it is unclear how much more could be accomplished through the WTO by adding new global restraints against outbreaks of major-power conflict.

In three cases in the 1980s where US-EC disputes moved outside the GATT process, they were typically resolved through bilateral mediation, usually after the United States sought an initial remedy through GATT dispute settlement procedures (box 7.2). Bilateral mediation contained the trade dispute to the product areas at issue and averted subsequent retaliation.

As discussed in chapter 6, this experience stands in contrast to that of the late 1920s and early 1930s, where European and US retaliatory trade barrier increases are thought to have contributed to (though not to fully explain) the rapid downturn in global income. Some go so far as to suggest that it is precisely the fear of recreating the events of the 1930s that has restrained retaliation and induced the major players to formally bind tariffs and commit to system principles.

Similarly, game theorists frequently focus on the need to establish cooperative agreements to prevent noncooperative outcomes (the experience of the 1930s is typically seen as the epitome of such an outcome). They see cooperative agreements such as the GATT and the WTO as useful in preventing an outbreak of retaliatory and noncooperative exclusionary behavior in the trading system (McMillan 1986; Abbott 1985; Hungerford 1991).

Game theory therefore suggests that the postwar trading system should not be evaluated only in terms of the amount of new market opening that has been achieved; one also has to ask how much market closing has been avoided. In other words, the trading system should not be evaluated relative to the status quo of the late 1940s, but instead relative to a world ridden by retaliatory trade barriers in which all semblance of international cooperation has collapsed.

Unfortunately, modern game theory cannot specify the form of international agreement that would best guarantee a strong trading system. International cooperation could take many forms, and there is no reason to defend the present system simply because it embodies a degree of cooper-

---

19. During the Uruguay Round negotiations, there were disturbing escalations in EU-US conflict over Airbus subsidies, beef hormones, oilseeds, and other matters.

Box 7.2   US-EC retaliation in the 1980s

Citrus-pasta war. In the early 1970s, the European Community lowered tariffs on citrus exports from several non-EC Mediterranean countries. In 1982, the United States asked a GATT panel to determine if this action was consistent with Article I. In March 1985 the Community blocked adoption of a panel report that said the EC preferential arrangements impaired US benefits under the article. On 13 July 1985, the United States raised tariffs on pasta (from 1 to 40 percent) and on pasta containing eggs (from 1 to 25 percent). The Community countered in October by raising tariffs on walnuts (from 8 to 30 percent) and on lemons (from 8 to 20 percent). The dispute was settled in August 1986, with a US agreement not to challenge future EC preferential arrangements with the Mediterranean countries and to drop the pasta tariffs and with an EC agreement to lower tariffs on US exports of grapefruit, lemons, and almonds.

EC enlargement. In 1986, the United States asked a GATT working party to examine the trade effect of Spain and Portugal joining the European Community, and it sought postponement of Spain's variable levies on corn and sorghum, which could have kept it out of the Spanish market. In March, the US threatened retaliation in white wine, beer, liquor, and cheese. In April, the Community countered with a list of corn gluten, feed, honey, and sunflower seeds. These restrictions went into effect in May with the failure of bilateral mediation. By July, an agreement was reached: the United States halted retaliation, and the Community agreed to delay imposing higher tariffs on US exports to Spain by six months and to purchase a quota of US products at a reduced tariff level.

Meat hormones. In 1989, the Community banned sale of hormone-enhanced meat, which excluded virtually all US meat exports (an estimated $100 million in lost exports). In negotiations under the Technical Barriers to Trade Agreement in 1988, the Community blocked a US request to establish a technical experts group, and the United States blocked an EC request for a GATT panel on the legality of the US retaliation. On 1 January 1989, the day the EC hormone ban went into effect, the United States imposed 100 percent tariffs on $100 million worth of boneless beef, pork, hams, shoulders, and other products. Counterretaliation was announced. Through a joint task force, the parties reached interim agreement in May on a certification system that would allow resumption of US shipments of hormone-free beef (accounting for 15 percent of its total exports to EC). Subsequently, the US Congress required US military bases in Europe to buy only US beef.

ation.[20] Other, more preferable cooperative arrangements may be available.

Some theorists (i.e., Rubinstein 1982) see collective agreements as supportable only if deviant behavior is sharply penalized. But Rubinstein implicitly argues that any cooperative outcome can be supported with such a penalty system, including those with less desirable properties. That is, the WTO may be better than no cooperation, but there are many pos-

---

20. Johnson (1976, 18), in discussing the GATT articles, argues that "the principle of non-discrimination has no basis whatsoever in the theoretical argument for the benefits of a liberal international order in general, or in any rational economic theory of the tariff bargaining process in particular."

sible cooperative arrangements to choose from, and each is supportable through an international legal structure.

A related view is that a clear, credible focal point to which all parties are willing to commit is necessary to attain a cooperative improvement on a noncooperative, retaliation-ridden world (McMillan 1989). Moreover, if the rules that define the focal point are viewed as inherently desirable, deviations will be less likely and may need to be sanctioned less severely through the agreed penalty system.

The GATT in 1947 can be seen in this light as such a focal point. Agreement on relatively weak system penalties was reflected in the dispute settlement provisions of Article XXII (consultation) and Article XXIII (nullification or impairment). However, member countries' limited recourse to these provisions increased the probability that the multilateral system would eventually erode.

Moreover, the relative inability of the negotiating process to respond to changing circumstances through new rule-writing efforts over seven negotiating rounds weakened joint commitment to the system.[21] The informality of process and conciliation within the GATT, often viewed by GATT aficionados as a major asset in avoiding escalation of conflict, may have added to the imprecision of the rules and further weakened joint commitment. In this view, by the late 1980s reestablishing the credibility of the WTO as a focal point was a critical objective.

Continuity of process is another feature said to be helpful in fending off trade conflicts. Under the so-called bicycle theory of the GATT (Bergsten 1975, 209–24; Destler 1986), virtually continuous trade negotiations over the postwar years have helped restrain retaliatory or deviant behavior. Individual countries will demonstrate commitment to either the current or a prospective future negotiation in order to achieve further gains from their trade partners' lowered barriers by holding off on their own barrier increases, and they will do so as long as negotiations are prospective or continuing, so as not to imperil the final cooperative agreement. Problems begin when the "bicycle" loses its forward momentum;[22] countries consequently lose the incentive to resist protectionist pressures. Hence, continuity in negotiating rounds is key in preventing an outbreak of global protection.

To the extent that any or all of these arguments are accepted, one could conclude that the WTO is preventing (and the GATT has prevented) increases in trade barriers. Ongoing multilateral negotiations helped repel barrier increases. The WTO continues, where the GATT left off, to provide

---

21. Congress dubbed the GATT "the General Agreement to Talk and Talk," while developing countries considered it a rich man's club.

22. Announcements at the 1991 OECD ministerial meeting stressing the importance of concluding the round were viewed as an attempt to avoid this outcome (*Financial Times*, 6 June 1991, 5).

a focal point for cooperation. And it represents the major global institutional arrangement for penalizing deviant behavior (if only weakly).

Unfortunately, however, many of the features that helped prevent retaliation in the past have also widened the gap between the multilateral and the overall trading system. Once they have committed to the focal point, politicians bend to domestic interest-group pressures, and in so doing incrementally erode the multilateral principles in ways that are often opaque.[23] Under a system with relatively weak penalty and enforcement mechanisms, such a process can continue for some time without seriously wounding the system, although at some point the cumulative erosion is severe enough that either joint action must be taken to reverse it or the system's value as a focal point is lost. In this sense, the creation of the WTO can be seen as joint action to reestablish a focal point for cooperation within the system.

In sum, evaluating the trading system's influence on postwar economic performance involves more than an attempt to measure how much of the trade growth that occurred can be attributed to trade liberalization. One also has to ask what the situation would have been in the absence of the GATT. As far as the WTO is concerned, we must also ask whether the WTO merely represents more of the same—the reestablishment under a new name of a weak focal point for cooperation—or strengthened arrangements that will revitalize the system. It is not yet clear which way the WTO will lean.

Strategic Considerations

It is hard to say whether trade wars would have occurred without the GATT. In the hegemonic world of the late 1940s and early 1950s, united by strategic rather than trade interests, the answer would be probably not. On the other hand, game theorists frequently stress the difficulties of establishing a focal point for cooperation in order to collectively avoid an inferior, noncooperative outcome. The GATT can fairly claim to have provided such a focal point; it is also an objective of the WTO to provide a focal point and thus reduce the risk of trade wars, though its ability to do so is at this point somewhat conjectural.

In the simplest construct—a two-country, non–zero sum game—trade barriers emerge as they did in the 1930s, representing classic noncooperative behavior (Johnson 1953–54; Gorman 1957). Successive barrier increases maximize the national gains from trade by improving the

---

23. Destler and Odell (1987) cite a number of cases of sectoral protection being accorded after intense political pressure by vested interests: footwear, steel, autos, and textiles. Grossman and Helpman (1992) consider the effects of special interest groups lobbying for protection and how these efforts may affect multilateral negotiations (see also Grossman and Helpman 1995).

country's terms of trade, and each country takes turns raising its barriers to the point at which incremental terms of trade gains just offset losses from forgone gains from trade.

When it takes a retaliatory step, each country assumes that its rival will not further raise barriers in response. Retaliation and counterretaliation occur until a noncooperative equilibrium is attained, typically with high trade barriers in both countries. At such an equilibrium, optimizing behavior by each country is consistent with the high barriers actually pursued by other countries—that is, no improvement in national welfare is obtainable through further terms of trade improvements from additional barrier increases (a Nash equilibrium).

While in reality it seems unlikely that increases in barriers would reach their full retaliatory limit, the need for institutional arrangements to ward off such a possibility, now embodied in the WTO, has always been deemed paramount. But the rules are not the only guarantor of a strong trading system in which trade-restricting measures are limited. Enforcement is also important, and its influence on the system before the Uruguay Round's conclusion must be examined separately from that of the rules alone. Here again, the WTO and the new system of dispute settlement procedures will come into play.

GATT dispute settlement is widely argued to have been flawed.[24] Before revisions were made at the midterm review of the Uruguay Round, pursuing a dispute complaint was often a lengthy process. Complaints of violations (known as "nullification" or "impairment") could take place only after consultations proved unsuccessful. GATT articles were in some places vague and in others verbose, leaving room for substantial ambiguity of interpretation, and accumulated GATT jurisprudence had less solid foundations for the settlement of disputes than is true under domestic law.

Adoption of the reports of the GATT panel, once concluded, could be blocked by the defendant at the GATT Council. Moreover, even when defendants accepted a negative report against them, they sometimes complied only in cosmetic ways that did not meet the spirit of the decision (i.e., through renaming of programs, reclassification schemes, and other devices). If attempts at conciliation following acceptance of a panel report failed, complainants had to return to the GATT Council yet again to seek compensation, failing which limited retaliation through a withdrawal of equivalent concessions could be allowed.

After a flurry of early cases, the frequency of disputes taken to the GATT fell sharply, only to escalate in more recent years (table 7.1). Nonetheless, GATT has not sanctioned retaliation in any recent case, and only once during its history (the 1953 Netherlands-US dispute).

---

24. Hudec (1992, 15) cites a number of cases with "bad" decisions.

Table 7.1 Multilateral dispute settlement, 1948–89

Period	Number of complaints	Number of panels initiated	Decisions reached
1948–59	53	25	20
1960–69	7	5	5
1970–79	32	22	16
1980–89	115	59	45

Source: Hudec (1992, 11).

Many participants in this process have claimed that the GATT's strength lay in its ability either to resolve trade disputes through mediation or to at least prevent their escalation. But it remained something of a puzzle as to why the multilateral system was not able to generate rules and disciplines that could be more strongly enforced and potentially help generate stronger economic performance. Given all this, it is perhaps not surprising that recourse to GATT dispute settlement, while accelerating during the Uruguay Round, remained relatively uncommon.[25] Japan filed its first formal request for a panel under the GATT only in 1990—the so-called screwdriver case, in which the European Community claimed circumvention of its antidumping duties against assembled Japanese products through Japanese imports of parts. The panel report supported the Japanese position (*Focus GATT Newsletter* 70, 1). Furthermore, major-power trade disputes, as discussed earlier, sometimes escalated outside the GATT process and were often resolved bilaterally.

More effective dispute settlement has long been viewed as crucial to the success of the multilateral system.[26] But all international law is by its nature weak compared with domestic laws backed by more vigorous court systems and penalties. Moreover, a weak system of trade rules may reflect the joint preferences of national governments. An eroding system of trade rules may have been what governments were most comfortable with in the postwar years, because it enabled them more freely to protect domestic industries while maintaining the appearance of international

25. Developing countries, for instance, rarely invoke dispute settlement procedures. A 1985 study of the GATT dispute settlement mechanism prepared for the US International Trade Commission found that only eight developing countries had ever filed GATT complaints (Bliss 1987, 45; Ching 1992). Data presented in Hudec, Kennedy, and Sgarbossa (1993, 29) show that since 1948, the United States, the European Community and EC members, Canada, and Australia filed 73 percent of the complaints. According to the authors, "The large majority of GATT contracting parties have never participated in the dispute settlement process" (30).

26. According to the Uruguay Round ministerial declaration, "negotiations shall aim to improve and strengthen the rules and the procedures of the dispute settlement process, while recognizing the contribution that would be made by more effective and enforceable GATT rules and disciplines" (GATT, "News of the Uruguay Round," October 1986, 4).

order. The postwar system of international trade rules may thus in part have been a show of multilateral order without the will to enforce it. Joint agreement to enforce trade rules with limited vigor is what Low (1993, 26–27) refers to as "the conspiracy of noncompliance." If this is an accurate picture of the system, then new arrangements under the WTO will do little to change things.

The idea that strength of the trading system is only loosely linked to system rules because of their weak enforcement is similar to the economists' argument that it is incentives, not institutions, that determine behavior and outcomes. Hence, one might argue that if the industrial countries had wanted to collectively reduce tariffs in the postwar years they would have done so with or without a GATT or a WTO. In this view, international trade arrangements need not be the determining factor.

Again, it is the role of GATT/WTO rules as a focal point for cooperation that is crucial: they have been a foundation on which countries wishing to achieve joint liberalization could build. The initial steps were small but established the credibility of the process, after which larger steps followed.[27] Early GATT negotiating rounds demonstrated the credibility of this joint commitment through agreement on extensive tariff bindings.[28] By the time the European Community had been formed and the United States had accepted that a tariff negotiation was needed to secure US access to EC markets, the ground was laid for the Dillon Round (the fifth) to achieve a further 8 percent tariff cut. This round provided the credibility and momentum needed to achieve the even larger 35 percent cuts in the subsequent Kennedy and Tokyo Rounds.

So why did weak enforcement occur, and will a stronger system of rules in the WTO make that much difference? As Jackson (1969, 1989, 1990a) has repeatedly pointed out, the GATT's temporary status weakened its credibility. The interplay of strategic and trade interests in the system over the years also fostered weak enforcement. In some ways, the commitment was as much to an alliance with the United States against communist advance as it was to the principles of the GATT system. The fact that some countries acted in a manner inconsistent with the principles mattered less than the survival of the alliance.[29]

Also, leaders in other countries were inclined to tolerate these actions in one country because it implicitly meant that they would be free to take similar actions. Moreover, if the hegemon violated the principle, it became

---

27. Credibility was especially important given the failure to launch the ITO.

28. At the first tariff negotiating round held in Geneva in 1947, the 23 original signatories agreed to lower or bind 50,000 tariffs (Kenwood and Lougheed 1983, 254; Dam 1970; Jackson 1969; Irwin 1995).

29. This is clearly the case in the acceptance of the US agriculture waiver in 1955 and formation of the European Community in 1957.

easier for everyone else to accommodate these actions (and copy them) rather than challenge them and undermine their strategic relationships.[30]

Thus regional trade arrangements went largely unchallenged in the GATT because other countries wanted to reserve the right to form similar arrangements at a later time or did not wish their own arrangements to be scrutinized. GATT-incompatible voluntary export restraints (VERs) proliferated and went unchallenged. Developed countries only loosely enforced Article XVIII-B on balance of payments with developing countries as partial compensation for the lack of challenge to VERs. Market-sharing arrangements evolved in textiles and apparel and implicitly in steel. Side deals in negotiations were sometimes used to prevent system strengthening (i.e., EC and US accommodations on agriculture in the Kennedy and Tokyo Rounds) as well as to achieve it.

As concerns over both the strength of system rules and their enforcement grew, attempts to remedy the situation through the GATT structure became more problematic. Negotiations became increasingly difficult to execute. The attempt to achieve a comprehensive safeguards code in the Tokyo Round was but a forerunner to the wider difficulties in the Uruguay Round.[31] These struggles signaled both the difficulty of repairing the existing multilateral system and the risk of acceleration of erosion in that system.

If stronger trade rules could have prevented these problems in the past, then the WTO offers countries an opportunity to recommit to a single focal point for international cooperation and thus avoid them in the future. But would stronger rules have made a difference? System rules written without the initial exceptions probably would have helped. But such rules may have been politically unattainable. Some of the exceptions in the GATT were (and still are) viewed as necessary in order to reach domestic political agreement (from affected firms and workers) on the need to liberalize.[32] In any case, stronger rules with even weaker enforcement may well have led to swifter and more widespread erosion. Weak enforcement, in turn, may be a reflection of an overly ambitious system whose rules, depending on the behavior of the larger players in the system, could probably never have been fully enforced.

---

30. For example, acceptance in the early 1960s of the US Short and Long Term Agreements in textiles with Japan would eventually lead to the MFA, implemented by six other industrial countries. Other industrial countries also followed the US lead in implementing voluntary export restraints in autos, footwear, and consumer electronics.

31. Merciai (1981, 55–57) discusses the positions of the main participants in the Tokyo Round (see also Robertson 1977, 47–53; Wolff 1983).

32. Baldwin (1988, 23–28) discusses the effects of domestic opposition to liberalization, specifically how it led the United States to insist on an escape clause to satisfy domestic interests that "no industry would be seriously injured by duty cuts." See also extensive discussion of the political dimensions to US trade policymaking in Destler (1986).

If the trading system is credited with achieving good macroeconomic performance and overall stability of the international environment, it matters little if weak rules are weakly enforced. But absent strong economic performance and in the face of a more unstable international environment, the WTO will have to turn to enforcement of trade rules to strengthen the trading system.

Summary

At the beginning of the Uruguay Round, the multilateral system as represented by the GATT was perceived as being in need of renewal. The establishment of the WTO—with its legal and procedural changes, including a strengthened dispute settlement mechanism, and its inclusion of services, intellectual property, and investment measures—reflected the negotiators' effort to address perceived weaknesses. The hope was that a strengthened and renewed system would result and the multilateral "bicycle" would continue down the path of liberalization and generation of economic growth.

Yet many of the pressures that led to the erosion of the system in the 1970s and 1980s remain, and some of the changes could actually weaken it. This could be the case, for instance, if there is an overload of new dispute cases. Also, bringing more nontrade issues into the WTO could result in higher trade barriers and reduced trade growth.

There is no denying that changes have been made to create a stronger focal point for international cooperation. Only time will tell whether these changes were sufficient to close the system gap or whether a vastly different, multitiered system will emerge, with the Uruguay Round marking the turning point.

Prospects for the Trading System

We have thus far discussed the many diverse factors that must be weighed in evaluating the Uruguay Round outcomes. We now conclude by projecting directions the system will likely take and identifying changes that will have the greatest impact on future trade liberalization.

The multilateral component of the trading system has long been identified in terms of three constituent parts: a global trade constitution, which sets out the terms of the general agreement; an ongoing negotiating process dedicated to achieving fresh trade liberalization; and an institutional structure for enforcing disciplines through dispute settlement and mediation. We see the Uruguay Round as providing a distinct break in the evolution of the multilateral system, especially as far as process is concerned, with corresponding implications for the wider global trading system.

The first four GATT rounds were concerned largely with tariff bindings and only achieved tentative initial liberalization; the next three rounds were to varying degrees preoccupied with tariff cuts, as the United States sought to come to terms with market-access issues in Europe following the Treaty of Rome. The latest and eighth round was a radical departure, encompassing a bewildering array of topics. It was relatively little concerned with tariffs but much concerned with system strengthening. At an institutional level, the creation of the World Trade Organization (WTO) is the most major change of the postwar years. And parallel to the round, and partly driven by it, there has been a surge in regional trade arrangements and a growth in pressures for linkage of trade policy to nontrade objectives.

The future for the wider trading system thus is different from that which faced the world before the Uruguay Round. There is now the potential for reverse liberalization: instead of a steady reduction of trade barriers, with debate centering on how much and how fast they should fall in given sectors, barriers could actually rise to accommodate nontrade objectives. Future trade policy debate will partly focus on rules allowing new uses of the old barriers. Continuing regional pressures raise the prospect of a widening two-tier system, with trade conflicts and accommodations of various kinds between the large blocs and overlapping and different arrangements between larger and smaller countries within blocs. Also, important drivers of trade growth lie beyond formal system arrangements—cross-border investment flows and unilateral trade liberalization.

If there were to be another trade round, it would likely be dominated by reciprocity-based initiatives for which the Uruguay Round blazed the trail by creating new negotiation possibilities—in such areas as tariffs, agriculture, and services. We believe these would figure more prominently than the current leading issues of trade and environment and competition policy. In addition to differences in substance, the momentum and process of future liberalization negotiations will, in our view, differ from that of earlier rounds.

Changes in institutional arrangements from the round, reflected in the World Trade Organization (WTO), will affect the management of global trade arrangements chiefly through biennial ministerial conferences, at which progress in the implementation of the agreements can be assessed and issues of interpretation can be clarified. In and of itself, the creation of the WTO does relatively little to change the multilateral negotiating process, nor does it modify the forces that influence the launch or successful conclusion of a future round.

The WTO and Future Negotiating Rounds

There will likely be another negotiating round in the WTO, although such a round may not be launched for quite some time. The Uruguay Round provided a continuity of process—the continued momentum needed to propel the "bicycle" of multilateral trade negotiations—that is a precondition for future rounds.

Several events during the eight GATT rounds added fresh momentum to liberalization at crucial points. Perhaps the key event was the formation of the European Community in the late 1950s along with US recognition of the need to negotiate access in European markets. This sparked three major tariff negotiations: the Dillon Round, the Kennedy Round, and the Tokyo Round. The Dillon Round lasted 18 months and at the time was viewed as having achieved tariff cuts of around 8 percent on a request-and-offer basis. The success of the Dillon Round and the continuing US concern about European market access resulted in the four-year Kennedy Round, with a formula-based tariff-cutting approach that eventually achieved tariff cuts of some 35 percent. The perceived success of the Kennedy Round in turn prompted the Tokyo Round, which echoed the preceding round in offering further tariff cuts of 35 percent.[1]

Similarly, the circumstances that surrounded the Uruguay Round could sustain the momentum of liberalization for the next few decades: concern over fragmentation of the global economy following the fall of the Berlin Wall in 1989, and the end of the Cold War, which was seen as dissolving the strategic glue that had held the trading system in an anticommunist alliance. Without it, some believed, multilateral cooperation on trade could not continue. According to this view, Europe and Japan somewhat reluctantly agreed to negotiate GATT with the United States and offered trade concessions in exchange for US troops being based on their soil. But cooperation since 1989 has continued nonetheless, and in the final stages of the Uruguay Round negotiations the key players reaffirmed the multilateral system.

An unwillingness to let the round fail and thereby damage the multilateral trading system led Germany and subsequently France to make the necessary concessions in agriculture. The added prospect of an Asia-Pacific trade alliance under the Asia Pacific Economic Cooperation forum (APEC) fueled these pressures. In its final stage, the Uruguay Round forced participants to declare in favor of the multilateral system. They revealed a preference: the multilateral system was worth a great deal to them. Even if the agreements lack some substance, the significance of the commitment to the process is clear. It sowed the seed for further negotiations.

Moreover, participants were willing to give a little to maintain the vitality of the system and thus to ensure continued stability and security. This drove the acceptance of the Dunkel text in December 1993 and the acceptance of the Uruguay Round agreements in Marrakesh in April 1994. Participants confronted the possibility of a system breakdown, backed away, and concluded the round and in doing so provided the bedrock for multilateral cooperation for decades to come.

Having said this, it is also our belief that establishing the WTO did little to alter the prospects for a new round. The WTO does provide important new procedures for monitoring and interpreting the Uruguay Round agreements through the ministerial meetings, which may mitigate tensions that surface as the details are worked out. But such meetings will not generate the agenda, timetable, process, or modalities necessary at the

---

1. The Tokyo Round was officially launched in 1973 and ended in 1979. However, not much was achieved in the early years, mainly because the United States did not receive negotiating authority until 1975. Further delays meant serious negotiations did not start until 1977. The Tokyo Round agenda reflected efforts to further the extensive tariff liberalization achieved in the Kennedy Round and extend liberalization to nontariff barriers and agriculture (Winham 1986).

launch of new negotiations. Indeed, these cannot be prespecified at these meetings; nor are they prespecified within the current structure of the WTO.[2] A future round would inevitably be launched under the auspices of the WTO, but the WTO itself does not make such a launch more probable than it would have been under previous GATT arrangements.[3]

The time required to launch a round is an important factor for new negotiations. It will take 10 years to complete the implementation of Uruguay Round agriculture and textiles provisions, and it seems unlikely that a new round could be launched before this time.[4] There is to be a mini-negotiation in agriculture after five years to seek exchanges of concessions within agriculture. We anticipate this will be relatively unsuccessful because of the inability to make cross-deals involving other areas; nonetheless, the agreement mandates this negotiation. Regional negotiations, especially in APEC, may further complicate the process. In addition, each successive GATT round has lasted longer and has taken longer to launch, and we anticipate the same trend would continue in a future round. Memory of the difficulties involved in the early and middle stages of the Uruguay Round will likely add to the delay in launching a round.

Some have suggested that there will be a move toward permanent negotiation under the WTO, and therefore negotiating rounds will become unnecessary. But as we noted, the planned biennial ministerial meetings, which would be the likely vehicle for permanent negotiation, are not sufficient for this purpose. The first few will be more concerned with implementation of the Uruguay Round and the resolution of disputes. It may be that a round could be launched at a ministerial meeting 10 years hence, but then these meetings would merely be playing roles similar to those of preceding GATT launches, midterm reviews, and concluding meetings in the Uruguay Round. A move to permanent negotiation we therefore see as unlikely; more likely is permanent monitoring and interpretation of existing agreements.

---

2. There are a few sectors where negotiations have been prespecified. Negotiations have already restarted on unfinished business from the Uruguay Round in the areas of basic telecommunications, maritime transport, financial services, and movement of labor. Provisions were included in the Uruguay Round for negotiations in agriculture to take place in five years. However, these developments are not, in and of themselves, enough to constitute permanent multilateral trade negotiations.

3. This is not meant to diminish the importance of the WTO as a continuing focal point and forum for multilateral trade negotiations. The institution is no more likely to compel leaders to expend the political will it takes to launch and conclude a round.

4. In an effort to maintain the momentum of trade liberalization at the G-7 meeting in July 1994, President Clinton attempted to launch a round of multilateral trade negotiations focusing on financial services, telecommunications, and investment rules. He was unsuccessful.

Agenda of a Future Negotiation

The content of future multilateral trade negotiations must at this point be somewhat speculative. Right after the wrap-up of the Uruguay Round, there were several forecasts that a future round would be a Green Round. It was argued that competition policy would be the second outstanding issue, with investment and labor standards following.

We do not dispute that there are pressures for clarification of trade rules in the environmental area. As we indicate in chapter 5, the central issues in trade and environment relate to the interpretation of existing trade rules—in particular, GATT Article XX—and how these rules may be modified. But these debates are not oriented toward reciprocity-based trade negotiations, the traditional mode for GATT rounds. Issues that lend themselves to this sort of negotiation have led past rounds, and any future round will be no exception.

The same proviso applies to talks on competition policy, where the issues relate to the potential trade effects from limited harmonization of domestic policies. Driving this debate are US and European concerns over exclusion from Japanese and other Asian markets that they believe stems from weak enforcement of competition laws. Thus, stronger enforcement of national laws, as well as issues of extraterritoriality and, from the developing-country side, control of collusion within national markets would be the focus of discussions. Again, as with trade and environment, competition policy negotiations would not fundamentally be reciprocity-driven, involving an exchange of barrier reductions in one country for those in another. Hence, while both trade and environment and competition policy could well be significant elements, a future negotiation centered largely on these issues is unlikely.

As we have argued, it is in tariffs and agriculture and to a lesser extent services (and perhaps investment) that countries will find the basis of the agenda for a future, reciprocity-based negotiation. Just as the unresolved issues of the Tokyo Round formed the core of the agenda for the Uruguay Round, the unresolved issues of the Uruguay Round could form the core of this new round.

The conversion of previously unbound, nontransparent protective measures in agriculture into bound (albeit high) tariffs opens the door to a major reciprocity-based negotiation of potentially large proportions. The sharp increase in coverage of tariff bindings in developing countries—from a little over 20 percent to almost 80 percent, with even higher coverage for economies in transition—also opens up the possibility of tariff-based negotiations on the largest scale yet. Because many of these tariff items relate to rapidly growing markets, the interest of the developed world in such negotiations is clear. In addition, if the Multi-Fiber Arrangement (MFA) is eliminated, as promised in the Uruguay Round, tariffs would remain as the binding instrument on trade in key apparel items and would represent both the highest tariff items in developed countries and the ones of most interest and importance to developing countries. Again, we see this as another possible starting point for a reciprocity-based negotiation.

In services, the tentative steps taken thus far could be amplified in subsequent negotiations. And in the investment area, the further narrowing of allowable investment restrictions under the trade-related investment measures (TRIMs) provisions could provide room for negotiation.

Environment for a Future Global Trade Negotiation

As we have noted, the most important driver behind a possible future negotiating round is the key players' perception that the system is valuable and that fresh liberalization is central to maintaining it. The successful conclusion to the Uruguay Round contradicted the view that multilateral negotiations would fall apart with the absence of the strategic underpinnings of the Cold War and showed that, because of these countries' concerns over trade performance and overall economic growth and prosperity, external policy remains crucial.

A future negotiation will become increasingly more entangled in nontrade objectives. The Uruguay Round agreements on intellectual property set the precedent by allowing cross-retaliation on goods trade for violation of intellectual property norms. The so-called 'new-new' issues widely touted as candidates for becoming lead issues of a new negotiation—trade and environment, labor standards, and human rights—fit the same mold. Trade policy could become the policeman for enforcing far-reaching rules to achieve nontrade objectives.

The changing global role of the fast-growing East Asian economies would be part of the backdrop to new negotiations. Malaysia and Thailand may grow by more than 8 percent in 1994 in real terms, China by almost 12 percent, and Indonesia by perhaps 7 percent (Dowling 1994, 2). Continued growth by these economies over the next 10 to 15 years will swing the center of global economic activity further toward Asia, heighten US and European concerns over market access in Asia, and subsequently increase their appetite for arrangements to pin down access in these growing markets. Developments within APEC may catalyze multilateral negotiations on these issues, as it did in the final stage of the Uruguay Round. European concerns over APEC could eventually even prove strong enough to fuel a new round.

Trade arrangements for China will also be a question. China had asked to become one of the founding members of the WTO.[5] The United States in turn

---

5. Negotiations for China to rejoin the GATT began in 1987. There was no agreement on the terms of China's accession and the talks were put on hold when the GATT session ended in

indicated that if this were to be the case China should be admitted as a developed country and thus face the stricter disciplines and obligations attending this classification.[6] At the heart of US concerns is a fear of rapid surges of Chinese exports in many product ranges. Over the last four years, China has emerged as the largest shipper of apparel to both US and European markets. Thus, issues related to China's status and trade arrangements with Asia in general will increasingly preoccupy makers of trade policy.

Conclusions

Viewed positively, the Uruguay Round has strongly reaffirmed the key players' multilateral commitment and set the ground rules for decades to come. Viewed negatively, the Uruguay Round has been a torturous affair for many of those involved. Originally meant to last four years, it took more than seven. Originally meant to yield an early harvest, it yielded relatively little until the final days. Originally meant to provide far-reaching changes in trade policy and a whole range of disciplines, it fell short of expectations.

None of this detracts from its overriding significance both for the short-term conduct of trade and the future directions for the world trading system. We believe that the Uruguay Round, merely by concluding, renewed the credibility of the multilateral trading system, which was in danger of further sharp erosion. It also provided an initial set of system rules in such areas as services, investment, and intellectual property, which, while substantively light, provides the beachhead from which liberalization in these areas can advance further. And it has sown the seeds for future negotiations through extensive bindings and added transparency.

Tariffication in agriculture, new and extensive tariff bindings in developing countries, and the conversion of quotas in textiles and apparel into bindings all create major opportunities for new exchanges of reciprocal concessions. The Uruguay Round was, in the final analysis, a reciprocity-driven trade round like all that preceded it, only more complex. Textiles and apparel were traded for intellectual property concessions by developing countries; tariff concessions were also reciprocally bargained. Furthermore, the Uruguay Round has made possible new, more extensive reciprocal exchanges of concessions in the future. It may be years before the fruits of these labors are apparent, but this does not diminish the round's positive, lasting contribution to the future of the global trading system.

December 1994. In July 1995 China was granted observer status, and working party discussions on China's membership resumed.

6. China has insisted that it is entitled to join as a developing country and have access to the privileges accorded to developing-country members (such as the balance of payments provision).

APPENDICES

The Uruguay Round Agreements

Agriculture

The agreement has four main components: the agreement on agriculture, concessions and commitments made on market access, domestic support and export subsidies, and the agreement on sanitary and phytosanitary measures. It also encompasses the separate ministerial decision concerning least-developed and net food-importing developing countries.

Agreement on Agriculture

This agreement brought agricultural trade within the rules and disciplines of the General Agreement on Tariffs and Trade (GATT) and recognized agricultural reform as a long-term process.

The agreement on agriculture also specified that member states had to make binding commitments in the areas of market access, domestic support, and export competition and reach an acceptable agreement on sanitary and phytosanitary measures. The implementation period was set at six years for developed countries and ten years for developing countries. In contrast, least-developed countries would be exempt from making reduction commitments. All commitments would be included in members' schedules of agricultural concessions and commitments.

Market Access

Under market-access conditions, participants of the round agreed to convert all nontariff barriers to tariffs that provide equivalent levels of protection. These tariffs were to then be reduced by an average of 36 percent for developed countries and 24 percent for developing countries. In addition, a minimum-access tariff quota of 3 percent was established, to be increased to 5 percent by the end of the implementation period.

Two conditions were added. The "special safeguard" provision for products subject to tariffs allowed "additional duties to be applied in case shipments at prices denominated in domestic currencies [would] fall below a certain reference level or in case of a surge of imports" (GATT 1994a, 46). The second proviso, the "special treatment" clause, allowed a country to maintain import restrictions to the end of the implementation period but under strictly defined conditions.

Agreement on Domestic Support and Export Subsidies

In this agreement, developed countries committed to decrease domestic agricultural support by reducing the total aggregate measurement of support (AMS) by 20 percent from the base period of 1986–88. Developing countries, however, only had to commit to 13.3 percent reductions and least-developed countries were exempt.

Reductions apply to all support provided on a product-specific basis and to other forms of support that are not specifically exempted. Policies that qualified for exemption from total AMS reduction commitments included "green box" policies, general government services (i.e., research, training, and infrastructure), and direct payments to producers (i.e., decoupled income support, structural adjustment assistance, environmental programs, and regional assistance); direct payments under production-limiting programs; certain government assistance measures encouraging agricultural and rural development in developing countries; and other support making up a small proportion of the production value of individual products or the total agricultural production value (in the case of non–product specific support). In the last proviso, the de minimis provision was 5 percent in the case of developed countries and 10 percent for developing countries.

Export Subsidies

Developed countries committed to reducing the value of direct export subsidies over six years by 36 percent below the 1986–90 base period and also to reducing the volume of subsidized exports by 21 percent. Developing countries made a similar commitment but only to reductions of two-thirds those of developed countries over 10 years. Developing countries are exempt from commitments to reduce the costs of marketing exports of agricultural products or internal transport subsidies. Least-developed countries are again exempt.

"Peace" provisions, applicable for nine years, are also included in the agreement. Member states agreed to exercise due restraint in applying countervailing duties against products included in the reform process.

Agreement on Sanitary and Phytosanitary Measures

This agreement covered food safety as well as animal and plant health regulations. It also recognized that individual governments had the right to use sanitary and phytosanitary measures, though only to the extent necessary, to protect human, animal, or plant life or health. Countries were encouraged to base these measures on international standards, guidelines, and recommendations with the understanding that higher standards could be imposed if there was sufficient scientific justification. Additionally, the agreement contained provisions on control, inspection, and approval procedures as well as transparency requirements. A Committee on Sanitary and Phytosanitary Measures was established to enforce these measures.

Possible Negative Effects of the Reform Program on Least-Developed and Net Food-Importing Developing Countries

This agreement recognized that because of the reforms, least-developed and net food-importing developing countries could face higher prices for food imports. It subsequently set out the objectives for providing food aid and for ensuring that increasing proportions of basic foodstuffs would be provided in full grant form.

Textiles and Apparel

The objective of the textiles and apparel agreement was to integrate textile and clothing sectors into the GATT by phasing out the Multi-Fiber Arrangement (MFA). Ultimately, all non-MFA restrictions not justified under a GATT provision would be phased out or brought into conformity with the GATT.

Integration was to take place in four stages over 10 years beginning 1 January 1995. Stage one (1 January 1995–31 December 1997) requires each country to integrate products from a list representing 16 percent of the total volume of 1990 imports.[1] In addition, annual quota growth rates must be at least 16 percent higher than those allowed under the MFA. In

---

1. For each of the first three stages, products must be integrated from tops and yarns, fabrics, made-up textile products, or clothing categories.

stage two (1 January 1998–31 December 2001), products that accounted for at least 17 percent of 1990 imports will be integrated and annual growth rates increased by 25 percent. In stage three (1 January 2002–31 December 2004), products that accounted for at least 18 percent of 1990 imports will be integrated and annual growth rates increased by 27 percent. In the final stage (1 January 2005), all the remaining products would be fully integrated.

Transitional Safeguard Mechanism

The safeguard mechanism will be applied to products not yet integrated into the GATT at any stage. This condition allows for safeguard action against an individual exporting country as long as the importing country demonstrates that overall imports in such increased quantities would cause (or threaten to cause) serious damage to the domestic industry. Members must also show sharp and substantial increases in imports. These safeguard restraints could remain in place for up to three years without extension or until the product was integrated into GATT. Special treatment is given to countries that have not been MFA members since 1986, new entrants, small suppliers, and least-developed countries.

A textiles monitoring body was established to enforce provisions on transshipment, rerouting, false declaration of country or place of origin, and falsification of official documents.

Antidumping

The Agreement on Implementation of Article VI revised the Tokyo Round Antidumping Agreement and specified methodology for determining dumping, including criteria for allocating an exporter's costs of production when exported prices must be compared with "constructed" values because there are no significant home-country sales of the product in question.

The agreement also strengthens the requirement that the importing country establish a causal relationship between the dumped imports and the subsequent injury to its domestic industry. In such cases, the agreement set up clear procedures on initiating antidumping cases and conducting investigations. These new guidelines allowed all interested parties the chance to present evidence.

Under this new provision, antidumping measures expired after five years unless it was determined that dumping and injury would likely recur. The de minimis provision required that the investigation of antidumping cases could be terminated if it was determined that the margin of dumping was less than 2 percent (expressed as a percentage of export price of the product) or if the volume of the dumped exports was negligible.

Agreement on Subsidies and Countervailing Measures

Subsidies

This agreement established the three categories of subsidies as prohibited, actionable, and nonactionable. Prohibited subsidies are those contingent on export performance or on use of domestic over imported goods. Actionable subsidies cause adverse effects on other member countries, including serious prejudice to the interests of another member. Serious prejudice is presumed to exist if the total ad valorem subsidy of a product exceeds 5 percent. Subsidizing members must prove that the subsidies in question did not cause serious prejudice to an affected member. The last category, nonactionable subsidies, includes nonspecific subsidies, specific subsidies for individual research, and precompetitive development, assistance to disadvantaged regions or assistance for adapting existing facilities to meet new environmental laws or regulations.

Countervailing Measures

This agreement set out disciplines for initiation of countervailing cases, for the investigations by domestic authorities, and on the rules of evidence. The measures also outlined the disciplines on the calculation of the amount of a subsidy and the basis for determination of injury to domestic industry. Under the de minimis provision, countervailing cases must be terminated if a subsidy is less than 1 percent ad valorem or if the volume of subsidized imports is negligible. A timetable for investigations and the duration of duties was established.

Countervailing measures provided for least-developed and developing countries with GNPs per capita incomes of less than $1,000, exempting them from disciplines on prohibited export subsidies and allowing them to have time-bound exemptions on other prohibited subsidies. Other allowances on export subsidies were made for developing countries and economies in transition.

Safeguards

The Uruguay Round agreement prohibited gray-area measures used to shelter domestic industries from imports. Members could not seek, take, or maintain any voluntary export restraints, orderly marketing arrangements, or other similar measures on either imports or exports. All such measures are to be eliminated or phased out within four years after entry into force of the World Trade Organization (WTO). Each importing member is allowed, for a limited time, an exception for one specific measure, subject to the mutual agreement of the affected exporter. The phase-out date for that measure is 31 December 1999. All existing safeguard measures under Article XIX of GATT 1947 must be terminated eight years after the date the measure is first applied or five years after entry into force of WTO, whichever date is later.

Safeguard actions will be applied, in principle, on the basis of nondiscrimination. However, provisions allow for departures from such an approach after consultations with the recently established Safeguards Committee. Criteria were also set for establishing "serious injury" and determining the impact of imports.

These safeguard measures cannot be applied to a product from a developing country if the developing country's share of imports of the product is less than 3 percent and if developing-country members with less than 3 percent of the import share can collectively account for less than 9 percent of the total imports of the product.

The agreement set time limits for safeguard measures. Four years is the maximum, but eight years is possible if authorities prove the necessity of an extension.

The agreement set out the requirements for the investigation of safeguard actions. Consultation and compensation provisions were also included. Conditions included allowing for zero compensation in the first three years of safeguard action.

TRIPs and TRIMs

Agreement on Trade-Related Aspects of Intellectual Property Rights (TRIPs)

Part one of the trade-related aspects of intellectual property rights (TRIPs) set out general provisions and basic principles, including national treatment for intellectual property and MFN.

Part two of the TRIPs agreement addressed copyrights, computer programs, trademarks and service marks, geographical indications, patents, integrated circuits, and antidumping practice in contractual licenses. Members were required to adhere to substantive provisions of the Berne Convention (Paris, 1971) on copyrights. As under the convention, computer programs are protected as literary works. The agreement defined types of trademarks and service marks eligible for protection and the minimum rights to be accorded to them. Protection guidelines were set for geographical indicators. Members must adhere to substantive provisions of the Paris Convention (1967) on patents and, furthermore, must grant product and process inventions 20 years of protection. Members agreed to protect integrated circuit designs for 10 years, and based provisions on the Washington Treaty on Intellectual Property in Respect of Integrated Circuits. Where anticompetitive practices in licensing arrangements have an adverse impact on competition, countries have the right to seek consultations to ensure compliance with national regulations.

Part three of the agreement obliged members to ensure domestic enforcement of intellectual property rights. It established a Council for Trade-Related Aspects of Intellectual Property Rights. Disputes arising from the agreement will be settled under integrated WTO procedures, which allows for retaliation in the goods sectors.

Developed countries were given a year to conform to the agreement, developing countries were allowed five years, and least-developed countries ten years. Developing countries with no current system for protecting product patents in the area of technology have ten years to introduce protection but must accept filing of patent applications in areas of pharmaceutical and agricultural chemicals.

Agreement on Trade-Related Investment Measures (TRIMs)

Under these conditions, members agreed not to apply any TRIM inconsistent with GATT Article III (national treatment) and Article XI (quantitative restrictions). A list of such TRIMs were agreed upon and included local-content requirements and trade-balancing requirements.

The agreement required notification of these TRIMs and their elimination within two years for developed countries and within five years for developing countries; least-developed countries had seven years. The agreement also established a Committee on TRIMs.

General Agreement on Trade and Services (GATS)

The services agreement consisted of three parts. The Framework Agreement contained the basic obligations applying to all members while the National Schedules of Commitment contained specific national commitments to be the subject of future negotiations. The last part included a number of annexes that addressed individual service sectors. Negotiations on telecommunications, audiovisual, and maritime services were to resume after the ministerial signing in Marrakesh on 15 April 1994.

The Framework Agreement consisted of six parts. Part one (scope and definition) specified services to which the agreement applied. Part two (general obligations and disciplines) set out the MFN obligation.[2] Other obligations and disciplines included transparency, provisions to increase participation of developing countries, treatment of services in economic integration (i.e., such as free trade areas), and the role of business practices and emerging safeguard measures, including provisions for security exceptions. Negotiations on trade-distorting subsidies in services were deferred.

Part three (specific commitments) contained provisions on market access and national treatment, which were not incorporated as general obligations. These commitments were made in national schedules. Part four (progressive liberalization) established the basis for further liberalization. The withdrawal or modification of commitments in schedules could take place after three years, but any action had to be negotiated with affected parties to agree on compensation.

Part five (institutional provision) dealt with institutional issues, including consultation and dispute settlement. A Council on Services was established. Part six (final provisions) covered circumstances in which benefits of the agreement could be denied. This section also included definitions of terms used throughout the agreement and stated that the annexes were to be considered an integral part of the agreement.

The annexes consisted of six parts. The Annex on Article II Exemptions dealt with exemptions from MFN treatment. The Annex on Movement of Natural Persons Supplying Services under the Agreement allowed for free movement of service providers under specific commitments. However, the agreement did not apply to measures affecting employment, citizenship, residence, or permanent employment.

The Annex on Financial Services described the rights of parties to protect investors and deposit holders and to ensure the stability and integrity of the financial system. The Annex on Telecommunications dealt with access to and use of public telecommunications and services. Parties were required to offer access to reasonable and nondiscriminatory terms for services. Technical cooperation for developed countries was also encouraged.

The Annex on Air Transportation excluded traffic rights and directly related activities. Agreements could only apply to aircraft repair and maintenance services, marketing of air transport services, and computer reservation services. The annex would be reviewed after four years. The Annex on Negotiation of Basic Telecommunications included exemptions from MFN obligations regarding basic telecommunications.

---

2. It was recognized that MFN treatment may not be possible in every sector. Exemptions were to be specified in an annex and reviewed after five years; they are to last no longer than ten years.

The World Trade Organization and Dispute Settlement

The World Trade Organization (WTO) encompassed all agreements and arrangements concluded under GATT auspices and other agreements and ministerial decisions resulting from the Uruguay Round. These would be binding on all WTO members. GATT 1947 was considered as legally distinct from GATT 1994.

Plurilateral trade agreements included agreements on trade in civil aircraft, government procurement, dairy, and bovine meat. These were only binding on their signatories.

The WTO has numerous functions. It facilitates the implementation, administration, and operation and furthers the objectives of the agreement establishing the WTO and the plurilateral agreements. The WTO is the forum for further multilateral trade negotiations and administers both the Understanding on Rules and Procedures Governing the Settlement of Disputes and the trade policy review mechanism (TPRM).

The WTO is to cooperate with the International Monetary Fund (IMF) and the World Bank and its affiliated agencies. The organization is headed by biennial ministerial conferences with the first to be held in Singapore in 1996.

A General Council was established to oversee the operation of the WTO and to act as a Dispute Settlement Body (DSB) and a Trade Policy Review Body. A Goods Council, a Services Council, and a TRIPs Council were established.

The WTO is open for original membership for two years after the 1 January 1995 entry into force. The organization requires original members to have schedules of market-access concessions and specific services commitments; least-developed countries have an additional year to submit their schedules.

Dispute Settlement

Dispute settlement procedures were revised in a number of ways. A Dispute Settlement Body was formed and exercises the authority of the General Council, the Subsidiary Councils, and the Committees of the Agreements.

Members must enter into consultations within 30 days of another member's request for them. If a dispute is not resolved after 60 days of the request for consultation, the complaining party can request a panel. But if the request for a consultation is turned down, the complaining party immediately requests a panel. Panel reports are adopted unless the DSB rejects it by consensus.

To expedite dispute settlements, specific timetables and procedures were set out for panels. Timetables for adoption and implementation of a panel report were also detailed.

An Appellate Body was established, with appeals limited to issues of law covered in the panel, and timetables for the appeal were also set out.

Under certain circumstances, concessions could be suspended under another agreement but not in the same sector as the dispute. Several provisions cover considerations to be given to the specific interests and particular problems of developing and least-developed countries in the event one is a party to a dispute. New rules and procedures would be reviewed within 4 years after the WTO entered into force.

Other Uruguay Round Results

Under the Tariff Reductions on Industrial Products provision, members agreed to arrange reductions of at least one-third, and tariffs are to be eliminated in some sectors in developed countries (including steel, wood and wood products, and pharmaceutical). Reductions are to be implemented in five equal increments, except as otherwise noted. These reductions will be recorded in national schedules of concessions annexed to the Uruguay Round protocol. Developing countries bound a significant number of tariffs and lowered many as well. Another important result was the General Agreement on Tariffs and Trade 1994.

Texts on interpretation of the following GATT articles included:

- Understanding on the Interpretation of Article II.1(b)

- Understanding on the Interpretation of Article XVII

- Understanding on the Interpretation of Balance of Payments Provisions

- Understanding on the Interpretation of Article XXIV

- Understanding on the Interpretation of Article XXV

- Understanding on the Interpretation of Article XXVIII

- Understanding on the Interpretation of Article XXXV

In addition, negotiations resulted in agreements on technical barriers to trade, implementation of Article VII (customs valuations), preshipment inspection, rules of origin, and import licensing procedures.

The Agreement on Technical Barriers to Trade sought to ensure that technical standards, testing procedures, and certification procedure did not create unnecessary barriers to trade. This provision also recognized countries' rights to protect such things as human, animal, and plant life or health and to protect the environment. It further encouraged countries to use international standards where appropriate. A Code of Good Practice for the Preparation, Adoption, and Application of Standards was also open to acceptance by private- and public-sector bodies and was included in the annex.

B

Chronology of the Uruguay Round

July 1985

After a lengthy and bitter session of the GATT Council, the United States calls for a vote on a proposal to convene a special session of the Contracting Parties to consider launching a new round of trade negotiations.

September 1985

A special session is convened, at which it is agreed that a group of senior officials should be established to report to the November 1985 session of Contracting Parties on proposed negotiations.

November 1985

The Contracting Parties agree to establish a preparatory committee with a mandate "to determine the objectives, subject matter, modalities for and participation in the multilateral trade negotiations" (GATT *Basic Instruments and Selected Documents*, 32nd supp., 1986, 10). It was also agreed that a ministerial meeting would be held in September 1986 to adopt a program for negotiations.

15–20 September 1986

A special session of the Contracting Parties is convened in Punta del Este, Uruguay. The ministers adopt a Ministerial Declaration to launch the Uruguay Round, the eighth round of GATT multilateral trade negotiations. The declaration includes a standstill and rollback provision to prevent GATT-inconsistent, trade-restrictive measures from being introduced during the round. The negotiations are considered the most ambitious ever, consisting of 15 negotiating groups.[1] The deadline for the conclusion of the Uruguay Round is set for December 1990.

5–8 December 1988   A midterm review is held in Montreal. Heading into the final days of the meetings, agreements are reached in all groups except agriculture, trade-related intellectual property (TRIPs), textiles and clothing, and safeguards. Although the ministers were expected to agree to disagree in agriculture and TRIPs and accept agreements in other areas, a number of developing countries refuse this outcome on the grounds that agriculture could be resolved if the United States and the European Community could muster the political will. All agreements are held over until April 1989 pending further consultations. However, improvements in the dispute settlement mechanism and a trade policy review mechanism are implemented immediately.

5–8 April 1989   Meetings are held in Geneva to complete the midterm review. Decisions are reached in agriculture, TRIPs, textiles and clothing, and safeguards and are released along with decisions in other areas "on hold" from the Montreal meeting in December. Progress in agriculture is achieved when agreement is reached on some elements of long-term reform as well. Similarly, progress occurs with the short-term freeze of support levels and on a work program for issues relating to sanitary and phytosanitary regulations.

3–7 December 1990   A ministerial meeting is held in Brussels. Negotiators are unable to agree on a final package to complete the Uruguay Round, largely due to an

1. The 15 negotiating groups are tariffs, nontariff measures, natural resource–based products, textiles and clothing, agriculture, tropical products, GATT articles, MFN agreements and arrangements, safeguards, subsidies and countervailing measures, trade-related intellectual property (TRIPs), trade-related investment measures (TRIMs), dispute settlement, functioning of the GATT system, and services.

impasse in agriculture between the United States and the European Community. The United States and the Cairns Group of agricultural exporting countries stick to proposals of a 90 percent reduction in export subsidies and a 75 percent reduction in domestic supports over a 10-year period beginning in 1991 with a 1990 base year. The European Community sticks to a proposed 30 percent reduction in overall support over five years beginning in 1991 from a 1986 base with limited commitments on export subsidies and increased imports, as well as a "rebalancing proposal" to allow increased border protection for certain cereal feed substitutes. It is agreed to continue negotiations in Geneva.

26 February 1991   Arthur Dunkel, chairman of the Trade Negotiations Committee (TNC) and GATT director general, announces that the Uruguay Round negotiations are back on track. However, agriculture is again the stumbling block to restarting negotiations. The deadlock is overcome when members agreed to negotiate domestic support, market access, export competition, and sanitary and phytosanitary measures. Negotiations are to proceed according to the work program.

25 April 1991   Dunkel announces a restructuring of the negotiating groups from 15 to 7 in order to encourage substantive negotiations.[2] The negotiations continue to proceed, though largely at a technical level.

24 May 1991   The US Congress votes to extend fast-track negotiating authority for another two years, thus providing the Uruguay Round negotiations with a possible two-year extension.

20 December 1991   Dunkel proposes a draft Final Act. In the case of agriculture, antidumping, and subsidies, compromise positions are constructed by the GATT Secretariat. The draft Final Act is not embraced by the Uruguay Round participants and negotia-

2. The groups were restructured as market access, textiles and clothing, agriculture, rule making, TRIPs, institutions, and services.

tions again grind to a halt. Dunkel also announces that he will step down once his term ends 31 December 1992.

13 January 1992	The TNC meets to confirm their support for continued negotiations—using the draft Final Act as a basis—to conclude the Uruguay Round. A four-track negotiating approach is adopted that requires market-access concessions in track one, services commitments in track two, legal drafting in track three, and, as a safeguard, work at the TNC level in case the draft Final Act needs to be changed in track four.
20 November 1992	The United States and the European Community finally reach an agreement on agriculture. Among the compromises reached in the Blair House Accord is the European Community's agreement to cut subsidized agricultural exports by 21 percent in volume over six years, value by 36 percent, and internal supports by 20 percent. The agreement averts a trade war between the United States and the European Community.
26 November 1992	The TNC reactivates the Uruguay Round negotiations after the US-EC agricultural agreement. The four-track approach initiated in January is retained and negotiators hope to conclude negotiations by the end of 1992.
28 February 1993	The US fast-track negotiating authority expires.
June 1993	The US fast-track negotiating authority is renewed in order to complete the Uruguay Round. The new deadline is 15 December 1993.
1 July 1993	Former EC Competition Policy Director Peter Sutherland of Ireland takes over as new GATT director general and chairman of the TNC.
7 July 1993	The Group of Seven (G-7) meeting is held in Tokyo. Just prior to the summit, Quad members—the United States, the European Community, Japan, and Canada—announce a draft market-access agreement that includes substantial tariff and nontariff reductions.
31 August 1993	Sutherland relaunches round negotiations because much work remains to be done in market

access and to a greater degree in agriculture, textiles and clothing, and services.

19 November 1993	Sutherland calls in the United States and the European Union to bring to the table a "decisive contribution" in order to conclude the Uruguay Round.
10–13 December 1993	An around-the-clock meeting is held between the heads of delegations in an effort to conclude the round.
15 December 1993	The Uruguay Round concludes after the United States and the European Union come to last-minute agreements. Conditions include tariffication of nontariff barriers, a phase-out of the Multi-Fiber Arrangement (MFA), establishment of a General Agreement on Trade in Services (GATS), and the establishment of the World Trade Organization (WTO) to supersede the GATT. A ministerial meeting is set for Marrakesh, 12–15 April 1994, in order to sign the final agreements and determine the work program. US negotiating authority expires.
12–15 April 1994	The ministerial meeting is held in Marrakesh. The final document totals more than 26,000 pages including text, concessions, and schedules. Two committees are formed: one to manage the transition and subsequent implementation of the WTO and another to examine the links between trade and the environment.
7 October 1994	The US congressional vote to ratify the Uruguay Round agreements is delayed until after the 8 November midterm elections. In the United States, opposition to the GATT deal mounts over sovereignty concerns and budget issues. Meanwhile, other major countries await US ratification before proceeding with their own.
29 November 1994	The US House of Representatives passes the Uruguay Round agreements, 288 to 146.
1 December 1994	The US Senate votes 76 to 24 in favor of the Uruguay Round. Successful ratification clears the way for other countries to ratify the agreements.
1 January 1995	The WTO goes into effect.

C

Regionalism in the Postwar Trading System

1947   Article XXIV, which allows formation of customs unions and free trade areas under certain conditions, is included in the General Agreement on Tariffs and Trade (GATT).

1957   The Treaty of Rome, effective 1 January 1958, establishes the European Economic Community (EEC). The treaty is a customs union between Belgium, Luxembourg, France, the Netherlands, Germany, and Italy.

1959   The Stockholm Convention establishes the European Free Trade Association (EFTA) to go into effect 1 July 1960. Members include Austria, Denmark, Norway, Portugal, Sweden, Switzerland, and the United Kingdom.

1960   The Montevideo Treaty establishes the Latin American Free Trade Association (LAFTA), comprising Brazil, Chile, Peru, Uruguay, and Argentina.

The Central American Common Market (CACM) is formed. Members include Costa Rica, El Salvador, Guatemala, Honduras, and Nicaragua.

1962   The African Common Market establishes a customs union between Algeria, the United Arab Republic, Ghana, Guinea, Mali, and Morocco.

1963   The Yaoundé Convention, a meeting between the EEC and former French, Belgian, and Italian colonies in Africa, is convened. The convention gives these countries preferential access to the European Community and sets up the European Development Fund.

1964   The Central African Customs and Economic Union (UDEAC) is formed. Members include Cameroon, the Central African Republic, Congo, Gabon, Chad, and Equatorial Guinea.

1965   Canada and the United States sign the Automobile Products Trade Agreement (Auto Pact).

1967   The East African Economic Community (EAEC) is formed between Tanzania, Kenya, and Uganda.

The Association of Southeast Asian Nations (ASEAN) is formed. Members include Indonesia, Malaysia, the Philippines, Singapore, and Thailand (Brunei joins in 1988).

1969   The Yaoundé Convention is extended.

1973   The European Community is enlarged to include the United Kingdom, Ireland, and Denmark.

The Caribbean Community (Caricom) is formed among Antigua and Barbuda, Guyana, Jamaica, St. Kitts and Nevis, and Trinidad and Tobago. Subsequently, Belize, Dominica, Grenada, Montserrat, St. Lucia and St. Vincent, and the Grenadines join in 1974 and Bahamas in 1983.

1975   The Yaoundé Convention is superseded by the Lomé Convention, which extends preferential arrangements to include former colonies of Britain as well as countries in the Caribbean and Pacific.

The Economic Community of West African States (ECOWAS) is formed. Members include Benin, Burkina Faso, Cape Verde, Côte d'Ivoire, Gambia, Ghana, Guinea, Guinea-Bissau, Liberia, Mali, Mauritania, Niger, Nigeria, Senegal, Sierra Leone, and Togo.

The Bangkok Agreement is signed between Bangladesh, India, Lao People's Democratic Republic, the Philippines, South Korea, Sri Lanka, and Thailand. The agreement established a preferential trade arrangement between member states.

1977   ASEAN becomes a preferential trade arrangement between Indonesia, Malaysia, the Philippines, Singapore, and Thailand. Brunei subsequently joins in 1984.

1979   The second Lomé Convention is agreed between the EEC and members of the African-Caribbean-Pacific (ACP).

1980   The Latin American Integration Association (LAIA) is established. Members include Argentina, Bolivia, Brazil, Chile, Colombia, Ecuador, Mexico, Paraguay, Peru, Uruguay, and Venezuela.

The South Pacific Regional Trade and Economic Agreement (SPARTECA) is formed. Australia and New Zealand are granted preferential, nonreciprocal access to the markets in the Cook Islands, Fiji, Kiribati, Niue, Papua New Guinea, Solomon Islands, Tonga, Tuvalu, and Western Samoa.

1981   Greece joins the European Community.

The Preferential Trade Area for Eastern and Southern Africa is formed. Members include Angola, Burundi, Comoros, Djibouti, Ethiopia, Kenya, Lesotho, Malawi, Mauritius, Mozambique, Rwanda, Somalia, Sudan, Swaziland, Tanzania, Uganda, Zambia, and Zimbabwe. Namibia joins in 1993.

1983   Australia and New Zealand form the Closer Economic Relationship (CER) to provide for a free trade agreement.

1984   The United States implements the Caribbean Basin Economic Recovery Act to extend duty-free treatment to 21 beneficiary countries in the region for 12 years.

The Third Lomé Convention is agreed upon between the EEC, members of the ACP, and Mozambique.

1985   The US-Israel Free Trade Area Agreement enters into force. The agreement states that all tariffs between the two countries will be eliminated over 10 years.

1986   Portugal and Spain join the European Community. The Single European Act is signed to provide for full European integration in 1992.

1989   The Canada-US Free Trade Agreement enters into force. Under terms of the agreement, all items between the two countries would be traded duty-free by 1998.

The Fourth Lomé Convention is agreed upon between members of the European Community, the ACP countries, and newcomers Dominican Republic, Haiti, and St. Kitts and Nevis.

1990   The European Community and EFTA undertake discussions on a European Economic Area (EEA), which would provide for freer movement of goods, services, capital, and people between the two associations.

The United States announces the Enterprise for the Americas initiative to explore a hemisphere-wide free trade zone between countries of North, Central, and South America.

1991   The United States, Mexico, and Canada enter discussions on a North American free trade area, leading eventually to the signing of NAFTA.

Andean Pact members Bolivia, Colombia, Ecuador, Peru, and Venezuela sign an accord to implement a free trade zone by the end of 1995.

The Treaty of Asuncion is signed between Brazil, Argentina, Uruguay, and Paraguay to form Mercosur, the South American Common Market. Their aim is to create a duty-free common market by the end of 1994.

Chile and Mexico sign a Free Trade Accord, which is to eliminate all nontariff barriers. Other conditions included a common tariff of 10 percent to apply to 95 percent of trade, effective January 1992, and a tariff reduction to zero over a four-year period.

Turkey and EFTA sign a free trade agreement to go into force January 1992. Under terms of the agreement, the EFTA is to eliminate duties on imports of industrial goods (excluding textiles) and processed farm products.

The European Community and EFTA finalize EEA to go into effect 1 January 1993.

The ASEAN Free Trade Agreement (AFTA) is formed. The group agrees to a 15-year period in which to create a single ASEAN market.

The EFTA signs trade cooperation accords with Bulgaria, Romania, and three Baltic states.

The European Community signs association accords with Poland, Hungary, and the Czech and Slovak Republics. The countries agree to work toward free trade within 10 years.

1992   El Salvador, Guatemala, and Honduras agree to form a free trade zone. Working toward establishing uniform tariffs on imports, the countries agree to allow unrestricted movement of most goods, capital, and labor.

The NAFTA negotiations conclude. The agreement, effective 1 January 1994, provides for the elimination of tariffs in stages over a period of no more than 10 or 15 years, including a phase-out of tariffs on textiles and apparels. Side agreements are subsequently negotiated on labor and environment.

Implementation of EEA, due to go into effect 1 January 1993, is delayed when Switzerland votes against joining.

Poland, Hungary, Slovakia, and the Czech Republic establish a regional trade zone under the Central European Free Trade Agreement (CEFTA). Their aim is to gradually eliminate tariffs over the next 17 years and become more compatible with the European Community and EFTA.

EFTA concludes free trade agreements with Romania and Poland.

Switzerland, Sweden, Norway, and Finland each conclude free trade agreements with Estonia, Latvia, and Lithuania.

The Czech and Slovak Federal Republics and the EFTA conclude a free trade agreement.

1993   Hungary and the EFTA conclude a free trade agreement that extends free trade in a range of goods, including processed agricultural goods, industrial goods, and fish.

Bulgaria and the EFTA conclude a free trade agreement that extends free trade in processed farm goods, industrial goods, and fish products.

Chile and Venezuela sign a free trade agreement. Under terms of the agreement, import tariffs are expected to be eliminated on 90 percent of products by 1997.

Chile and Bolivia sign a bilateral agreement to reduce tariffs.

The South Asian Preferential Trading Agreement is established with the aim of forming a common market between Bangladesh, Bhutan, India, Maldives, Nepal, Pakistan, and Sri Lanka.

Nicaragua, Honduras, El Salvador, and Guatemala reach an agreement to liberalize trade. As a result, barriers to trade in textiles, shoes, and leather goods are to be reduced.

The Group of Three (Mexico, Venezuela, and Colombia) sign a free trade agreement to go into effect in June 1994. The agreement covers market access, rules of origin, investment, government procurement, and intellectual property.

Chile and Colombia sign a free trade agreement that eliminates most nontariff barriers and reduced tariffs.

Guatemala, Honduras, El Salvador, Nicaragua, Costa Rica, and Panama sign an agreement toward freer trade and increased integration.

Turkey and the European Community negotiate a timetable leading to a customs union between the two countries by 1995.

Slovenia negotiates free trade agreements with both the Czech Republic and the Slovak Republic.

1994   The EEA comes into effect, creating a free trade area between the European Union and the EFTA countries of Austria, Finland, Norway, Sweden, and Iceland.

Sweden, Finland, Austria, and Norway negotiate full membership into the European Union. Referendums in Sweden, Finland, and Austria confirm membership in the European Union to go into effect 1 January 1995. Norway rejects membership in the European Union but expects to remain in the EEA.

Mexico and Costa Rica conclude a free trade agreement to go into effect January 1995. The agreement eliminates tariffs and most nontariff barriers and includes provisions for intellectual property rights, labor mobility, dispute settlement, and national treatment for investment.

Andean Pact members agree to a common external tariff. The four-tier tariff would go into effect January 1995.

Colombia and Caricom conclude a free trade agreement to go into effect January 1995. As a result, Colombia would gradually reduce tariffs on Caricom products over a 3-year period while Caricom would gradually reduce tariffs on Colombian products over a 5-year period.

Mercosur members reach a compromise agreement on a common tariff structure allowing a customs union to go into effect January 1995.

Asia Pacific Economic Cooperation (APEC) members agree to accelerate the liberalization of trade and investment measures within the group. Members would begin liberalizing tariff and other barriers in the year 2000 while developed-country members would achieve an open market by 2010. The developing countries would have until 2020 to complete their liberalization. APEC members includes Australia, Brunei, Canada, Chile, Hong Kong, Indonesia, Japan, Malaysia, Mexico, New Zealand, Papua New Guinea, People's Republic of China, the Philippines, Singapore, South Korea, Taiwan, Thailand, and the United States.

Chile is formally invited to begin negotiations to join NAFTA.

At the Summit of the Americas held in Miami (9–11 December 1994), 34 countries in North, Central, and South America and the Caribbean jointly agree to negotiate a Free Trade Area of the Americas by 2005.

1995   The European Union and Turkey agree on a customs union accord effective 1 January 1996. Under its terms, tariffs are to be eliminated and a common tariff established on products from outside the customs union. In addition, some EU agricultural restrictions would still apply to Turkish exports.

Chile begins negotiating its accession to NAFTA. Negotiations are expected to be completed by the end of 1995.

Estonia, Lithuania, and Latvia sign association agreements with the European Union. The agreements provide trade and cooperation deals and possible future EU membership.

Vietnam joins ASEAN and is given a longer implementation period to fulfill ASEAN liberalization timetables.

The International Trade Organization (ITO) of the 1940s

Drafting of the Charter

In December 1945, the United States presented its proposals for the expansion of world trade and employment to the United Nations' Economic and Social Council (ECOSOC) as the basis for discussion of an international organization to govern world trade.[1] The ECOSOC, in turn, appointed a preparatory committee with members from 17 countries (including six underdeveloped ones) to prepare a draft agreement for an international organization. Over the next two years, the committee met three times to redraft and revise the document. On 21 November 1947, representatives of over 50 countries (including 32 underdeveloped ones) met in Havana for the International Conference on Trade and Employment to discuss and negotiate a further 800 amendments. On 24 March 1948, the conference concluded, and the Charter of the International Trade Organization was signed by 53 countries.

ITO Charter Contents

In addition to those articles that made up Parts I–III of the General Agreement on Tariffs and Trade (GATT), which were taken from the ITO chap-

---

1. The US State Department under Cordell Hull was responsible for the drafting of an institution to govern world trade under the Bretton Woods system. The drafting of the World Bank and the International Monetary Fund was initiated much earlier under Secretary Henry Morgenthau Jr. and Harry Dexter White of the Treasury Department (Gardner 1956; Brown 1950; Diebold 1952; Wilcox 1949; Dam 1970; Jackson 1969).

ter on commercial policy, the ITO included chapters on Employment and Economic Activity, Economic Development and Reconstruction, Restrictive Business Practices, and Intergovernmental Commodity Agreements. There were also institutional provisions covering membership, structure and administration, amendment or withdrawal, and a review of the charter (see Brown 1950 and Wilcox 1949 for detailed analysis).

A Chapter-by-Chapter Review

Chapter 2: Employment and Economic Activity

This chapter recognized the international implications of domestic measures taken to avoid unemployment or underemployment. Through this chapter each member pledged to take action to achieve and maintain full employment and increase demand. Members also agreed to avoid measures that would result in balance of payments problems for other countries. In the event of persistent balance of payments difficulties, the members agreed to exchange information and engage in consultations that would lead to the affected countries taking measures to correct the situation.

This chapter also recognized that "all countries have a common interest in the achievement and maintenance of fair labor standards related to productivity and, thus, in the improvement of wages and working conditions as productivity may permit" (Wilcox 1949, 233–34). Accordingly, each member was to take the necessary steps to eliminate unfair labor conditions.

Chapter 3: Economic Development and Reconstruction

Under this chapter, each member agreed to develop its own resources, to increase productivity, and to cooperate with other states through international agencies in promoting general economic development. Members were not to impose restrictions on exports necessary for development, nor were members to impose restrictions on those imports. According to the provisions of this chapter, each developing country was to decide which industries to promote. Subsidies to new industries were permitted. Developing countries were also permitted to impose new tariffs or raise existing ones on commodities not already covered by a trade agreement. Members were required to obtain prior approval before using a new form of protection it had previously agreed not to use. According to Wilcox (1949), the charter established "a new principle in international affairs: that such restrictive measures as import quotas and mixing regulations [were] not to be employed, without international sanction, for the development of infant industries" (Wilcox 1949, 60).

Chapter 5: Restrictive Business Practices

Members agreed to take all necessary measures, by legislation if need be, to ensure within its jurisdiction that companies and enterprises, both public and private, did not engage in practices that would inhibit competition, restrict access to markets, or promote monopolistic control in international trade. This applied whenever such practices interfered with the expansion of production or trade, or the achievement of any objective of the charter. In the event of a member's complaint, the ITO would investigate, hold hearings, and, if the complaint was found to be valid, would request concerned members to take remedial action. The ITO would also be able to recommend remedial actions.

Chapter 6: Intergovernmental Commodity Agreements

Through the provisions in this chapter, members agreed that intergovernmental commodity agreements would be confined to primary commodities. The agreements were to be open to participation on an equal basis by any member of the ITO and the terms of the agreement made public at all stages.

Agreements that regulated production, exports, imports, or prices would be confined to commodities produced under strictly specified conditions and to periods of unmanageable surplus and widespread distress. The agreements were to be limited in duration and subject to review and also were to assure adequate supply. Consuming and producing countries were to have an equal voice. Each participating country in the agreement was to adopt an economic adjustment program designed to make a continuation of the agreement unnecessary.

Chapter 7: Structure of the ITO

The ITO was to consist of three branches:

- a conference of all member states, each casting a single vote;

- an executive board, which would conduct ongoing administration and consist of 18 members, 8 of whom would always represent the countries of chief economic importance, including the United States;

- and a director general, who would carry out the detailed operations, along with a staff and a small number of specialized commissions of technical experts.

The ITO was to be considered a UN organization and thereby funded according to UN principles.

Dispute Settlement

Disputes arising among members of the ITO were to be settled by direct consultation, by arbitration, or by the decision of the executive board. Members could appeal the rulings of the board to the conference and, on legal questions, the organization or any of its members could request an advisory opinion from the International Court of Justice (ICJ). The organization would be bound by the Court's opinions.

If, after the complaints procedure, it was determined that a member had not lived up to its obligations, the complaining member or members would not be bound to their corresponding obligations and would be able to take measures to restore the balance of interest between the parties to the dispute. The ITO would retain the power to place limits on retaliation to avoid disputes escalating into trade wars.

Why the ITO Was Not Ratified

The charter for the ITO was submitted to the US Congress in mid-1948 after the Havana Conference. In December 1950, however, it was announced that the charter would not be resubmitted to the US Congress for ratification. Thus, even though Congress did not formally reject the ITO, any hope for the establishment of an ITO was eliminated. US failure to garner support for the ITO was significant because it had been the driving force behind the Bretton Woods institutions and had advocated a third pillar alongside the International Monetary Fund (IMF) and the World Bank.

US failure to ratify the ITO charter can be traced to a number of reasons. To start with, there were changes in the world political situation and the situation in the United States between the time negotiations for an international trade organization were initiated in 1945 and when the charter was considered for ratification in 1948–50.

Initial attempts at negotiating an ITO began in 1945 as a US loan to Britain was being negotiated. Therefore, an ITO was seen as an extension of the negotiations that established the IMF and the Bank that would subsequently help dismantle the discriminatory, restrictive trade practices believed to have contributed to the Depression and World War II. By 1948, when the Havana Charter was signed, the transition from wartime to peacetime economies was proving more difficult and expensive than expected. In the United States, Congress was debating the Marshall Plan, which would provide funds for European integration and recovery. By 1949, Congress was occupied with the North Atlantic Treaty and Military Defence Assistance Program, so again consideration of the charter was delayed. By 1950, two tariff negotiating rounds conducted under the GATT had been held, and the ITO had been overtaken by events.[2]

An additional factor in the decision not to resubmit the charter was the lack of support for it by business groups in the United States. The "perfectionists" in the United States felt the charter contained too many loopholes and escape clauses to be effective. The charter was the result of several drafting sessions involving negotiations and compromises. Consequently, the United States had to accept some items it was not entirely comfortable with, while having to insist on others remaining in the charter. This led to escape clauses and exemptions for balance of payments problems, infant industries, and agriculture. According to this group, the charter was not liberal or international enough. However, the "protectionist" groups in the United States felt the charter did not give them enough protection; consequently, they would not support the charter either.[3]

By late 1950, it was felt there was insufficient support for the charter in Congress, and in December it was quietly announced that the charter for the ITO would not be resubmitted for congressional approval.

The GATT's Relationship to the ITO

The GATT was intended to be a temporary trade agreement pending ratification of the ITO. Its purpose was to oversee the Geneva, Annecy, and Torquay multilateral tariff negotiations. The articles of the GATT were drafted in such a way that the participants, especially the United States, would not have to seek approval from their legislatures, as the GATT was

---

2. In Geneva 1947, at which time the United States was unsuccessful in its attempts to abolish the Imperial Preference. Movement on preferences was thought necessary to generate support for the ITO. Another round was held in Annecy, France, in 1949 and yet another round was under way in Torquay, England, in 1950–51.

3. By 1950, tariff cuts made in Geneva 1947 were beginning to affect domestic producers and protectionist pressure was the strongest it had been since World War II. Groups normally supportive of liberal trade were against the charter, including the National Association of Manufacturers, the National Foreign Trade Council, the US Chamber of Commerce, and the US Council of the International Chamber of Commerce (Gardner 1956). Diebold (1952) discusses the "perfectionists" versus the "protectionists."

to be eventually superseded by the ITO. Consequently, the GATT was put into effect according to the Protocol of Provisional Application.[4]

GATT Article XXIX (2) (Relation of this Agreement to the Havana Charter) stated that "part II [Articles III–XXIII] of this Agreement shall be suspended on the day on which the Havana Charter enters into force." At the end of the Havana Conference in 1948, a resolution was adopted establishing an Interim Commission for the International Trade Organization (ICITO). This commission would be responsible for the preparations leading to the implementation of the Havana Charter. The secretariat services for the GATT continued to be supplied by the Interim Commission until the WTO went into effect in January 1995.

---

4. See Jackson (1990a) for a discussion of the problems this creates and why there is a need for the GATT to be applied "definitively."

References

Abbott, K. W. 1985. "The Trading Nation's Dilemma: The Functions of the Law of International Trade." *Harvard International Law Journal* 26 (Spring): 501–32.

Aldcroft, D. H. 1977. *From Versailles to Wall Street, 1919–1929.* Berkeley: University of California Press.

Anderson, A. D. M., and A. M. Rugman. 1989. "The Canada-US Free Trade Agreement: A Legal and Economic Analysis of the Dispute Settlement Mechanisms." *World Competition Law and Economics Review* 13, no. 1.

Anderson, K. 1992. "Effects on the Environment and Welfare of Liberalizing World Trade: The Cases of Coal and Food." In K. Anderson and R. Blackhurst, *The Greening of World Trade Issues.* Hertfordshire, UK: Harvester Wheatsheaf.

Anderson, K. 1995. "The Entwining of Trade Policy with Environmental and Labor Standards." In Will Martin and L. Alan Winters, *The Uruguay Round and the Developing Economy.* Part of the World Bank Discussion Paper Series No. 307. Washington: World Bank.

Anderson, K., and R. Blackhurst, eds. 1993. *Regional Integration in the Global Trading System.* Hertfordshire, UK: Harvester Wheatsheaf for the GATT.

Arnold, M., and C. Bronckers. 1988. "The EEC's New Trade Policy Instrument: Some Comments on Its Application (Reg. 2641/84)." *Journal of World Trade,* vol. 22, no. 6: 19–38.

Asia Pacific Economic Cooperation (APEC). 1994. *Achieving the APEC Vision: Free and Open Trade in the Asia Pacific.* Second Report of the Eminent Persons Group. Singapore: APEC.

Atlantic Council of the United States. 1976. *GATT Plus—A Proposal for Trade Reform.* New York: Praeger Publications.

Bagwell, K., and R. W. Staiger. 1993. *Multilateral Tariff Co-operation During the Formation of Regional Free Trade Areas.* NBER Working Paper No. 4364. Cambridge, MA: National Bureau of Economic Research.

Baldwin, R. E. 1970. *Nontariff Distortions of International Trade.* Washington: Brookings Institution.

Baldwin, R. E. 1988. *Trade Policy in a Changing World Economy.* Chicago: University of Chicago Press.

Baldwin, R. E. 1989. "The Growth Effects of 1992." *Economic Policy* (October): 247–83.

Baldwin, R. E. 1992. "Measurable Dynamic Gains from Trade." *Journal of Political Economy* 100, no. 1 (February): 162–74.

Barbier, E., B. Aylward, J. Burgess, and J. Bishop. 1991. "Environmental Effects of Trade in the Forestry Sector." London: International Institute for Environment and Development. Photocopy.

Barbier, E., J. Burgess, T. Swanson, and D. Pearce. 1990. *Elephants, Economics, and Ivory.* London: Earthscan.

Bayard, T. O., and K. A. Elliott. 1994. *Reciprocity and Retaliation in U.S. Trade Policy.* Washington: Institute for International Economics.

Beath, J. 1990. "Innovation, Intellectual Property Rights and the Uruguay Round." *The World Economy* 13, no. 3 (September): 411–26.

Beghin, J., D. Roland-Holst, and D. van der Mensbrugghe. 1994. "A Survey of the Trade and Environment Nexus: Global Dimensions." *OECD Economic Studies*, no. 23: 167–92.

Bergsten, C. F. 1975. *Toward a New International Economic Order: Selected Papers of C. Fred Bergsten, 1972–74.* Lexington, MA: Lexington Books.

Bergsten, C. F. 1990. "The World Economy after the Cold War." *Foreign Affairs* 69, no. 3: 96–112.

Bergsten, C. F. 1994. "APEC and World Trade: A Force for Worldwide Liberalization." *Foreign Affairs* 73, no. 3: 20–27.

Bergsten, C. F., and W. R. Cline. 1983. "Trade Policy in the 1980s: An Overview." In W. R. Cline, *Trade Policy in the 1980s.* Washington: Institute for International Economics.

Bergsten, C. F., E. Davignon, and I. Miyazaki. 1986. *Conditions for Partnership in International Economic Management.* New York: Trilateral Commission.

Bergsten, C. F., and M. Noland. 1993. *Reconcilable Differences? United States–Japan Economic Conflict.* Washington: Institute for International Economics.

Blackhurst, R., A. Enders, and J. François 1995. "The Uruguay Round and Market Access: Opportunities and Challenges for Developing Countries." Paper presented at the Uruguay Round and the Developing Economies, a World Bank conference, 26–27 January, Washington.

Bliss, J. C. 1987. "GATT Dispute Settlement Reform in the Uruguay Round: Problems and Prospects." *Stanford Journal of International Law* 23: 31–56.

Boddez, T. M., and M. J. Trebilcock. 1993. *Unfinished Business: Reforming Trade Remedy Laws in North America.* Policy Study 17. Toronto: C. D. Howe Institute.

Bollard, A., and D. Mayes. 1992. "Regionalism and the Pacific Rim." *Journal of Common Market Studies* 30: 195–209.

Boner, R., and R. Krueger. 1991. *The Basics of Antitrust Policy: A Review of Ten Nations and the European Communities.* World Bank Technical Paper, no. 160. Washington: World Bank.

Bordo, M. 1995. "Is There a Good Case for a New Bretton Woods International Monetary System?" *The American Economic Review* 85, no. 2: 317–22.

Braga, C. P. 1995. "Trade-Related Intellectual Property Issues: The Uruguay Round Agreement and Its Economic Implications." Paper presented at the Uruguay Round and the Developing Economies, a World Bank conference, 26–27 January, Washington.

Brand, R. 1990. "Private Parties and GATT Dispute Resolution: Implications of the Panel Report on Section 337 of the US Tariff Act of 1930." *Journal of World Trade* 24, no. 3: 5–30.

Brandao, A., and W. Martin. 1993. *Implications of Agricultural Trade Liberalization for the Developing Countries.* World Bank Working Paper No. WPS 1116. Washington: World Bank.

Bretton Woods Commission. 1994. *Bretton Woods: Looking to the Future.* Commission Report. Washington: Bretton Wood Commission.

Broadman, H. G. 1994. "GATS: The Uruguay Round Accord on Trade in Services in the Uruguay Round." *The World Economy* 17, no. 3: 281–92.

Bronz, G. 1956. "An International Trade Organization: The Second Attempt." *Harvard Law Review* 69: 440–82.

Brown, W. A. Jr. 1950. *The United States and the Restoration of World Trade*. Washington: Brookings Institution.

Brunner, K., ed. 1981. *The Great Depression Revisited*. Boston, MA: Martinus Nijhoff Publishing.

Bryant, R. C., and E. Hodgkinson 1989. "Problems of International Cooperation." In R. C. Cooper et al., *Can Nations Agree? Issues in International Economic Cooperation*. Washington: Brookings Institution.

Calleo, D. P. 1987. *Beyond American Hegemony: The Future of the Western Alliance*. New York: Basic Books.

Camps, M., and W. Diebold Jr. 1986. *The New Multilateralism*. New York: Council on Foreign Relations.

Camps, M., and C. Gwin. 1981. *Collective Management. The Reform of Global Economic Organizations*. New York: McGraw-Hill.

Canada. 1993a. *An Overview of Canada's Competition Act*. Ottawa: Consumer and Corporate Affairs.

Canada. 1993b. *The North American Free Trade Agreement: The NAFTA Manual*. Ottawa: Department of Foreign Affairs and International Trade.

Canada, Royal Commission on the Economic Union and Development Prospects for Canada. 1985. Report volume 1. Ottawa: Ministry of Supply and Services.

Charnovitz, S. 1986. "Fair Labor Standards and International Trade." *Journal of World Trade Law* 20, no. 1: 61–78.

Charnovitz, S. 1992. "Environmental and Labor Standards in Trade." *The World Economy* 15, no. 3: 335–56.

Ching, M. 1992. "Evaluating the Effectiveness of the GATT Dispute Settlement System for Developing Countries." *World Competition Law and Economics Review* 16, no. 2: 81–112.

Cline, W. R. 1987. *The Future of World Trade in Textiles and Apparel*. Washington: Institute for International Economics.

Cline, W. R., Noboru Kawanabe, T. O. M. Kronsjo, and Thomas Williams. 1978. *Trade Negotiations in the Tokyo Round: A Quantitative Assessment*. Washington: Brookings Institution.

Cloud, D. S. 1994. "Critics Say GATT Threatens U.S. Sovereignty." *Congressional Quarterly Weekly Report* 52, no. 29 (23 July): 2005–10.

Commission of the European Communities. 1991. *Report on United States Trade Barriers and Unfair Practices 1991*. Brussels: Directorate-General for Economic and Financial Affairs.

Commission of the European Communities. 1992. *Report on United States Trade and Investment Barriers 1992: Problems of Doing Business with the US*. Brussels: Directorate-General for Economic and Financial Affairs.

Commission of the European Communities. 1993. *European Economy Annual Report for 1993*, no. 54. Brussels: Directorate-General for Economic and Financial Affairs.

Commission of the European Communities. 1994. *Report on United States Barriers to Trade and Investment 1994*. Brussels: Directorate-General for Economic and Financial Affairs.

Commonwealth Secretariat. 1982. *Protectionism: Threat to International Order*. London: Marlborough House.

Congressional Research Service. 1988. *Congressional Research Service Review* 9, no. 6 (June).

Conybeare, J. 1987. *Trade Wars: The Theory and Practice of International Commercial Rivalry*. New York: Columbia University Press.

Cooke, P. 1989. "Recent Developments in the Prudential Regulation of Banks and the Evolution of International Supervisory Regulation." Remarks at the Joint Universities Conferences on Regulating Commercial Banks, 1–2 August, Canberra.

Copie, F. 1992. "Trade Wars: A Repetition of the Inter-War Years?" In *Current Controversies*, no. 2. London: Institute of Economic Affairs.

Cox, D., and R. Harris 1985. "Trade Liberalization and Industrial Organization: Some Estimates for Canada." *Journal of Political Economy* 93, no. 1: 115–45.

Dam, K. W. 1970. *The GATT: Law and International Economic Organization*. Chicago: University of Chicago Press.

Deardorff, A. V., and R. M. Stern. 1986. *The Michigan Model of World Protection and Trade.* Cambridge, MA: MIT Press.

Deardorff, A. V., and R. M. Stern. 1990. *Computational Analysis of Global Trading Arrangements.* Ann Arbor: University of Michigan Press.

deMelo, J., and A. Panagariya, eds. 1993. *The New Regionalism in Trade Policy.* Washington: World Bank.

Destler, I. M. 1986. *American Trade Politics: System under Stress.* Washington: Institute for International Economics.

Destler, I. M., and J. Odell. 1987. *Anti-Protection: Changing Forces in United States Trade Politics.* Washington: Institute for International Economics.

Diebold, W. Jr. 1952. *The End of the ITO.* Essays in International Finance No. 16. Princeton, NJ: Princeton University.

Diebold, W. Jr. 1988. "The History and the Issues." In W. Diebold Jr., *Bilateralism, Multilateralism and Canada in US Trade Policy.* Cambridge, MA: Ballinger.

Dowling, M. J. Jr. 1994. "Outlook for Asia." Paper presented at the Seventh Workshop on Asian Economic Outlook, 26–28 October, Asian Development Bank, Manila.

Data Resources Incorporated (DRI). 1993. "Impacts of Trade Liberalization under the Uruguay Round." A study prepared for the Office of the United States Trade Representative. Washington: DRI/McGraw-Hill.

Dymond, W. 1989. "Lord Ronald and United States Trade Policy." Occasional Paper. Centre for Trade Policy and Law. Ottawa: Carleton University.

Enders, E. A., and R. J. Wonnacott. 1994. "The Liberalization of East-West European Trade: Hubs, Spokes and Further Complications." Photocopy.

Erzan, R., and G. Karsenty. 1989. "Products Facing High Tariffs in Major Developed Market-Economy Countries: An Area of Priority for the Developing Countries in the Uruguay Round?" *UNCTAD Review* 1, no. 1: 51–74.

Esty, Daniel. 1994. *Greening the GATT: Trade, Environment, and the Future.* Washington: Institute for International Economics.

European Commission. 1995. *European Economy Annual Economic Report for 1995*, no. 59. Brussels: Directorate-General for Economic and Financial Affairs.

European Community. 1989. *EEC Competition Policy in the Single Market.* Luxembourg: Office for Official Publications of the European Communities.

Evans, J. W. 1971. *The Kennedy Round in American Trade Policy.* Cambridge, MA: Harvard University Press.

Faull, J. 1993. "Playing by the Rules: A Guide to Competition Law around the World." *International Financial Law Review 12, Special Supplement* (May): 3–23.

Feketekuty, G. 1993. "Reflections on the Interaction between Trade Policy and Competition Policy." Ottawa: Centre for Trade Policy and Law, Carleton University. Photocopy.

Finger, J. M. 1990. "Subsidies and Countervailing Duties." In H. Edward English, *Pacific Initiatives in Global Trade.* Halifax: Institute for Research on Public Policy.

Finger, J. M. 1995. "Legalized Backsliding: Safeguard Provisions in the GATT." Paper presented at the Uruguay Round and the Developing Economies, a World Bank conference, 26–27 January, Washington.

Foreman-Peck, J. 1983. *A History of the World Economy.* Brighton, UK: Wheatsheaf Books.

François, J. F., H. M. Arce, K. Reinert, and Joseph E. Flynn. 1996. "Commercial Policy and the Domestic Carrying Trade." *Canadian Journal of Economics* 29, no. 1 (February): 181–98.

François, J. F., B. McDonald, and H. Nordström. 1994. "The Uruguay Round: A Global General Equilibrium Assessment." Paper presented at Challenges and Opportunities for East-Asian Trade, National Centre for Development Studies, Canberra, 13–14 July. Photocopy.

François, J. F., B. McDonald, and H. Nordström. 1995. "Assessing the Uruguay Round." Paper presented at the Uruguay Round and the Developing Economies, a World Bank conference, 26–27 January, Washington. Photocopy.

Frankel, Jeffrey A. 1996. *Regional Trading Blocs in the World Economic System*. Washington: Institute for International Economics. Forthcoming.

Friedman, M., and A. J. Schwartz 1965. *The Great Contraction: 1929–1933*. Princeton, NJ: Princeton University Press.

Fujimura, J. 1994. *Global Strategies and Foreign Direct Investment: Implications for Trade and the Canadian Economy*. Policy Staff Paper No. 9417. Ottawa: Department of Foreign Affairs and International Trade.

Funabashi, Y. 1988. *Managing the Dollar: From the Plaza to the Louvre*. Washington: Institute for International Economics.

Gardner, R. 1956. *Sterling-Dollar Diplomacy*. Oxford, UK: Clarendon Press.

General Agreement on Tariffs and Trade (GATT). 1990. *International Trading Environment*. Report by the Director-General. Geneva: GATT.

General Agreement on Tariffs and Trade (GATT). 1991. "Trade and Environment." Factual Note by the Secretariat. Geneva: GATT.

General Agreement on Tariffs and Trade (GATT). 1993a. *International Trade and the Trading System: Report by the Director General 1992–1993*. Geneva: GATT.

General Agreement on Tariffs and Trade (GATT). 1993b. "An Analysis of the Proposed Uruguay Round Agreement, with Particular Emphasis on Aspects of Interest to Developing Economies." GATT Secretariat, 29 November.

General Agreement on Tariffs and Trade (GATT). 1993c. *Trade Policy Review Mechanism: European Communities*, vol. 1. Geneva: GATT.

General Agreement on Tariffs and Trade (GATT). 1994a. "Uruguay Round: Final Act." Marrakesh, 15 April. Photocopy.

General Agreement on Tariffs and Trade (GATT). 1994b. "Trade and the Environment." 17 February. Geneva: GATT.

General Agreement on Tariffs and Trade (GATT). 1994c. *Trade Policy Review Mechanism: Australia*, vol. 1. Geneva: GATT.

Gitli, E., and G. Ryd. 1992. "Latin American Integration and the Enterprise for the Americas Initiative." *Journal of World Trade* 26, no. 4: 25–45.

Giunta, T., and L. Shang. 1993–94. "Ownership of Information in a Global Economy." *The George Washington Journal of International Law and Economics* 27, nos. 2 and 3: 327–58.

Goldin, I., O. Knudsen, and D. van der Mensbrugghe. 1993. *Trade Liberalization: Global Economic Implications*. Washington: World Bank; Paris: OECD Development Center.

Goldin, I., and D. van der Mensbrugghe. 1995. "The Uruguay Round: An Assessment of Economywide and Agricultural Reforms." Paper presented at the Uruguay Round and the Developing Economies, a World Bank conference, 26–27 January, Washington.

Gorman, W. M. 1957. "Tariffs, Retaliation and the Elasticity of Demand for Imports." *Review of Economic Studies* 25: 133–62.

Graham, Edward M., and J. David Richardson. 1996. *Global Competition Policy*. Washington: Institute for International Economics.

Griffin, J. P. 1994. "An Analysis of the Draft Anti-Trust Enforcement Guidelines for International Operations." *World Competition* 18, no. 2: 5–34.

Grinols, E. 1989. "Procedural Protectionism: The American Trade Bill and the New Interventionist Mode."*Weltwirtschaftliches Archiv (Review of World Economics)* 125, no. 3: 501–21.

Grossman, G., and E. Helpman. 1994. "Protection for Sale." *American Economic Review* 84, no. 4 (September): 833–50.

Grossman, G., and E. Helpman. 1995. "Trade Wars and Trade Talks." *Journal of Political Economy* 103, no. 4: 675–708.

Grossman, G., and A. Krueger. 1991. *Environmental Impacts of a North American Free Trade Agreement*. NBER Working Paper No. 3914. Cambridge, MA: National Bureau of Economic Research.

Haaland, J., and T. C. Tollefssen. 1994. *The Uruguay Round and Trade in Manufactures and Services: General Equilibrium Simulations of Production, Trade and Welfare Effects of Liberalization*. Centre for Economic Policy Research Discussion Paper No. 1008. London: CEPR.

Hamilton, B., and J. Whalley. 1983. "Optimal Tariff Calculations in Alternative Trade Models and Some Possible Implications for Current World Trading Arrangements." *Journal of International Economics* 15, no. 3/4 (November): 323–48.

Hamilton, C., ed. 1990. *The Uruguay Round: Textiles Trade and the Developing Countries.* Washington: World Bank.

Hamilton, C., and J. Whalley. 1987. "A View from the Developed World." In J. Whalley, *Dealing with the North: Developing Countries and the Global Trading System.* London, Canada: Centre for the Study of International Economic Relations, University of Western Ontario.

Hamilton, C., and J. Whalley. 1990. "Safeguards." In J. J. Schott, *Completing the Uruguay Round: A Results-Oriented Approach to the GATT Trade Negotiations.* Washington: Institute for International Economics.

Hamza, M. A. B. 1987. *Guidebook for the GSTP: The Global System of Trade Preferences among Developing Countries—Origin, Dimensions, Negotiations, and Prospects.* Geneva: UN Conference on Trade and Development.

Hansen, A. 1938. *Full Recovery or Stagnation?* New York: W. W. Norton.

Harrison, G. W., T. F. Rutherford, and D. G. Tarr. 1995. "Quantifying the Uruguay Round." Paper presented at the Uruguay Round and the Developing Economies, a World Bank conference, 26–27 January, Washington.

Harrold, P. 1995. "The Impact of the Uruguay Round on Africa: Much Ado about Nothing?" Paper presented at the Uruguay Round and the Developing Economies, a World Bank conference, 26–27 January, Washington.

Hart, M. M. 1987. "GATT Article XXIV and Canada–United States Trade Negotiations." *Review of International Business Law* 1, no. 3 (December): 317–55.

Hart, M. M. 1991. "A North American Free Trade Agreement: The Elements Involved." *The World Economy* 14, no. 1: 87–102.

Hathaway, D., and M. Ingco. 1995. "Agricultural Liberalization and the Uruguay Round." Paper presented at the Uruguay Round and the Developing Economies, a World Bank conference, 26–27 January, Washington.

Haveman, J. D. 1992. "Some Welfare Effects of Dynamic Customs Unions Formation." Purdue University. Photocopy.

Hertel, T., W. Martin, K. Yanagishima, and B. Dimaran. 1995. "Liberalizing Manufactures Trade in a Changing World Economy." Paper presented at the Uruguay Round and the Developing Economies, a World Bank conference, 26–27 January, Washington.

Hindley, B. 1994. "Safeguards, VERs, and Anti-Dumping Action." *The New World Trading System: Readings.* Paris: Organization for Economic Cooperation and Development.

Hoekman, B. M. 1993. *Developing Countries and the Uruguay Round Negotiations on Services.* Discussion Paper Series No. 822. London: Centre for Economic Policy Research.

Hoekman, B. M. 1995. "Tentative First Steps: An Assessment of the Uruguay Round Agreement on Services." Paper presented at the Uruguay Round and the Developing Economies, a World Bank conference, 26–27 January, Washington.

Hoekman, B. M., and P. C. Mavroidis. 1994. "Competition, Competition Policy and the GATT." *The World Economy* 17, no. 3: 121–50.

Hoekman, B. M., and P. Sauvé. 1994. *Liberalizing Trade in Services.* World Bank Discussion Papers No. 243. Washington: World Bank.

Horlick, G. N. 1993. "How the GATT Became Protectionist: An Analysis of the Uruguay Round Draft Final Antidumping Code." *Journal of World Trade* 27, no. 5: 5–17.

Horlick, G. N., and P. Clarke. 1994. "The 1994 WTO Subsidies Agreement." *World Competition* 17, no. 4: 41–54.

Houthakker, H., and S. Magee. 1969. "Income and Price Elasticities in World Trade." *Review of Economics and Statistics* 51, no. 2: 111–25.

Hudec, R. E. 1989. "The Structure of South-South Trade Preferences in the 1988 GSTP Agreement: Learning to Say MFMFN." In J. Whalley, *Developing Countries and the Global Trading System,* vol. 1. London: MacMillan.

Hudec, R. E. 1992. "The Judicialization of GATT Dispute Settlement." In M. Hart and D. Steger, *In Whose Interest? Due Process and Transparency in International Trade*. Ottawa: Centre for Trade Policy and Law.

Hudec, R. E., D. L. M. Kennedy, and M. Sgarbossa. 1993. "A Statistical Profile of GATT Dispute Settlement Cases: 1948–1989." *Minnesota Journal of Global Trade* 2, no. 1: 1–113.

Hufbauer, G. C. 1989. "Beyond GATT." *Foreign Policy, no. 77* (Winter): 64–76.

Hufbauer, G. C. 1990. "Subsidies." In J. J. Schott, *Completing the Uruguay Round: A Results-Oriented Approach to the GATT Trade Negotiations*. Washington: Institute for International Economics.

Hufbauer, G., and J. J. Schott. 1985. *Trading for Growth*. POLICY ANALYSES IN INTERNATIONAL ECONOMICS 13. Washington: Institute for International Economics.

Hufbauer, G. C., and J. J. Schott. 1992. *NAFTA: An Assessment*. Washington: Institute for International Economics.

Hufbauer, G. C., J. J. Schott, and K. A. Elliott. 1990. *Economic Sanctions Reconsidered: History and Current Policy*. Washington: Institute for International Economics.

Hull, C. 1948. *The Memoirs of Cordell Hull*, vol. 1. New York: MacMillan.

Hungerford, T. 1991. "GATT: A Cooperative Equilibrium in a Non-Cooperative Trading Regime?" *Journal of International Economics* 31: 357–69.

Ikenberry, G. J. 1989. "Rethinking the Origins of American Hegemony." *Political Science Quarterly* 104, no. 3: 375–400.

International Monetary Fund (IMF). 1994. "Trade Agreement Mandates Broad Changes." *IMF Survey* 23, no. 1 (10 January): 2–4.

Irwin, D. 1995. "The GATT in Historical Perspective." *The American Economic Review* 85, no. 2 (May): 323–34.

Jackson, J. H. 1969. *World Trade and the Law of GATT*. Indianapolis: Bobbs-Merrill.

Jackson, J. H. 1989. *The World Trading System*. Cambridge, MA: MIT Press.

Jackson, J. H. 1990a. *Restructuring the GATT System*. London: Pinter for the Royal Institute of International Affairs.

Jackson, J. H. 1990b. "Reflections on Restructuring the GATT." Paper for the Institute for International Economics, 25 June, Washington. Photocopy.

Jackson, J. H. 1993. "Regional Trade Blocs and GATT." *The World Economy* 16, no. 2: 121–31.

Jackson, J. H. 1994. "Dispute Settlement Procedures." In *The New World Trading System: Readings*. Paris: OECD.

Jackson, J. H. 1995. "The World Trade Organization: Watershed Innovation or Cautious Small Step Forward?" In S. Arndt and C. Milner, *The World Economy Global Trade Policy 1995*. Oxford, UK, and Cambridge, MA: Blackwell.

Johnson, H. G. 1953–54. "Optimum Tariffs and Retaliation." *Review of Economic Studies* 21: 142–43.

Johnson, H. G. 1976. "Trade Negotiations and the New International Monetary System." In G. and V. Curzon, *Commercial Policy Issues*, no. 1. Leiden: A. W. Sitjhoff.

Jones, K. 1989. "Voluntary Export Restraint: Political Economy, History and the Role of the GATT." *Journal of World Trade Law* 23, no. 3: 125–40.

Julius, D. 1990. *Global Companies and Public Policy*. London: Royal Institute of International Affairs.

Keesing, D. B., and M. Wolf. 1980. *Textile Quotas against Developing Countries*. Thames Essay No. 23. London: Trade Policy Research Centre.

Kennan, J., and R. Riezman. 1990. "Optimal Tariff Equilibria with Customs Unions." *Canadian Journal of Economics* 23: 70–83.

Kenwood, A. G., and A. Lougheed. 1983. *The Growth of the International Economy, 1820–1980*. London: George Allen and Unwin.

Keohane, R. O. 1984. *After Hegemony: Cooperation and Discord in the World Political Economy*. Princeton, NJ: Princeton University Press.

Kindleberger, C. P. 1973. *The World in Depression, 1929–1939*. London: Allen Lane Penguin Press.

Kirmani, N., P. Molojani, and T. Mayer. 1984. *Effects of Increased Market Access on Exports of Developing Countries*. IMF Staff Papers 31. Washington: IMF.

Komuro, N. 1995. "The WTO Dispute Settlement Mechanism: Coverage and Procedures of the WTO Understanding." *Journal of World Trade* 29, no. 4: 5–96.

Krugman, P. R. 1991. "Is Bilateralism Bad?" In E. Helpman and A. Razin, *International Trade and Trade Policy Review*. Cambridge, MA: MIT Press.

Laird, S., and A. Yeats. 1987. "Tariff-Cutting Formulas and Complications." In J. M. Finger and A. Olechowski, *The Uruguay Round: A Handbook on the Multilateral Trade Negotiations*. Washington: World Bank.

Laird, S., and A. Yeats. 1988. "Trends in Non-Tariff Barriers of Developed Countries 1966–1986." World Bank Policy, Planning, and Research Working Paper WPS 137. Washington: World Bank.

Lavergne, R. 1983. *The Political Economy of U.S. Tariffs: An Empirical Analysis*. Ottawa: North-South Institute.

League of Nations. 1942. *Commercial Policy in the Interwar Period: International Proposals and National Policies*. Geneva: League of Nations.

League of Nations. 1945. *Commercial Policy in the Post-war World*. Geneva: League of Nations.

Leamer, E. 1984. *Sources of International Comparative Advantage: Theory and Evidence*. Cambridge, MA: MIT Press.

Leonard, R., and E. Christensen. 1991. Testimony on Behalf of the Community Nutrition Institute before the International Trade Commission Hearing on Economic Effects of a Free Trade Agreement between Mexico and the United States, 12 April.

Levinson, A. 1994. "Environmental Regulation and Industry Location: International and Domestic Evidence." University of Wisconsin. Photocopy.

Lewis, W. A. 1970 [1949]. *Economic Survey 1919–1939*. London: George Allen and Unwin.

Low, P. 1992. "Trade Measures and Environmental Quality: The Implications for Mexico's Exports." In P. Low, *International Trade and the Environment*. World Bank Discussion Paper 159. Washington: World Bank.

Low, P. 1993. *Trading Free: The GATT and US Trade Policy*. New York: Twentieth Century Fund Press.

Low, P., and A. Subramanian. 1995. "TRIMs in the Uruguay Round: An Unfinished Business?" Paper presented at the Uruguay Round and the Developing Economies, a World Bank conference, 26–27 January, Washington.

Low, P., and S. Yeats. 1995. "Non-Tariff Measures and Developing Countries: Has the Uruguay Round Leveled the Playing Field?" *The World Economy* 18, no. 1: 51–70.

Ludlow, R. 1989. "The Future of the International Trading System." *The Washington Quarterly* 12, no. 4 (Fall): 157–69.

Madden, P. 1994. *The Road From Marrakesh: Regulating World Trade for Sustainable Development*. London: Christian Aid.

Madden, P., and J. Madeley. 1993. *Winners and Losers: The Impact of the GATT Uruguay Round on Developing Countries*. London: Christian Aid.

Malmgren, H. B. 1983. "Threats to the Multilateral System." In W. R. Cline, *Trade Policy in the 1980s*. Washington: Institute for International Economics.

Mander, D., and P. Perkins. 1994. "Trade Disputes and Environmental 'Regulatory Chill:' The Case of Ontario's Environmental Levy." *World Competition* 18, no. 2: 57–76.

Mark, J. 1985. "The Multi-Fibre Arrangement: Unraveling the Costs." Briefing. Ottawa: North-South Institute.

McMillan, J. 1986. *Game Theory in International Economics*. New York: Harwood.

McMillan, J. 1989. "A Game-Theoretic View of International Trade Negotiations: Implications for the Developing Countries." In J. Whalley, *Developing Countries and the Global Trading System*, vol. 1. London: Macmillan.

Merciai, P. 1981. "Safeguard Measures in GATT." *Journal of World Trade Law* 15, no. 1: 41–66.

Messerlin, P. 1989. "The EC Antidumping Regulations: A First Economic Appraisal, 1980–1985." *Weltwirtshaftliches Archiv* (Review of world economics) 125, no. 3: 563–87.

Messerlin, P. 1990. "The Anti-dumping Regulations of the European Community 'Privatization' of Administered Protection." In M. Trebilcock and R. York, *Fair Exch Reforming Trade Remedy Laws*. Toronto: C. D. Howe Institute.

Nam, C. 1987. "Export Promoting Subsidies, Countervailing Threats, and the General Agr ment on Tariffs and Trade." *World Bank Economic Review* 1, no. 4: 727–74.

Nguyen, T., C. Perroni, and R. M. Wigle. 1991. "The Value of the Uruguay Round Success." *The World Economy* 14, no. 4: 359–74.

Nguyen, T., C. Perroni, and R. M. Wigle 1993. "An Evaluation of the Draft Final Act of the Uruguay Round." *Economic Journal* 103, no. 421 (November): 1540–49.

Nguyen, T., C. Perroni, and R. M. Wigle. 1995. "A Uruguay Round Success?" *The World Economy* 18, no. 1: 25–30.

Nierop, T., and S. DeVos. 1988. "Of Shrinking Empires and Changing Roles: World of Trade Patterns in the Post-War Period." *Tijdschrift voor Economische en Sociale Geografie* 79, no. 5: 343–64.

Organization for Economic Cooperation and Development (OECD). 1966. *Economic Growth 1960–1970*. Paris: OECD.

Organization for Economic Cooperation and Development (OECD). 1985. *Costs and Benefits of Protection*. Paris: OECD.

Organization for Economic Cooperation and Development (OECD). 1992. *OECD Economic Studies*, No. 19 (Winter). Paris: OECD.

Organization for Economic Cooperation and Development (OECD). 1993. *Assessing the Effects of the Uruguay Round*. Paris: OECD.

Organization for Economic Cooperation and Development (OECD). 1994. *Managing the Environment: The Role of Economic Instruments*. Paris: OECD.

Oye, K. 1990. "When Sanctions Brought Free(er) Trade Discriminating Liberalization in the 1930s." MIT. Photocopy.

Page, S., and M. Davenport. 1994. *World Trade Reform: Do Developing Countries Gain or Lose?* ODI Special Report. London: Overseas Development Institute.

Pearce, D. 1991. "Deforesting the Amazon: Towards an Economic Solution." *Ecodecision* 1, no. 1. Toronto: Environment and Policy Society and Royal Society of Canada.

Pearce, D., S. Fankhauser, N. Adger, and T. Swanson. 1992. "World Economy, World Environment." *The World Economy* 15, no. 3: 295–313.

Perroni, C. 1995. "The Uruguay Round and Its Impact on Developing Countries: An Overview of Model Results." Report prepared for an UNCTAD project on the impact of the Uruguay Round on Developing Countries. Photocopy.

Perroni, C., and J. Whalley. 1994. *The New Regionalism: Trade Liberalization or Insurance?* NBER Working Paper No. 4626. Cambridge, MA: National Bureau of Economic Research.

Perroni, C., and R. M. Wigle. 1994. "International Trade and Environmental Quality: How Important are the Linkages?" *Canadian Journal of Economics* 27, no. 3 (August): 551–67.

Petersmann, E. U. 1993. "International Trade Law and International Environmental Law: Prevention and Settlement of International Environmental Disputes in GATT." *Journal of World Trade* 27, no. 1: 43–81.

Peterson, C. 1992. "Trade Conflict and Resolution Methodologies." *American Economic Review* 82, no. 2 (May): 62–66.

Piggott, J., J. Whalley, and R. M. Wigle. 1992. "International Linkages and Carbon Reduction Initiatives." In K. Anderson and R. Blackhurst, *The Greening of World Trade Issues*. Hertfordshire, UK: Harvester Wheatsheaf.

Pomfret, R. 1988. *Unequal Trade: The Economics of Discriminatory International Trade Policies*. London: Blackwell.

Preeg, E. H. 1970. *Traders and Diplomats*. Washington: Brookings Institution.

Rappoport, R., and E. White. 1994. "Was the Crash of 1929 Expected?" *American Economic Review* 84, no. 1 (March): 271–81.

Reichman, J. H. 1993. *Implications of the Draft Trips Agreement for Developing Countries as Competitors in an Integrated World Market*. Discussion Paper No. 73. Geneva: UN Conference on Trade and Development.

Report of the Group of Experts. 1995. "Competition Policy in the New Trade Order: Strengthening International Cooperation and Rules." Luxembourg: Office of Official Publications of the European Communities.

Robertson, D. 1977. *Fail Safe Systems for Trade Liberalization*. London: Trade Policy Research Centre.

Rousslang, D. J., and J. W. Suomela. 1985. "The Trade Effects of a U.S. Import Surcharge." *Journal of World Trade Law* 19, no. 5: 441–50.

Rubin, A. 1994. "Trade: Dole, Clinton Compromise Greases Wheels for GATT." *Congressional Quarterly* 52, no. 46 (26 November): 3405.

Rubinstein, A. 1982. "Perfect Equilibrium in a Bargaining Model." *Econometrica* 50, no. 1: 97–109.

Samples, K., M. Gowen, and J. Dixon. 1986. "The Validity of the Contingent Valuation Method for Estimating Non-Use Components of Preservation Values for Unique Natural Resources." Paper presented to the American Agricultural Economics Association, July, Reno, Nevada.

Sauvé, P. 1995. "Assessing the General Agreement on Trade in Services: Half-Full or Half-Empty?" *Journal of World Trade* 29, no. 4: 125–45.

Schott, J. J., assisted by Johanna W. Buurman. 1994. *The Uruguay Round: An Assessment*. Washington: Institute of International Economics.

Schultz, J. 1994. "Environmental Reform of the GATT/WTO International Trading System." *World Competition* 18, no. 2: 77–113.

Shoven, J., and J. Whalley. 1992. *Applied General Equilibrium*. Cambridge, UK: Cambridge University Press.

Shrybman, S. 1989. "International Trade and the Environment." Paper prepared for the Canadian Environmental Law Association, Toronto.

Sistema Econômico Latino-Americano (SELA). 1990. "The Bush Enterprise for the America's Initiative: A Preliminary Analysis by the SELA Permanent Secretariat." Caracas (September).

Staiger, R. W., and F. A. Wolak. 1994. *Measuring Industry Specific Protection: Antidumping in the United States*. NBER Working Paper No. 4696. Cambridge, MA: National Bureau of Economic Research.

Stern, R. M. 1990. "Symposium on TRIPS and TRIMS in the Uruguay Round: Analytical and Negotiating Issues: Introduction and Overview." *The World Economy* 13, no. 4: 493–96.

Stern, R. M., and D. L. Hummels. 1990. "Evolving Patterns of North American Merchandise Trade and Foreign Direct Investment, 1960–1990." Symposium on Analytical and Empirical Studies of North American Trade and Investment Relations. Proceedings printed in *The World Economy* 17, no. 1.

Stewart, T. P., ed. 1993. *The GATT Uruguay Round: A Negotiating History 1986–1992*, vol. 1 and 2. Boston: Kluwer Law and Taxation Publishers.

Stoeckel, A., D. Pearce, and G. Banks. 1990. *Western Trade Blocs: Game, Set or Match for Asia-Pacific and the World Economy*. Canberra: Centre for International Economics.

Tangermann, S. 1994. "An Assessment of the Agreement on Agriculture." In *The New World Trading System: Readings*. Paris: Organization for Economic Cooperation and Development.

Tharakan, P. K. M. 1993. "Contingent Protection: The U.S. and the EC Anti-dumping Actions." *The World Economy* 16, no. 5: 575–600.

Tobey, J. 1990. "The Effects of Domestic Environmental Policies on Patterns of World Trade: An Empirical Test." *Kyklos* 43, no. 2: 191–209.

Trebilcock, M., and R. York, eds. 1990. *Fair Exchange: Reforming Trade Remedy Laws*. Toronto: C. D. Howe Institute.

Trela, I. 1994a. "Agricultural Trade Liberalization in the Uruguay Round: Implications for Developing Countries." Report prepared for an UNCTAD project on the impact of the Uruguay Round on developing countries. Photocopy.

Trela, I. 1994b. "Phasing Out the MFA in the Uruguay Round: Implications for Developing Countries." Report prepared for an UNCTAD project on the impact of the Uruguay Round on developing countries. Photocopy.

Trela, I., and J. Whalley. 1990. "Unraveling the Threads of the MFA." In C. Hamilton, *The Uruguay Round: Textiles Trade and the Developing Countries*. Washington: World Bank.

Tumlir, J. 1985. *Protectionism Trade Policy in Democratic Societies*. Washington: American Enterprise Institute for Public Policy Research.

Uimonen, P. 1994. "Trade Rules and Environmental Controversies During the Uruguay Round and Beyond." International Monetary Fund. Photocopy.

United Nations (UN). 1992. *World Investment Report: Transnational Corporations as Engines of Growth*. New York: United Nations.

UN Conference on Trade and Development (UNCTAD). 1990. *Agricultural Trade Liberalization in the Uruguay Round: Implications for Developing Countries*. New York.

UN Conference on Trade and Development (UNCTAD). 1994. *The Outcome of the Uruguay Round: An Initial Assessment*. Supporting Papers to the Trade and Development Report. New York.

US Congressional Budget Office. 1979. "The Effects of the Tokyo Round of Multilateral Trade Negotiation on the US Economy: An Updated View." Background paper, July.

US Executive Office of the President, Office of the Special Representative for Trade Negotiations. 1967. *Report on United States Negotiations*. Washington.

US International Trade Commission (USITC). 1984. *Annual Report of the President of the United States on the Trade Agreements Program*. 1983, 27th Issue. Washington.

US International Trade Commission (USITC). 1986. *Annual Report of the President of the United States on the Trade Agreements Program*, 1984–1985, 28th issue. Washington.

US International Trade Commission (USITC). 1987. *Operation of the Trade Agreements Program 38th Report, 1986*. Washington.

US International Trade Commission (USITC). 1990. *Operation of the Trade Agreements Program, 41st Report, 1989*. Washington.

US International Trade Commission (USITC). 1991. *The Likely Impact on the United States of a Free Trade Agreement with Mexico*. USITC Publication 2353. Washington.

US International Trade Commission (USITC). 1992. *The Year in Trade: Operation of the Trade Agreements Program 43rd Report, 1991*. Washington.

US International Trade Commission (USITC). 1993. *The Year in Trade: Operation of the Trade Agreements Program 44th Report, 1992*. USITC Publication 2640. Washington.

US International Trade Commission (USITC). 1995. *The Economic Effects of Anti-dumping and Countervailing Duty Orders and Suspension Agreements*. Investigation No. 332–344. Washington.

US Tariff Commission. 1949. *Operation of the Trade Agreements Program, July 1934 to April 1948*. Washington.

US Trade Representative (USTR). 1993. *1993 National Trade Estimate Report on Foreign Trade Barriers*. Washington.

Vermulst, E., and B. Driessen. 1995. "An Overview of the WTO Dispute Settlement System and Its Relationship with the Uruguay Round Agreements." *Journal of World Trade* 29, no. 2: 131–762.

Vermulst, E., and P. Waer. 1995. "The Post Uruguay Round EC Anti-Dumping Regulation." *Journal of World Trade* 29, no. 2: 53–76.

Viner, J. 1950. *The Customs Union Issue*. Lancaster, PA: Carnegie Endowment for International Peace.

Walters, A. 1994. "Do We Need the IMF and the World Bank?" London: Institute of Economic Affairs.

Weintraub, S. 1991. "Free Trade in North America: Has Its Time Come?" *The World Economy* 14, no. 1: 57–66.

Whalley, J. 1985. *Trade Liberalization among Major World Trading Areas*. Cambridge, MA: MIT Press.

Whalley, J. 1989a. "Developing Countries and the New Bilateralism." Paper prepared for a project on Trade Issues in Development, North-South Institute, Ottawa.

Whalley, J., ed. 1989b. *The Uruguay Round and Beyond*. The Final Report from the Ford Foundation Project on Developing Countries and the Global Trading System. London: Macmillan.

Whalley, J. 1991. "The Interface between Environmental and Trade Policies." *Economic Journal* 101, no. 405: 180–89.

Whalley, J. 1993. "Regional Trade Arrangements in North America: CUSTA and NAFTA." In J. deMelo and A. Panagariya, *New Dimensions in Regional Integration*. Washington: World Bank.

Whalley, J. 1995. "Developing Countries and System Strengthening in the Uruguay Round." Paper prepared for a World Bank conference on the Uruguay Round and the Developing Economies, 26–27 January, Washington.

Whalley, J. 1996. "Quantifying Trade and Environment Linkages Through Economywide Modeling." In M. E. Bredahl, N. Ballenger, J. C. Dunmore, and T. L. Roe, *Agriculture, Trade, and the Environment: Discovering and Measuring Critical Linkages*. Oxford: Westview Press.

Whalley, J., and R. M. Wigle. 1991. "The International Incidence of Carbon Taxes." In R. Dornbusch and J. Poterba, *Global Warming: Economic Policy Responses*. Cambridge, MA: MIT Press.

Whitchard, O. G. 1988. "US Multinational Companies: Operations in 1986." *Survey of Current Business* 68, no. 6 (June): 85–96.

Whitman, M. v. N. 1975. "Leadership without Hegemony: Our Role in the World Economy." *Foreign Policy*, no. 20 (Fall): 138–64.

Wilcox, C. 1949. *A Charter for World Trade*. New York: Macmillan.

Winham, G. 1986. *International Trade and the Tokyo Round Negotiation*. Princeton, NJ: Princeton University Press.

Winston, C. 1993. "Economic Deregulation: Days of Reckoning for Microeconomists." *Journal of Economic Literature* 31, no. 3: 1263–89.

Winters, A. 1993a. "The European Community: A Case of Successful Integration?" In J. deMelo and A. Panagariya, *New Dimensions in Regional Integration*. Washington: World Bank.

Winters, A. 1993b. "Expanding E.C. Membership and Association Accords: Recent Experience and Future Prospects." In K. Anderson and R. Blackhurst, *Regional Integration in the Global Trading System*. Hertfordshire, UK: Harvester Wheatsheaf for the GATT.

Wolff, A. W. 1983. "Need for New GATT Rules to Govern Safeguard Actions." In W. R. Cline, *Trade Policy in the 1980s*. Washington: Institute for International Economics.

Wonnacott, R. J. 1990. "US Hub-and-Spoke Bilaterals and the Multilateral Trading System." C. D. Howe Institute Commentary, no. 23 (October). Toronto: C. D. Howe Institute.

Wonnacott, R. J. 1993. "Hemispheric Trade Liberalization: Is the NAFTA on the Right Track?" C. D. Howe Institute Commentary, no. 49 (June). Toronto: C. D. Howe Institute.

World Bank Group. 1994. *Learning From the Past, Embracing the Future*. Washington.

World Trade Organization (WTO). 1995. *Regionalism and the World Trading System*. Geneva: WTO Secretariat.

Zerby, J. 1990. *Prospects for Trading Blocs in the Asia-Pacific Region*. Montreal: Centre for International Business Studies, University of Montreal.

Index

Other Publications from the Institute for International Economics

BOOKS

IMF Conditionality
John Williamson, editor/*1983*   ISBN cloth 0-88132-006-4   695 pp.

Trade Policy in the 1980s
William R. Cline, editor/*1983*
(out of print)   ISBN paper 0-88132-031-5   810 pp.

Subsidies in International Trade
Gary Clyde Hufbauer and Joanna Shelton Erb/*1984*
                              ISBN cloth 0-88132-004-8   299 pp.

International Debt: Systemic Risk and Policy Response
William R. Cline/*1984*   ISBN cloth 0-88132-015-3   336 pp.

Trade Protection in the United States: 31 Case Studies
Gary Clyde Hufbauer, Diane E. Berliner, and Kimberly Ann Elliott/*1986*
(out of print)   ISBN paper 0-88132-040-4   371 pp.

Toward Renewed Economic Growth in Latin America
Bela Balassa, Gerardo M. Bueno, Pedro-Pablo Kuczynski,
and Mario Henrique Simonsen/*1986*
(out of stock)   ISBN paper 0-88132-045-5   205 pp.

Capital Flight and Third World Debt
Donald R. Lessard and John Williamson, editors/*1987*
(out of print)   ISBN paper 0-88132-053-6   270 pp.

The Canada-United States Free Trade Agreement:
The Global Impact
Jeffrey J. Schott and Murray G. Smith, editors/*1988*
                              ISBN paper 0-88132-073-0   211 pp.

World Agricultural Trade: Building a Consensus
William M. Miner and Dale E. Hathaway, editors/*1988*
                              ISBN paper 0-88132-071-3   226 pp.

Japan in the World Economy
Bela Balassa and Marcus Noland/*1988*
                              ISBN paper 0-88132-041-2   306 pp.

America in the World Economy: A Strategy for the 1990s
C. Fred Bergsten/*1988*   ISBN cloth 0-88132-089-7   235 pp.
                              ISBN paper 0-88132-082-X   235 pp.

Managing the Dollar: From the Plaza to the Louvre
Yoichi Funabashi/*1988, 2d ed. 1989*
                              ISBN paper 0-88132-097-8   307 pp.

United States External Adjustment and the World Economy
William R. Cline/*May 1989* ISBN paper 0-88132-048-X   392 pp.

Free Trade Areas and U.S. Trade Policy
Jeffrey J. Schott, editor/*May 1989*   ISBN paper 0-88132-094-3   400 pp.

Dollar Politics: Exchange Rate Policymaking in the United States
I. M. Destler and C. Randall Henning/*September 1989*
(out of print)   ISBN paper 0-88132-079-X   192 pp.

Latin American Adjustment: How Much Has Happened?
John Williamson, editor/*April 1990*
                              ISBN paper 0-88132-125-7   480 pp.

The Future of World Trade in Textiles and Apparel
William R. Cline/*1987, 2d ed. June 1990*
ISBN paper 0-88132-110-9   344 pp.

**Completing the Uruguay Round: A Results-Oriented Approach
to the GATT Trade Negotiations**
Jeffrey J. Schott, editor/*September 1990*
ISBN paper 0-88132-130-3   256 pp.

Economic Sanctions Reconsidered (in two volumes)
  Economic Sanctions Reconsidered: Supplemental Case Histories
  Gary Clyde Hufbauer, Jeffrey J. Schott, and Kimberly Ann Elliott/*1985, 2d ed.*
  December 1990   ISBN cloth 0-88132-115-X   928 pp.
                          ISBN paper 0-88132-105-2   928 pp.

  Economic Sanctions Reconsidered: History and Current Policy
  Gary Clyde Hufbauer, Jeffrey J. Schott, and Kimberly Ann Elliott/*December 1990*
                          ISBN cloth 0-88132-136-2   288 pp.
                          ISBN paper 0-88132-140-0   288 pp.

Pacific Basin Developing Countries: Prospects for the Future
Marcus Noland/*January 1991*   ISBN cloth 0-88132-141-9   250 pp.
(out of print)   ISBN paper 0-88132-081-1   250 pp.

Currency Convertibility in Eastern Europe
John Williamson, editor/*October 1991*
ISBN paper 0-88132-128-1   396 pp.

International Adjustment and Financing: The Lessons of 1985-1991
C. Fred Bergsten, editor/*January 1992*
ISBN paper 0-88132-112-5   336 pp.

North American Free Trade: Issues and Recommendations
Gary Clyde Hufbauer and Jeffrey J. Schott/*April 1992*
ISBN paper 0-88132-120-6   392 pp.

Narrowing the U.S. Current Account Deficit
Allen J. Lenz/*June 1992*
(out of print)   ISBN paper 0-88132-103-6   640 pp.

The Economics of Global Warming
William R. Cline/*June 1992* ISBN paper 0-88132-132-X   416 pp.

U.S. Taxation of International Income: Blueprint for Reform
Gary Clyde Hufbauer, assisted by Joanna M. van Rooij/*October 1992*
                          ISBN cloth 0-88132-178-8   304 pp.
                          ISBN paper 0-88132-134-6   304 pp.

Who's Bashing Whom? Trade Conflict in High-Technology Industries
Laura D'Andrea Tyson/*November 1992*
ISBN paper 0-88132-106-0   352 pp.

Korea in the World Economy
Il SaKong/*January 1993*
ISBN paper 0-88132-106-0   328 pp.

Pacific Dynamism and the International Economic System
C. Fred Bergsten and Marcus Noland, editors/*May 1993*
ISBN paper 0-88132-196-6   424 pp.

Economic Consequences of Soviet Disintegration
John Williamson, editor/*May 1993*
ISBN paper 0-88132-190-7   664 pp.

Measuring the Costs of Protection in Japan
Yoko Sazanami, Shujiro Urata, and Hiroki Kawai/*January 1995*
ISBN paper 0-88132-211-3   96 pp.

Foreign Direct Investment in the United States, Third Edition
Edward M. Graham and Paul R. Krugman/*January 1995*
ISBN paper 0-88132-204-0   232 pp.

The Political Economy of Korea-United States Cooperation
C. Fred Bergsten and Il SaKong, editors/*February 1995*
ISBN paper 0-88132-213-X   128 pp.

International Debt Reexamined
William R. Cline/*February 1995*
ISBN paper 0-88132-083-8   560 pp.

American Trade Politics, Third Edition
I. M. Destler/*April 1995*   ISBN paper 0-88132-215-6   360 pp.

Managing Official Export Credits: The Quest for a Global Regime
John E. Ray/*July 1995*   ISBN paper 0-88132-207-5   344 pp.

Asia Pacific Fusion: Japan's Role in APEC
Yoichi Funabashi/*October 1995*
ISBN paper 0-88132-224-5   312 pp.

Korea-United States Cooperation in the New World Order
C. Fred Bergsten and Il SaKong, editors/*February 1996*
ISBN paper 0-88132-226-1   144 pp.

Why Exports Really Matter!   ISBN paper 0-88132-221-0   34 pp.
Why Exports Matter More!   ISBN paper 0-88132-229-6   36 pp.
J. David Richardson and Karin Rindal/*July 1995; February 1996*

Global Corporations and National Governments
Edward M. Graham/*May 1996*   ISBN paper 0-88132-111-7   168 pp.

Global Economic Leadership and the Group of Seven
C. Fred Bergsten and C. Randall Henning/*May 1996*
ISBN paper 0-88132-218-0   192 pp.

The Trading System after the Uruguay Round
John Whalley and Colleen Hamilton/*July 1996*
ISBN paper 0-88132-131-1   224 pp.

SPECIAL REPORTS
1   **Promoting World Recovery: A Statement on Global Economic Strategy**
    by Twenty-six Economists from Fourteen Countries/*December 1982*
    (out of print)   ISBN paper 0-88132-013-7   45 pp.
2   **Prospects for Adjustment in Argentina, Brazil, and Mexico:**
    Responding to the Debt Crisis   (out of print)
    John Williamson, editor/*June 1983*   ISBN paper 0-88132-016-1   71 pp.
3   **Inflation and Indexation: Argentina, Brazil, and Israel**
    John Williamson, editor/*March 1985*   ISBN paper 0-88132-037-4   191 pp.
4   **Global Economic Imbalances**
    C. Fred Bergsten, editor/*March 1986*   ISBN cloth 0-88132-038-2   126 pp.
                                  ISBN paper 0-88132-042-0   126 pp.
5   **African Debt and Financing**
    Carol Lancaster and John Williamson, editors/*May 1986*
    (out of print)   ISBN paper 0-88132-044-7   229 pp.

WORKS IN PROGRESS

Private Capital Flows to Emerging Markets after the Mexican Crisis
Guillermo Calvo, Morris Goldstein, and Eduard Hochreiter

Trade, Jobs, and Income Distribution
William R. Cline

Trade and Labor Standards
Kimberly Ann Elliott and Richard Freeman

Regional Trading Blocs in the World Economic System
Jeffrey A. Frankel

Transatlantic Free Trade Agreement
Ellen Frost

Forecasting Financial Crises: Early Warning Signs for Emerging Markets
Morris Goldstein and Carmen Reinhart

Overseeing Global Capital Markets
Morris Goldstein and Peter Garber

Global Competition Policy
Edward M. Graham and J. David Richardson

Flying High: Civil Aviation in the Asia Pacific
Gary Clyde Hufbauer and Christopher Findlay

Toward an Asia Pacific Economic Community?
Gary Clyde Hufbauer and Jeffrey J. Schott

The Economics of Korean Unification
Marcus Noland

The Case for Trade: A Modern Reconsideration
J. David Richardson

Crawling Bands: Lessons from Chile, Colombia, and Israel
John Williamson

For orders outside the US and Canada please contact:

Longman Group UK Ltd.   Telephone Orders: 0279 623923
PO Box 88, Fourth Avenue   Fax: 0279 453450   Telex: 81259
Harlow, Essex CM 19 5SR   UK

Canadian customers can order from the Institute or from either:

RENOUF BOOKSTORE   LA LIBERTÉ
1294 Algoma Road   3020 chemin Sainte-Foy
Ottawa, Ontario K1B 3W8   Quebec G1X 3V6
Telephone: (613) 741-4333   Telephone: (418) 658-3763
Fax: (613) 741-5439   Fax: (800) 567-5449

Visit our website at: http://www.iie.com   E-mail address: orders@iie.com